ADVANCE PRAISE

This book took my breath away. Lynn is authentic, courageous, smart, and filled with heart. She is brave to bare her soul, knowing it will help people everywhere. I think of that young girl, sister, woman, wife, and mother reading Lynn's book and how they might appreciate that they, too, can—and will—overcome life's obstacles and emerge with spirit, love, resilience, and purpose.
—Denise D. Resnik, CEO of DRA Collective and nonprofit leader

An extraordinary story about one woman overcoming multiple traumas through unrelenting resilience. I'm confident many people are going to see themselves in at least one part of her story and as a result, experience healing and inspiration.
—Dr. Steve Schein, Corporate Sustainability Strategist, Family Business Advisor, author of *A New Psychology for Sustainability Leadership*

I loved this book and could not put it down. Lynn has lived a life that has thrown her some unbelievably cruel and damaging experiences. In each chapter, she points out lessons you can learn from. I advise keeping a pen and paper handy when you read. How Lynn has come through all this turmoil and evolved into an extraordinary woman full of love, kindness, and compassion is astounding. She teaches us to accept, grow, and learn from what life throws at us.
—Peter H. Thomas, Founder of Century 21 Canada and LifePilot; Chairman Emeritus, The Entrepreneur Organization

Walking Through Pain to Purpose is a story of pain, turmoil, resilience, joy, and triumph. Lynn tells her story with vulnerability and candor in a way that anyone can relate to. Every page left me wanting more. She tenderly gives dignity to the unique beauty of children with autism and other developmental disorders. This book truly shows the beauty and strength of the human spirit.

—**Marcia Meyer, former CEO-PetsMart, Founder & President, The Be Kind Project**

Lynn Balter's memoir, *Walking Through Pain to Purpose*, is an extraordinary journey that allows us to reflect on our own lives—our triumphs, our sorrows, and most importantly, the reality that we each control our destiny in how we live and the power of the actions we take. That perseverance is the key to creating the life we want. A true page turner.

—**Renie Cavallari, best-selling, award-winning author of *HeadTrash*; Founder & CEO of Powered by Aspire, an award-winning leadership and innovation company; CEO of RCI Institute**

Walking Through Pain to Purpose is captivating, heartwarming, and inspiring. Lynn presents her own personal journey as she finds purpose and strength through her own pain. This book will motivate you to tap into your own strength and encourage you with the hope and faith we all need to get through life's most difficult times.

—**Stacy Fornara, Co-founder Bible.com, Founding member Entrepreneur Organization, Arizona Chapter**

This memoir is a masterpiece. From the moment I picked it up, I couldn't put it down. That Lynn could endure so much pain and come out the other end with such resilience and beauty is amazing. She's experienced life like no other. Her honesty is staggering. Bravo!

—**Rita Thomas, Health Coach, author of *LifeDiet* and *Recipes for Life*; Executive Director, The Thomas Foundation**

This book has hit a nerve and will be successful. A profound personal journey of survival, transcendence, and a deep observation of humanity. It will challenge and transform our beliefs and reframe what it means to live a truly inspired life.
—Patrice O'Donnell-Bonnell, CEO, PBSG Coaching

Reading this book was like watching a really good movie. It resonates so much that you can't seem to get it out of your head! The author's frank storytelling was even therapeutic. Lynn Balter is accomplishing amazing and positive changes. This book is captivating and brutally honest.
—Michelle Gianetti, Artist and Illustrator through the eyes of faith, creation, and evolution

A POWERFUL read! It's like my own life kept getting in the way, and all I wanted to do was read Lynn's book! She is a walking MIRACLE.
—Elaine Gauette, Retired high school counselor

Lynn Balter has opened her soul to us so we could see the crossroads and struggles she went through, yet through her faith and perseverance, she did not allow herself to just lie down. A true endorsement of what one can overcome and still win.
—Rosie Tutag, Pharmaceutical Newsletter Editor

When well-being and happiness don't come along in our lives, we can get stuck in the past and suffer every day, or we can keep going with positivism, knowing our own limitations to moving forward. *Walking Through Pain to Purpose* is proof of moving forward while giving back to family, others, and community. Lynn feels the pain and walks through it to be healed and create a higher purpose. In the overwhelming demands of life, she shows how to find a path to inner peace and balance.
—Mavi Farca, Spanish Teacher, Christ Church School

WALKING THROUGH PAIN TO PURPOSE

TURNING TRAUMA INTO TRIUMPH

A MEMOIR
LYNN BALTER

WALKING THROUGH PAIN TO PURPOSE

TURNING TRAUMA INTO TRIUMPH

A MEMOIR
LYNN BALTER

PEACOCK PROUD
P·R·E·S·S
Phoenix, Arizona

Walking Through Pain to Purpose: Turning Trauma into Triumph, A Memoir
Copyright © 2022 by Lynn Balter

First Published in the USA in 2022 by Peacock Proud Press, Phoenix, Arizona
    ISBN 978-1-957232-01-0 Hardback
    ISBN 978-1-957232-02-7 Paperback
    ISBN 978-1-957232-03-4 eBook
    Library of Congress Control Number: 2022906205

All rights reserved. No part of this publication may be reproduced, stored in, or introduced into a retrieval system, or transmitted, in any form, or by any means (electronic, mechanical, photocopying, recording or otherwise) without the prior written permission of the publisher. This book is sold subject to the condition that it shall not, by way of trade or otherwise, be lent, resold, hired out, or otherwise circulated without the publisher's prior consent in any form of binding or cover other than that in which it is published and without a similar condition, including this condition being imposed on the subsequent purchaser. All images and articles in this publication have been used with permission.

Editors
    Laura L. Bush, PhD, PeacockProud.com
    Charles Grosel, Write4Success.net

Cover and Interior Layout
    Jana Linnell

Portrait Photographer
    Karianne Munstedt, kariannemunstedt.com

DISCLAIMER: This is a work of nonfiction. The information is of a general nature to help readers know and understand more about the life of the author, Lynn Balter. Readers of this publication agree that Lynn Balter will not be held responsible or liable for damages that may be alleged or resulting directly or indirectly from their use of this publication. All external links are provided as a resource only and are not guaranteed to remain active for any length of time. The author cannot be held accountable for the information provided by, or actions resulting from accessing these resources.

TABLE OF CONTENTS

Dedications... 11
Preface: **What I Believe** 15
Chapter 1: **In the Desert**... 23
Chapter 2: **Family Pathology – The Journey Begins** 29
Chapter 3: **The Patterns Take Hold** 41
Chapter 4: **Adolescent Escape**.. 58
Chapter 5: **Life Interrupted**... 78
Chapter 6: **Life Lessons Follow You Everywhere** 92
Chapter 7: **Family and Business Don't Mix** 101
Chapter 8: **My Husband, My Teacher** 117
Chapter 9: **Twins R Us**.. 132
Chapter 10: **Autism is a Family Journey**............................. 139
Chapter 11: **The Nanny Wars and Other Battles**.................. 160
Chapter 12: **My Breast Cancer – The Whisper Becomes a Boulder** 181
Chapter 13: **Neil's Cancer – The Boulder Becomes a Brick Wall** 189
Chapter 14: **How Do You Get a Break Around Here?** 198
Chapter 15: **Traumatic Brain Injury – Lessons from Michael** 218
Chapter 16: **Healing Through Service**................................ 239
Chapter 17: **What Death Can Teach Us** 258
Chapter 18: **Finding Peace in the Midst of COVID and Cancer**................. 275
Chapter 19: **Writing to be Free** 286
Acknowledgments 299
About the Author... 301
Notes 303

DEDICATIONS

*I dedicate this book to the following friends and family
in my life that have turned tragedy into triumph
and their pain into purpose.*

Peter and Rita Thomas
Todd, son of Peter and Donna and Stepson of Rita Thomas, took his life on February 1, 2000, at age thirty-six. Peter and Rita created the Todd Thomas Foundation to celebrate Todd's life, honor his memory, and raise awareness about the magnitude of mental illness and the effect it has on individuals, as well as our society. The foundation also assists in decreasing the stigma associated with suicide and supports research for effective treatments. Peter and Rita have created and/or been influential in many business and philanthropic organizations over the years. They have made a difference in the lives of so many people. They live the example of giving back while Walking Through Pain to Purpose.

Denise Resnik
Denise Resnik cofounded the Southwest Autism Research & Resource Center (SARRC) in 1997. She has led the way to better understand and improve life for people with autism. She is also the Founder and CEO of First Place AZ in 2012: Developing supportive homes and communities for adults with autism, down syndrome, and other neurodiversities. First Place also provides a residential transition program for adults with autism. Denise and Rob Resnik's son Matt is an adult who was diagnosed

with autism in 1993. Denise has taken her role as Matt's mother beyond caring for her own son to become a catalyst for creating an entire community of support for thousands of individuals with autism and their families in Phoenix. The result of her work has been recognized by the PBS NewsHour as creating "the most autism friendly city in the world," influencing other communities everywhere.

Lisa Jan Cohen
The Kyah Rayne Foundation (KRF) was founded by Lisa Jan Cohen in 2019 to honor her daughter Kyah Rayne. KRF is dedicated to advancing food allergy awareness and education, and to increasing Epinephrine Auto-Injector access. Kyah was twenty-one years old when she died of fatal anaphylaxis in Lisa's arms, after experiencing just the taste of a peanut. Lisa has dedicated her life to food allergy education and advocacy. She continues to transform her pain with purpose by raising awareness for this common but overlooked disease.

Bob and Suzanne Wright
Inspired by their grandson who was diagnosed with autism, Suzanne and Bob Wright cofounded Autism Speaks in 2005. Guided by the Wright's leadership and vision, Autism Speaks has grown into the world's leading autism science and advocacy organization. The Wrights helped raise funding for groundbreaking science, effective advocacy, and extensive family services, enhancing the lives of people with autism and their families now and into the future.

Marcia Meyer
After observing the difficulty her special needs granddaughter was having in the public school system, Marcia Meyer founded the Be Kind People Project in 2012. Marcia's granddaughter, Grace, ultimately passed away at sixteen years old from a rare multisystem disorder in 2016. The Be Kind Project is and was created to initiate positive social change in schools and provide a framework for youth that will improve academic achievement, interpersonal relationship skills, accountability, behavior, personal health

and wellness, teacher appreciation, and the formation of enduring values. After Grace's death, a new entity was created within The Be Kind Project called Grace's Groupies that focuses on special needs children and offers one on one support in the classroom.

Jennifer Carroll

Jennifer Carroll was married to a successful entrepreneur. They raised two amazing kids, but she lost her husband, Phil, tragically to prostate cancer when he was just fifty-two. She authored a book, **Beyond Invincible**, honoring her late husband and to create a platform to speak about men's health and the need to get checked regularly for prostate cancer. She found purpose through her pain in sharing the philosophies she learned living large and living to give. Her journey of loss led her to become a voice of resilience and rediscovery.

Jennifer and her daughter, Jessica, host high-end events they call Fun Frisky Play Days! The dynamic duo, also known as J&J, gather illuminated ladies in community to rediscover themselves and learn how to play the J&J way (funfabfrisky.com). Jennifer also wrote the children's book, **Bigsbee's Unbee-lievable Journey to Fly!** It's a metaphorical life skills book encouraging children to begin with a dream, belong to a great group, be accepting of others, and believe in themselves.

Neil Balter

My wonderful husband, Neil, tirelessly dedicates his time, fundraising magic, and entrepreneurial skills in the fight against autism. Neil has also been an advocate to many families that have been diagnosed with autism or cancer. He has mentored countless entrepreneurs around the world as one of the founding members of Entrepreneurs Organization (EO), previously Young Entrepreneurs (YEO). He is always willing to help where he is needed and, by his example, has been an inspiration to me.

Janice Oliveto

My Aunt Janice, my father's sister, lost her son Nathan Grimm at eleven years old due to heart failure. Nathan was born with down syndrome and suffered through many heart surgeries through his short life. Not long after Nathan had passed, Aunt Janice adopted a special needs baby with down syndrome and autism. Her name is Natalie, and she is now twenty years old and living in California with her mom, my Aunt Janice. When I asked my aunt why she adopted and then raised Natalie, a child with special needs, she said, "Because I Know How."

Fransisca Gonzales

Fransisca has been our housekeeper for many years. She's part of our family and my hero. This courageous, loving woman had to leave her four young children under the care of her mother in Guatemala so that she could come to America and provide for her family. Over all these years, she sends every penny she has earned that she can spare to Guatemala to care for her family. Fransisca and her granddaughter Lizeth are legal here in the U.S. and continue to provide care to those they love that are living in the most malnourished and impoverished country in Latin America.

Cheryl and Tom Blair, *A Tribute of Prayer*

Cheryl and Tom Blair, my cousins, lost their son Tommy at twenty-nine years old, due to an unexplained cause that took his life. He had no conditions that the family was aware of. Cheryl and Tom have two extraordinary daughters and care for many young children in their childcare company. Tommy recently died, and although they will always feel the pain of losing their son, they live their lives in purpose, and we pray for their healing. May they find comfort in all they have to offer others in their example of faith and love.

Preface
WHAT I BELIEVE

I have unconsciously been preparing to write this book since I was a young girl and recently decided to put it on the page.

We all have a journey to enlightenment and self-discovery, but we each must undergo our own unique lessons to bring us closer to our most evolved selves. If we listen to the whispers of life, they will guide us. This book tells the story of my journey in this lifetime and the growth that came to me once I learned to be still and listen to those whispers. Sometimes the whispers become a thunderous roar. We have the choice to be still and listen and grow or to ignore the whispers and wait for the next, more painful lessons. Life is a learning curve. Writing this book gives me a chance to reflect on my life—where I've been and where I'm going, what I've learned and what I still need to learn. Writing this book has become a sacred act, an important stage of my journey to self-discovery.

I respect everyone's beliefs and honor the many ways each of us finds our truths. In this book, I express *my* beliefs, many of which I have learned from reading dozens of enlightened authors over the years. From the time I was a young girl, I have yearned for the spiritual and have been blessed to study many inspiring writers and teachers. As Lao Tzu is said to have observed, "When the student is ready, the teacher will appear."[1] Teachers have always miraculously appeared just when I needed them. I've been lucky that way.

In my beliefs, however, teachers aren't always the obvious ones, such as writers, mentors, coaches, therapists, clergy, and so on (although these figures do have much to offer). The kinds of teachers I'm talking about can be anyone in your life, including those you least expect—that sibling you never quite got along with, your parents, a friend you are drawn to and continue to have conflict with, a boss that tests your very being, ex-lovers and ex-spouses, lifelong spouses, difficult clients. Sometimes your relationships with these teachers are painful.

Events and circumstances can also be teachers—illnesses (our own or those of loved ones), unexpected lawsuits, car accidents, any of the curve balls life can throw at us. And though we often learn from the bad things that happen to us, teachers can also be positive figures—those joyful souls who just seem to know how to live a good life no matter what comes their way, the angels in our lives who with a gesture or a smile or a kind word cut through our pain to touch our hearts, the friend or family member who always has our back.

In short, teachers are anyone or anything that gives you pause to reflect, that helps you on your journey of self-development. Often, they don't even know they're your teachers. They teach by the fact of their existence and your relationship with them, or in the case of circumstances, in how you respond. They are more like soulmates—those souls put on earth to reach our deepest selves and provide, even without knowing it, what we need to keep evolving. Gary Zukav, spiritual teacher and author of four New York Times bestsellers, including *Seat of the Soul*, calls the realm where this takes place *Earth School*.[2] We can call it our lifetime.

Spirituality is often difficult to talk about because it's so personal and hard to define. To understand my story, you should know that this is what I believe:

- We are all One, part of the Divine Mind, the universal intelligence of souls. When we exist on this level, we are pure spirit without ego. We are soul.

- Between lifetimes, in our soul state, when we have the wisdom of our true selves, we choose our lessons and make agreements with other souls to bring us to further enlightenment in our next lifetime.

- Our souls are born into consciousness and over many different lives we try to learn lessons to bring us to a higher consciousness, to our true selves in human form.
- Every child comes into each lifetime completely whole. As life occurs, it chips away at our divine knowledge that we are all we need to be. Many of us spend our lifetimes trying to rediscover the wholeness we already had when we were children, the wholeness we have forgotten.
- The purpose of life is to learn to love one another and ourselves, to treat every soul with the knowledge that we are all One. Each of us begins our lifetime with the intention of learning the lessons that will develop that ability to love. We are often prevented from experiencing that kind of love by the wounds we have suffered in our human form, some of which we received in our past lifetimes.
- The lessons of this lifetime are different for everyone, and they often come with pain, sometimes great pain. One should not ignore this pain or try to escape it. Everything happens for a reason. The medicine is in the pain. Only by walking through the pain can we heal the wounds that prevent us from evolving into our true selves.
- We teach people how to treat us—by the way we react to them, by the boundaries we establish or don't establish, by the space we let them occupy in our heads (and our lives), and how healthy we are at expressing our own needs.
- We are accompanied by spiritual guides who protect us and keep us on track in learning the lessons of our lifetime.
- We heal ourselves in part by healing others and by providing service to other individuals or to society at large. It is important to distinguish between offering service, which is done with a healthy intention in aiding to the healing of others, and being a servant, which falls in the realm of unhealthy, enabling behavior.

The pain of life's lessons is God's way of grabbing our attention. God never gives up. We can spend many lifetimes in this earth school drawing closer to our true selves. In each lifetime, we all have a specific purpose to heal a wounded part of ourselves. God taps into that pain until we listen and begin to heal that part of our soul. Oprah Winfrey puts it this way:

> *Life whispers to you all the time. It whispers, and if you don't get the whisper, the whisper gets louder. I call it like a little pebble— a little thump—upside the head. The pebble or the thump upside the head usually means it's gone into a problem. If you don't pay attention to the problem, the pebble then becomes like a brick. The brick upside your head is a crisis, and if you don't pay attention to the brick upside your head, the crisis turns into a disaster and the whole house—the brick wall—comes falling down.*[3]

Pain is that brick to the head, which tries to get our attention before the walls fall in around us. But sometimes the walls must fall down before we get the message. Insights come when we are willing to see things from a new perspective. Each time we have an insight, our consciousness shifts and brings us closer to our true selves.

I'm writing my story not to tell you how to live your life, but to show you how I've lived mine, to share the lessons I've learned in this lifetime. Maybe you'll learn from some of my lessons by applying them to the times you've had to walk through pain. Medicine is in the pain if you are willing to experience it and let it heal you. Sometimes we don't understand the lesson until much later. But if we can be still and listen to the whispers, the pebbles and the bricks will less likely become the walls that fall on top of us.

Most of us must go through many lifetimes to walk through the pain intended for our growth. I'm sure I've lived many lifetimes and have many lifetimes ahead. It is our choice, through free will, to walk through the pain or not. When we let ourselves feel the pain and walk through it, we begin to heal. Additional healing occurs when we use our lessons to help others going through the same pain and hardship, when we can be of service. That's when walking through the pain creates an even higher purpose.

Each lesson for me has been a mountain to climb. I have tripped and fallen many times and slid back down the mountain only to start climbing again. Every fall was part of the lesson meant to heal a wounded part of myself and lead me to the freedom that follows. Are you ready to climb your mountains, to walk through your pain? Are you listening to the whispers of your lessons?

My Prayer for WALKING THROUGH PAIN TO PURPOSE

As I write this book, it is my prayer that I honor each amazing person in my life and respect their journey in telling my story. I speak my truth from my perspective, which may not be the same as those who have shared these experiences with me. I know that each person in my life does the best they can from their level of consciousness, just as I do.

In telling my story I don't intend to hurt anyone, but to tell my truth and the lessons I've learned from my soulmates and teachers honestly and in a loving and compassionate way. I will reveal only what is essential to my truth as I walk through pain to purpose. I am not writing this book to place judgment or blame. I am writing to seek and offer forgiveness with the understanding that we are here in earth school to help each other grow. We only suffer from others because they are suffering. This suffering shapes us, pushes us along our path. Each relationship is meant for us to learn and grow.

Every day I walk through my pain to my purpose and the peace and freedom it will ultimately bring. I tell my story to further heal myself and to reach out to others who may benefit from the lessons intended for me in this lifetime.

Amen.

Chapter 1
IN THE DESERT

On a chilly January night in Phoenix, Arizona, I arrived home from my job as a property manager at about six. Life was good. I had graduated from college a few years before and moved to Arizona to get a new start. After waitressing for about a year, I moved into property management and began managing apartment communities. I was in charge of my own life, free for the first time from my family's influence.

The complex I managed at the time was in a rougher area of the city, and it had been a long day. I lived at a different community in a nicer area with its own gated and monitored entrance. I couldn't wait to get home and relax for a bit before my boyfriend, Tom, came over. I planned to make a cozy, romantic dinner as it was stormy and cold outside. He was getting off work late, so I had plenty of time to warm the homemade chicken soup I had made the day before. I also had just enough time for a short nap before he arrived.

I was beat. I didn't even bother to undo the row of buttons that trailed down the back and up the hips of my dress. I always thought that dress had a ridiculous number of buttons, but I loved it anyway. I also felt a twinge of guilt every time I wore it. My father had bought it for me one Christmas when I knew he couldn't afford it. But I looked damn good in that dress, and I wanted to look good for Tom. I kept it on, fell onto my bed, and wrapped myself in the cozy afghan my grandmother had spent hours crocheting. My grandmother had always been a stable, secure presence in my life, and her afghan reminded me of that time.

I fell asleep within seconds, and slept so soundly I didn't even hear my roommate Judith come home and then go out to K-Mart. I learned about that later. As usual, she left through the sliding glass door and kept it unlocked. We both used the door as a shortcut for errands. We couldn't lock it from the outside, and we couldn't get back in if it was locked from the inside.

It was funny, we had lived together in a few different apartments, and we had always been sure to get a second-story apartment for safety, something women always have to think about. I was a property manager of apartment communities and very few women rented first floor units. This apartment was on the second floor like all the others.

Despite our efforts to stay safe, though, we often used this sliding door in the back instead of the front door. The back stairs led down to a narrow dead-end street outside the complex. The street was rarely used and opened onto a very empty, desolate desert that covered a few miles. The desert was barren and full of secret wonder. I loved to look out the window at its vast beauty, its solitary and calming energy. The beauty of the desert aside, it was also easier to park our cars on that street rather than inside the complex, since from the interior parking spots, we'd have to drive through the gate at the guard house for even the quickest of errands.

I had fallen into that early, luscious part of sleep where you have the sweetest of dreams when I was suddenly, violently yanked awake. Or was I? *What was that?* I thought, confused and loopy. *Am I awake? Is this real or still a dream?* Once I shook loose some of the cobwebs, I felt a sharp pressure against my throat. *Is that a knife? That's a knife!* My eyes sprang open, and I saw a hulking man in a black ski mask, who was, in fact, holding a knife to my throat.

"Do what I say, or I'll kill you," a gruff voice commanded.

The man pulled me out of bed brutally by the hair and dragged me across the room as if I were a ragdoll. I knew instantly I had lost control. He owned me to do with as he wished. I was fully awake now, adrenalin charging through me, but I had the presence of mind to realize that if I wanted to survive, I had to stay clearheaded.

"Stand up and move," he said, with a terrifying voice as he pressed the thick, jagged knife against my back. He yelled again to move and move quickly, or he would kill me.

"Help! Help me! Please someone help me!" I screamed instead, hoping someone in the nearby apartments could hear me. I had watched enough cop shows to know that if he took me out of the building, my chances of surviving shrunk drastically. I screamed and screamed, all the while trying desperately to twist out of his grip, but he was too strong.

"Scream again, and I'll kill you right now."

He pushed me violently through the dark hallway, then forced me through the living room and out the sliding glass door to the top of the narrow stairway that led out to the vast desert behind the apartment. As he shoved me down the stairs, I got far enough away from the knife that I could break and run. He caught me within seconds, though, and struck me hard about the face and head.

"If you fucking do that again, you'll die, bitch!" He hit me with each word.

"Please don't hurt me! Please don't hurt me," I begged. I didn't let myself think of anything except the hope—the belief—that I would get through this violent abduction. That I would be tough enough to survive.

I gave in and let him lead me away from the apartment. By this time, it was about 7:00 p.m. Darkness had fallen over the cold, windy desert. I learned later that the man in the mask had been stalking me for weeks and knew that my roommate had just gone out the patio door, leaving it unlocked, as he'd seen one of us do many times before. That I had fallen asleep just made it easier for him.

He dragged me farther and farther into the desert, getting us far away from anyone who might hear my pleas for mercy. It seemed as if we walked for hours, but it must have only been minutes. He seemed unnaturally large—at least six-foot-four and two hundred and fifty pounds. He spoke with what sounded to me like an Appalachian accent, so I guessed he was not well educated and likely had a hard and broken life. What hope did I have as a twenty-five-year-old woman who stood only five-foot-four and weighed a-hundred-and-five-pounds? Would I ever get home again? I was terrified I wouldn't survive if I didn't do what he said. Even if I did do what he said, I had to show him a reason to let me live.

I shuffled through the possibilities, then I said, "I'm pregnant. Please don't hurt the baby."

Of course I wasn't pregnant, but I'm sure I was convincing. I had learned how to survive early in life, and I had become quite the actress. *I am going to survive this*, I vowed. If he couldn't see me as a human being, maybe the life of a baby would melt his resolve—or maybe he would get turned off by the notion of raping a pregnant woman. I had to try. *God*, I prayed, *please let this work.*

He pulled me along, punching and slapping me all the while. Finally, we stopped, and he ripped off my dress, tearing through each button like a bear ripping through flesh. His roughness reminded me of the men at construction sites, hooting and howling as I walked by. As a property manager, I encountered these catcalls often. Men looked at me (and other women) as if they had the right to harasses me, to treat me like an object, with no regard for how I felt or the panic they created as I tried to get from one side of the site to the other. They didn't care. To them, it was a game. And now I was being stripped and beaten by a monster, and this was no game. He was doing with me as he pleased, and he made sure I knew my life and body were in his hands.

Meanwhile, and throughout the whole encounter, he wouldn't stop talking about why he had chosen me and the lengths he had gone to get me.

He had been stalking me for months, he told me. "I know everything about you. I know who you are. I know where you work. I know your boyfriend's name. I know where you go after work. I know which car is yours. And I know you can't get away from me." This was part of the power trip, no doubt, what got him off. He needed someone to know his story. He needed me to know his story. How strong and smart he was. How he could get anyone or anything he wanted. He talked and talked throughout the entire experience, bragging about how much control he had over me, using words that sickened me. It is hard for me to repeat many of the things he said. The foulness of the language repulses me to this day.

I was at his mercy. I felt that if I survived this, nothing would ever be the same again. I would never feel safe again.

And the talking. The talking. He even told me things you'd think he wouldn't want me to know because they could help identify him. He told me that he had broken out of jail with two other men in New Mexico. He boasted to me that the three of them shared his rage and went around the country raping women, like it was a fun game. "The police are getting closer to catching us," he told me, "so we decided to separate. The other two are in California." He went on to describe how he would identify his victim in each state and spend months stalking her before capturing her. Then he'd move onto the next state and the next victim.

At some point during this monologue, he pushed me to the ground and raped me, with violence and aggression. He continued to talk, each comment more vulgar than the last.

"You've been fucking since you were five. I know it. You like it. You're so fuckable," he said over and over. As he did so, I went inside of myself and went to God with a deep knowing that he was there, and I would be safe, no matter what the outcome. I went into my mind so deeply I left my body, hovering some distance above all that was happening. When I wasn't in my body, he couldn't hurt me the way he wanted to, the way he thought he was hurting me. I was no longer there. I was with our Lord, who had been with me since I was a very young girl. He had brought me through every challenge to that point in my life, and while I was with him, he let me know that he always would. I prayed to God for another reason. I had hurt my sister Lori in an argument the day before, and I prayed that I wouldn't die before telling her I was sorry.

I don't know how long I stayed in this suspended state. I was drawn back into my body when he said, "I'm done, bitch," in an emotionless tone. "If I decide to let you live, know that I can always find you if I want you again. For whatever reason."

"I won't say a thing," I said. "Never." I held my breath. *Is he going to let me live? I think he's going to let me live.* "I promise."

"Turn over and put your face in the dirt," he said, adjusting his pants. "Stay like that for thirty minutes, and you live. One movement before then, and you die. Got it?"

I nodded and turned on to my stomach, scraping my face and legs in the rocky soil, the taste of dust in my mouth. I had never felt so dirty in all my life.

Then he ran off. I heard the crunch of his heavy tread in the soil, the slap of the desert plants on his legs.

I don't know how long I stayed there before I pushed myself to my feet and ran as fast and as hard as I could back to the apartment, holding my dress closed, the loose ends flapping around my legs, looking over my shoulders as if he was right behind me. It was worse by far than being chased in any dream I had ever had.

When I got back to the apartment, I finally let myself think. I had been assaulted. I had been—let's call it what it was—raped. But I had survived. I had survived as God had said I would. He had answered my prayer, and I will be forever grateful. It wasn't my time to die that night. I was twenty-five years old, and I still had much work to do to fulfill my soul's purpose in this lifetime. And I had to apologize to my sister.

This is good, I said to myself. *I'm okay. I survived. All right. This is good. This is good. What do I do next? What do I do?*

That's when I went into shock.

Chapter 2
FAMILY PATHOLOGY – THE JOURNEY BEGINS

> *"Your soul and the souls of your parents agreed to your relationship in order to balance the energy that each needed to balance or to activate dynamics within each other that are essential to lessons that each much learn."* [4]
> —Seat of the Soul, Gary Zukav

Though I would not wish the experience of rape on anyone, I believe it was a life lesson—a very harsh one, one of those bricks to the head that Oprah talks about. Don't get me wrong. I am not making light of it. I was violently raped and experienced trauma because of it. But the patterns that led to my rape had been set in place long before that time.

I was born in 1959 and learned early that the world could be a scary place.

My mother was a volatile, impulsive, unpredictable woman. She could be sweet as pie one minute, loving and nurturing, and fly off the handle the next, enraged at some stupid kid thing one of us did that passed unnoticed the day before. We never knew which way she'd go. We learned to watch her carefully, like the weather, to keep her happy and run for cover when the storm came. As the oldest child, it often fell to me to do the impossible—control the weather.

One of my very first memories involved such a sudden storm.

We lived in Farmington, Michigan. I was five years old in 1964, a thin young girl with bright blue eyes from my mother's Irish family and dark, curly hair from my father's Italian one. My hair had a mind of its own, and I often had trouble keeping it neatly brushed, especially for school. I attended kindergarten at the neighborhood public school. I walked there every morning with my friends, beginning each day full of fun and adventure.

That morning was typical of a Michigan Fall, sunny and brisk. I was excited. I loved school. This was the first time I was out in the world. I felt independent and grown up. I couldn't wait to get out the door to have fun with my friends and teacher, Mrs. Norton, who was kind and gentle. It was such a happy place, that kindergarten room. Mrs. Norton paid attention to what made each of us different. She cared about how we felt. I loved the comfort of that classroom and the joy it brought to me. I could always count on Mrs. Norton to help me feel good.

As I walked down the hallway to the front door anticipating the fun I'd have that day, my mother shouted from behind me: "Stop. Stop. Where do you think you're going?" Her voice was like the sound of thunder that shook the sky so suddenly I thought the earth could break in two. My small body shook to its bones.

"You look terrible! Your hair is a mess! You can't go out the door like that," she yelled in a rage. Her eyebrows clinched and her skin boiled with a red fire that took my breath away. I couldn't imagine what I had done. I grew more and more terrified as she approached. The rage and panic contorted her face into someone I didn't know—and didn't want to know. She grabbed me by the shoulder with one hand, pulled my hair, then shoved me against the wall.

"I can't do everything around here. You better learn how to take care of yourself!" She grew louder with every word, holding on to my hair and shaking me hard.

"Why are you doing this?"

"I didn't do anything! STOP!" I yelled back, looking at her as if she had lost her mind. She usually didn't care how we looked unless we had to impress someone who mattered to her. But I had broken a cardinal rule. You never talked back to my mother.

"Who do you think you are, young lady?" With her free hand, she slapped me across the face with all her might; a starburst went off in my head. My cheek stung with pain as well as shame, and I knew suddenly that everything had changed. My sense of comfort and safety had been shattered. I was terrified. On that day, I became a scapegoat for my mother's pain. I don't remember how long I cried. I felt heartbroken and devastated. I would never really trust her in the same way again.

That was the first time I experienced that kind of terror. Other mothers seemed to make their children feel better. Why was mine different? I watched the other moms cuddle with their kids, but my mom didn't like to touch. There were no snuggles before bed or lying together and embracing each other. She was not the kind of mother who held you when you were scared or gave you big mommy kisses. Was it my fault? Was there something wrong with me? As I grew up, I knew I had to make her happy, but why was that? In other families, the mom's job was to make the kids happy.

But not in our family. That was my job. And I knew I could do it. I was strong and I could make it happen. I had to be strong to take care of her and my brothers and sisters. If I could only keep things in order, maybe we'd all be okay.

Later that day she did another surprising thing. She came to the school at recess and apologized. The memory of the visit is fuzzy, but I remember her walking up to the playground fence and calling to me. I was startled to see her standing there, almost terrified. She had come to my happy place—the place I could play and enjoy being a kid in the world of kids.

"Honey, I'm sorry. I didn't mean to hurt you," she announced.

"Okay, Mommy." I trembled, but with some relief.

It was the last time she ever apologized to me. I believe she really did feel bad, but she also came to make sure I didn't tell anyone, especially my father. What I learned that day was that if I wanted anything that looked like peace and quiet, I had to keep her secrets. For self-preservation, I decided to keep her secrets, to behave, to try to do good in her eyes. If I did what she expected, maybe she'd treat me better. Maybe she'd treat me like the other moms treated their kids.

My mom was very concerned about the image she presented to the world. I made a silent bargain with her that day. We would switch roles. I would take care of her; I would be the protector and defender of her image to the world. That fall day I began to develop my skill in people pleasing, and I became very good at it. I learned to live for the approval of others but especially Mom. I learned to hold things in, to keep my reactions to myself. I learned not to cry, not to say anything, to pretend everything was okay, to pretend I was okay, so Mom wouldn't explode. I learned to repress my feelings to the point where I doubted my feelings were real. I felt I had no choice. I was just a kid, and I was stuck. An adult can leave, but a child cannot.

That hallway where my mother—*my mother*—threw me against the wall and hit me still haunts me. I remember its stark white walls and the front door to freedom only steps away. The safety the front door represented felt well out of reach.

My mother had two other children by the time I was five, with another on the way. I was the oldest, my little sister was one-and-a-half years behind me, and my little brother was still a baby. When I was three, we had moved into a community of starter homes in Farmington. The neighborhood was filled with families and kids our age. It was a great place for kids, and a happy time for our family. We neighborhood kids shared each other's swing sets. We played tag and hide and seek. We rode our trikes and bikes on the sidewalks and up and down each other's driveways.

This was a happy time for my mother and father, too. They truly loved each other, that much no one ever doubted, and there were only the beginning signs of the depression that remained undiagnosed in Mom throughout her life, along with the erratic behavior that resulted. Given what I have learned since then, I believe she was clinically depressed and if not clinically narcissistic, then at least very self-centered. We've also discovered that more than one family member has had to battle with depression and related disorders.

I think Dad still had hope then, hope that it was all going to be okay, hope that there was nothing really wrong with Mom—that she would learn to be happy. My mother loved my father and she loved us, but she was unprepared for the role of mother and the pressures of caring for a family. It was all too much for her. She was an only child raised on a pedestal, never really having to think about anyone but herself until she was married. And once she was married, she wanted more than anything to show the world she was the great wife and mother she thought everyone expected her to be. When she couldn't actually be that kind of wife and mother, she pretended she was, and expected the rest of us to buy into the act as well.

Although Mom seemed unable to take care of children, she continued to have babies. Maybe it was her Catholic upbringing. Maybe she thought it would keep Dad in the marriage. Maybe it was because she had grown up as an only child and didn't want that for her children. I'll never be sure.

Meanwhile, my father must have been feeling the demands that come from being the sole breadwinner and having to provide for a family with a not entirely reliable but demanding wife and partner in my mother. He also faced great expectations from his family, which was very competitive about status, wealth, and success. His parents always put my father up against his older brother (my Uncle Russ), who, as far as they were concerned, was the bigger success in all the ways that mattered. My father spent his life in insecurity and self-doubt, trying to prove them wrong, trying to prove himself worthy of his family's love and admiration. Dad would repeat this pattern between me and my sister Lori, who was a year and a half younger than me. Dad unconsciously created the same dynamic of the adored oldest child while my sweet sister Lori experienced the same pain he had experienced, which was created by the comparison with his own daughters. That was *his* journey, the journey to self-worth, the lesson his soul was meant to learn in this lifetime. I have been very careful within the pages of this book to include only those patterns within our family that have affected me through my perceptions, but my sister Lori thought this dynamic recreated in our family of origin (from my father's side) was an important part of our journey in which we have repeated unconscious family patterns that can continue for many generations. My father passed down the pain in his journey to Lori (his daughter that he loved dearly), and she unintentionally repeated this pain.

I believe Mom and Dad were both trying to be good enough in their own ways, and despite my growing fear of Mom's blowups, I was mostly happy in that home.

When they were together, they always made holidays special and birthdays too. Every Thanksgiving Dad would take us to the J. L. Hudson Parade in Detroit and watch the wonder on our faces while our little toes grew numb from the freezing weather. We came home to a delicious meal Mom prepared with such love and care. Then the next month on Christmas morning we woke to piles of presents under the tree.

I vividly remember the party Mom hosted for my seventh birthday in 1966. We rarely had company, but Mom put on a beautiful party that day. She had even invited all of my friends' moms.

I felt so pretty. I scrubbed myself in the tub, shampooing and brushing my pixie haircut to perfection (my mom found the shorter hair easier to take of). I wore a flared princess dress, which was pink and white and embroidered with the most delicate lace flowers. My lace socks were pink and white as well and folded perfectly over black patent leather shoes.

Our little house had everything in place. The white and pink decorations—paper flowers, streamers, the tablecloth and napkins—matched my dress too. Even the cake Mom made from scratch had white and pink flowers. She always made the most delicious frosting. I couldn't wait to devour it.

We had Pin the Tail on the Donkey already to go and Musical Chairs set up in the middle of the living room. As my friends arrived, they stacked their presents on the dining room table. Then we gathered together to play, running through the house with my favorite songs from the Archies and the Monkeys playing in the background.

I was so happy. The house looked the way I wished it looked every day. Mom was beautiful that day too. At twenty-eight, she still had a waistline that looked great in her poufy purple dress that had a Jackie Kennedy elegance. I could tell she was happy too. She had done it just right. It was as if we were all in the middle of an episode of *Leave it to Beaver*. I felt like all the other little girls that day, cared for and carefree, with no worries in the world. It was a party just like the ones my friends had.

Although Mom and Dad rarely took pictures, there are some of that party in black and white with my friends and I wearing our fancy dresses, each of us smiling with a child's delight. I cherish those photographs. I couldn't count on which Mom I was going to get most days, but that day she shone like a star. Birthdays and holidays brought out the best in her, and that was a party for the ages.

Mom could also be kind and loving when you were sick or in the middle of a crisis or a difficult childhood calamity. Most days, though, I just tried to keep the peace. I had to ignore or accept her rages. There didn't seem to be another choice. Because I never knew when the screaming and chaos would begin, I survived one day at a time.

When I was young, more babies kept coming and more chaos followed with each one. The more children, the more overwhelmed Mom became. Our home grew dirtier and more unorganized with each child. Mold grew on our toys. Dishes were left piled in the kitchen for days, crusty with old meals. The sponges in the sink gave off a rancid odor that lingered throughout the entire kitchen. Baths were more of a weekly than daily activity, and my sister, brother, and I were often very dirty. I had scabs on my head that hurt, sometimes to the point of bleeding, when I tried to comb my hair. The laundry piled up for weeks with a rank and pungent odor. We wore clothes for days before changing. We looked like children raised by wolves and often acted that way as well. We fought constantly with each other and had no manners to speak of. Babysitters refused to take us on.

Because our family was growing and Dad was doing well at work, when I was in the fourth grade we moved into a grand Tudor-style house in an upscale neighborhood in a beautiful area of downtown Detroit. Dad had put himself through Engineering school and worked while married to Mom and became partner in an ever growing automotive engineering company. We even had a nanny, Peggy, whom we kids loved, but Mom barely tolerated. I had the feeling Mom resented Peggy. I believe having her there took away my mother's privacy and her actions at home would be revealed to another adult. It had to be a relief to have help with the many needs that children and a home require, but it would be harder to keep the secrets, the secrets that Mom did not even want to accept herself. Because of Peggy, though, our house was usually in order in those days; we even had a housekeeper. Peggy was good to all of us, and I felt safe there and well cared for, as did my siblings. Mom had my youngest sister in that home, which brought us up to five kids total.

I was ten years old, and I still loved school—this time Gesu Catholic, a parochial school founded in 1925. It followed all the Catholic school traditions, including teaching nuns and uniforms and strict rules you didn't dare disobey. If you did, you received a jug slip, which meant you were sent to the head sister who gave you a paddling on your bottom. I remember getting one good one. I was hanging out with a few girls who always got in trouble. They convinced me to take the winning art project one of them wanted. The teacher yelled, "You're a follower, not a leader!" Was she trying to snap me out of people pleasing even back then?

I always felt put together at Gesu because the uniform was easier to take care of than a bunch of different outfits, and Peggy kept us on track with bathing and lunches and so on. I had so many wonderful friends at Gesu. Some of us walked to school together, and we gathered at recess and lunch hour to play games like tag and hopscotch and kickball. Boys and girls had separate playgrounds. At that age we didn't mind. Once again, school was a safe zone. I felt independent. All I had to worry about there was schoolwork and my friends. It was a glorious release.

I remember that being the happiest time in my childhood. We were all together, and Peggy ran things smoothly and kept chaos to a minimum. Even Mom and Dad were involved with the church, teaching Confraternity of Christian Doctrine (CCD classes), which was religious education for children and teenagers who didn't attend parochial school.

All that changed after the field trip.

Our school often went on field trips with other schools in the district. These trips were big deals for us kids. This one was to a park with a lake for swimming, so we were all in our bathing suits. There must have been twenty busloads of kids from all the neighboring schools. When the doors to the buses opened, we were off and ready to enjoy our holiday.

Sometime that day, my sister Lori and I ventured off from the group to walk on a heavily wooded trail that looked like it would be fun to explore. We still wore our cute little two-piece bathing suits. Some boys noticed we were alone and followed us. I didn't think too much of it, though they seemed a little older than we were—after all, we went to school with older boys.

They started talking to us, and at first it seemed as if they just wanted to have some innocent fun. "Hey, you girls wanna hang out?" said one of the boys in a sweet voice.

I thought it was cool they were treating us as if we were older. What kid doesn't want that?

Then he followed up with, "We really like your bathing suits. Any chance we could all do some skinny dipping?" His sweet smile turned into a leer.

Our early warning system went to code red. We backed away.

"You really are pretty," he persisted. "Why don't you show us what's under those bathing suits?" The group of them, about four or five, pushed in around us and raked us over with their eyes. They became more aggressive, and we grew full on scared. I maneuvered to keep my sister behind me, not sure in my innocence what they had in mind but trying to protect her from whatever it could be.

That's when they went after me.

"Come on, come here, don't fight it! Let's have some fun, baby."

One of the boys grabbed my now trembling body and pushed me to the hard dirt ground.

"Help!" I yelled. "Help! Don't hurt me."

They took turns touching me and pulling at my bathing suit. With all their attention on me, my sister was able to get away and run for help. Meanwhile, the boys tried to kiss me. Their hands went everywhere on my arms and legs, under my bathing suit. I tried to protect myself, but there were too many of them, and they were stronger.

Finally, I heard what sounded like a group of adults coming down the path. The boys stopped and backed away. Now that they were about to be caught, the sweet-talking one begged me not to tell. "We didn't hurt you, right. Tell them we were just playing around and having fun," he said calmly, using that sweet voice of his, as if I was his best friend. But in his eyes was a cold steel threat to do what he said.

The other boys were more scared, less in control, and looked at me pleading with their eyes. "We're good, right? We're all good. Nothing happened here. Don't tell. Don't tell. Don't tell."

Led by my sister, who someone had wrapped in a towel, several teachers emerged along the path. One came to me, and the others tracked down the boys who belatedly tried to run. The sweet talker just stayed where he was, brazen in his confidence that I would do as he said.

The teacher comforting me got another towel from someone and wrapped it around me in a cocoon. "Are you alright?" she asked. What's going on here?" She looked from me to the boys and back again. The sweet talker kept his eyes on me.

"I'm fine, please just let me go home." Now that I was safe, I broke down and sobbed uncontrollably, my whole body shaking. The teacher picked me up and carried me over to my sister. I collapsed into my sister's arms and cried and cried.

I couldn't bear to tell the teachers what happened in part because I didn't know what happened. I didn't have the words to explain it. Now, of course, I realize how badly I had been violated. Even though they were kids, I had been sexually assaulted. Although they didn't go as far as intercourse, these boys had taken something very fundamental from me—my safety in the world, my body, myself, my soul. I had lost control, and I had felt helpless and overwhelmed. I tried to fight back, but it didn't matter.

At the same time, not being in control was all too familiar to me. With the lack of boundaries in our family and Mom's volatility, I felt that way just about every day. I had learned to take whatever came my way without complaint, to take care of everyone in my life, including adults. I had learned to be the peacemaker, the people pleaser, the one who smoothed and soothed everyone's feelings but my own.

If the teachers hadn't shown up when they did, I wonder if I would have ever told anyone. Would I have listened to those boys' pleas to protect them rather than myself? I had taught myself to suffer in silence, a pattern I had already become used to living by. Thank God my sister ran for help and told those teachers what happened. I don't know if they were ever punished; all I know was that I never had to see those boys again, at least in person. The memory of them is etched forever in my mind, though I was able to bury it deeply for a long time. It was only after the sexual assault I experienced as an adult in Arizona that I remembered more consciously the assault I experienced as a child on a field trip. See what I mean about patterns?

I didn't realize how deep the wounds of that early childhood event went for me. As a child I didn't have the capacity to process what those boys had done, and my parents were little help. I knew they were upset when they learned what happened, that they were angry and afraid, but they didn't have the strength to face it themselves, let alone provide me the tools I needed to articulate and process what happened. Neither of them wanted to talk about it, but my father found it particularly difficult, me being his cherished oldest daughter. I always had a special role. No other adult ever talked directly to me about it either. During my childhood, the training to ignore my own emotions was well underway. I followed my parents' implicit instructions to avoid talking about awful experiences—to ignore them, to tamp them down, to try to forget them—well before I was molested on that spring day in Detroit.

Soon after the field trip, and at least partly because of it, we moved from that beautiful house (and nanny) that I loved in Detroit to an even more upscale neighborhood in the Rolling Oaks subdivision in the suburb of Farmington Hills. My parents felt the new home and neighborhood were safer than Detroit. Mom, for one, had never really liked Detroit as much as the rest of us had, and used her genuine concern for our safety to insist we move. Dad loved that Detroit house, too, and didn't really want to move, but at the time, he loved my mother more than the house and still wanted to please her.

That didn't last the year.

Chapter 3
THE PATTERNS TAKE HOLD

After we moved from Detroit, the family seemed to spiral downward, and life unraveled again. My mother just didn't seem to have the capacity to take care of us and the house at the same time. Today, as a sixty-something woman with children of my own (twins no less), I have compassion for what it takes to raise and care for children. My father was always working, and my mother was on her own. We didn't have a nanny in the new house, and given her disposition, Mom could no longer cope.

My mother was exhausted by life, numb and vacant inside, without the capacity to awaken. Simple everyday things overwhelmed her. She wasn't even able to care for herself much of the time, becoming more overweight and unkempt as her sadness increased. Many days she stayed dressed in muumuu-style pajamas. The house was filthy. Instead of doing laundry or cleaning, she laid on the couch, eating from assorted chocolate boxes and watching *Days of Our Lives* and *General Hospital*. I cannot remember much about what was happening with my younger brothers and sisters. It's still quite a blur. Mom certainly had a lot of responsibility with a two-year-old, a five-year-old, a seven-year-old, a ten-year-old, and me at eleven. My heart bleeds for Mom when I try to understand how overwhelmed she must have been.

I was in sixth grade, helped as much as I could, and tried not to ask much for myself. The more I helped out and did as I was told, the better life was for all of us.

As things got worse for Mom, she and Dad fought more and more often. My father didn't understand why she couldn't do her job as wife and mother, as he saw it. Other women did it just fine. What was wrong with her? I remember Dad doing the grocery shopping after a full day of work, and with my help, making sure the kids got something to eat and made it to bed at night.

Dad grew more and more frustrated with Mom. Not only was Mom not pulling her weight in the house, as my dad saw it, she wasn't very affectionate with him or me. She was closed off emotionally to Dad and to me. I can't speak to how my siblings saw it, but I felt that we were all lost in a spiral of sadness. Soon Dad looked elsewhere for affection and support. I pieced much of this together later.

Mom found out about Karen when she overheard them on the phone.

"Who were you talking to?" she yelled in fury.

I was home and could hear the explosion from the kitchen. Dad was upstairs. I heard him hang up abruptly.

"I knew you were seeing her. I could feel it. Who the hell do you think you are? We have five children. You fucking son of a bitch. I've given you everything. You're never here and now I know why. I hate you!"

The house shook with her anger, and I shook with fear. I wasn't sure whether to run or go and help her. This was much more than her normal everyday anger. This was pure rage. Her voice had hysteria I had never heard before. I could hear her pain.

"I can't take this anymore," Dad yelled, running down the stairs. "I'm leaving. And I want a divorce."

As he ran through the house, I tried to grasp what was happening. He saw me in the foyer as he made his way to the front door. He looked at me with such desperation, such compassion, because he knew he had to leave me there. Then he got into his car and drove away. I watched from the living room window, our security vanishing with the receding taillights.

Mom came running toward me like a mad woman, her rage bleeding through her skin in a color red I had never seen before. She was in such a frenzy that I didn't know what she might do next. I was scared.

"Do something!" she yelled at me. "Fix this. Make him come back!"

From an early age, it was my job to fix things. But Mom also knew I was Dad's treasured little girl. If he came back for anything, it would be me. I had a special relationship with Dad that she did not, the cherished oldest daughter. She wanted him to look at her the way he looked at me, to hold her the way he held me, to love her the way he loved me. I could feel the resentment from her. It was a deep, unconscious anger toward me that would manifest over the years in different ways. Maybe Mom kept having more children, so he would stay with her out of obligation to the children.

Meanwhile, she just wanted me to get him back. I was frozen in horror. I couldn't speak as she yelled, "Make him come back! Make him come back!" over and over.

He never did come back, though. I didn't even ask him to. It never occurred to me that I had a voice. He had escaped, and I was trapped there, eleven years old.

Things got a little hazy after Dad left. The next thing I remember is that Mom left as well, and Grandma, Dad's mom, moved in to take care of us. Grandma shopped for food and fed us. She did laundry. She made sure we showered and bathed, scrubbing the young ones herself. She brushed our hair. She made sure we got to school and bed on time. She cleaned that whole house, scrubbing down floors and walls, dusting, vacuuming. Best of all, she hugged us tight and told us it would be all right. All the things Mom never seemed to have the capacity to do. In many ways, it was a vacation for us.

Later I learned Mom had gone to seek help (I still don't know where), and she was prescribed Librium until she was able to accept what had happened. She never talked about that part of her life, and we never asked. Even as a child, I knew that she needed to grieve. We were all about to enter a new beginning, a beginning that would prove to be quite difficult for all of us.

After Mom returned several weeks later, it got even harder. Mom was devastated and heartbroken, angry and now severely depressed. She rarely got off the couch, and couldn't take care of herself, let alone her children. My father had worked all the time and had rarely been at home before he left, but he was our father and in his own way, he was there for us. He counteracted Mom's chaos and helped us feel somewhat safe. Once he was gone, everything went topsy turvy. We didn't know what we were going to eat one meal to the next, cereal mostly, which was easy for us to prepare on our own. Mom also taught me to cook a few basic dishes, like Sloppy Joes and hot dogs. Occasionally, Mom would come up for air and prepare a meal. She was a good cook when she put her mind to it, but these times were far and few between. The house became an unruly hurricane of destruction and chaos without any structure or order.

Karen, the woman Dad left Mom for, was his secretary at his engineering firm. I would visit Dad's office now and then. I was always so impressed with the many men drawing on the massive design boards, standing on stair steps to reach the diagrams and complete the automotive parts to perfection. This was before the invention of AutoCAD and other drafting software used from the 1950s to 1980s. Dad was always dressed in an impeccable suit each day as he sold his tools to Fischer Body, General Motors, Ford, and others. During my visits, I always enjoyed spending time with Karen. She ended up being the kindest woman Dad became involved with after Mom, but they never married. Dad needed a warm and loving woman to take care of him in a way Mom didn't. Karen fit the bill. That relationship was never going to last, though, because it didn't fit the patterns Dad was used to. Ultimately, Dad needed to be the one taking care of his partner, not the other way around. In the self-help literature, he was a classic codependent enabler—until he couldn't take it anymore and moved on.

Karen was kind to me, too, and took care of me to the extent she was able to as a not-quite-step mother. She understood what I had been through with the divorce, and the conditions under which I was still living with my mother. She saw me when I visited Dad. She asked me how I felt and what I needed. She listened when I spoke. She treated me like a child in the best sense. She nurtured me and comforted me. She taught me about hygiene and how to better care for myself. She didn't expect me to take care of her, to prepare meals, to clean the house, to fix things. It was a relief. Karen had three children of her own that she cared for so well. Watching her care for her own children warmed my heart.

At the same time, I felt guilty that I loved Karen and the normalcy she represented. I never spoke to Mom about my feelings for Karen. It would have been too painful for her. I would never have hurt her like that. Although I loved the peace and tranquility of my visits with Dad and Karen, I felt sad for Mom. I would never have left her for Dad. I had to take care of her. It was my destiny, my responsibility. That's what I believed with all my heart.

Not surprisingly, I found it hard to let go when my dad ended his relationship with Karen when I was thirteen. For years afterward I prayed they'd get back together, but of course they never did. I also prayed that he'd find someone else like Karen, but he never did that either. None of the women who came after Karen had her compassion and empathy. They all wanted Dad's sole attention for themselves. They saw me and my siblings as nothing but a threat.

People hurt others when they have so much pain it spills over. Mom was heartbroken and had been suffering well before the divorce. The divorce itself profoundly exacerbated her already fragile condition. She was wounded so deeply that she didn't have the capacity to see that she was destroying herself and the people she loved the most. Though I hated to see her suffer, there was nothing much I could do to help. I was just a kid.

Mom was the only child of a strong—some would say overbearing—mother who gave birth to Mom later in life. Grandma knew this would likely be her one shot at motherhood, and maybe that's why she did everything for Mom—spoiled her, really. Mom did virtually nothing for herself other than hanging out with her friends and attending school. She had no chores, no responsibilities, no siblings she had to share with. My mother told me stories over the years. If she asked for toys or clothes, she got them. Life revolved around my mother. Grandma took care of her every need. One day, Mom showed me her scrapbooks from high school and all the things her mother had saved for her over the years. I remember wondering what it felt like to get such attention from your mother. I don't think it ever occurred to my mother that I envied that attention, that I wanted to feel that special to her as well.

By the time I knew her, Mom's mom was an older grandmother, a slim, small woman, but formidable. She wore her silver hair up and was always impeccably dressed. She walked with an air of cold confidence. Like Mom, she didn't like touching and was not physically affectionate. I never remember her hugging me or putting me on her lap (though I do remember getting a few spankings from her). She never played with me. As with my own mother, I mostly just tried to do as I was told and keep her happy. I never felt very close to her, but I did know that she loved me in her distant, imperious way.

That's also how she treated her husband—Mom's father, my grandfather. Grandma ran the house with an iron fist, and she expected Grandpa to do as he was told. I remember him as a gentle and kind man, but Grandma was inevitably disappointed with everything he did. I cringed at the demeaning way she treated him, how she called him names, called him weak, scolded him as if he were a naughty child. Grandpa worked for Michigan Consolidated Gas, where he put in long days for little money delivering appliances throughout the Detroit area. He never complained, but escaped through alcohol, another pattern passed down through the generations of our family.

He treated me well, though. He was a jolly old guy with a big belly and a smile that made a rainy day sunny. He took me on long car rides, and we played games like checkers and Go Fish. He snuggled with me and held me with the kind of love that made everything seem perfect in the world. He was a wonderful grandfather, and I loved him very much.

Grandma's love was more complicated. She loved her grandchildren in a formal, abstract way, and I suppose she even loved my grandfather, but she aimed most of her love toward her daughter—my mother—and aimed is the right word, because she wielded love like a weapon. It was a smothering, all-encompassing kind of love that demanded reciprocation. If she was going to devote herself exclusively to my mother, then she expected my mother to do the same. That's why Grandma grew angrier and angrier every time Mom got pregnant and had another baby. Her grandchildren and her son in law were not what she had in mind for her daughter—they demanded too much attention and too much care. I think Grandma knew in her own way that she had not prepared my mom for what was necessary to raise her ever growing family. Grandma was concerned about her daughter's well-being and wanted Mom to have the ability to put herself and her own mother first.

Once Dad left, Mom was alone with us five children, and we were alone with her. Her mother had unconsciously crippled her by doing too much. Mom had never learned the tools to live the life she wanted to create for herself. She wanted to be taken care of, that was all she knew. She wanted a husband who would support her no matter what. My father did neither of these. He had needs of his own—for love, for affection, for companionship, for someone who held up her end of the bargain—that my mother couldn't provide. My father was not her father, who had essentially given up and given in to my grandmother and stayed in an unhealthy and dysfunctional home where he did as he was told and received no respect.

I know why Mom fell in love with Dad. He was kind, attractive, driven, and full of life, with curly brown hair, deep brown eyes, and a smile that lit up a room. He wasn't a large man, standing at five-ten and about one hundred and sixty pounds, but he dressed impeccably and carried himself accordingly. His crisp manner always reminded me of Johnny Carson. Dad was classy and at ease at fancy events and nice restaurants. He had become a master engineer and had started up several automotive design companies over the years. But he also loved to read and learn about a wide range of topics, especially those of a spiritual nature.

Dad had joined the army after high school and married Mom shortly after he mustered out at twenty-one, as they did in those days. As I mentioned, he put himself through college while working full time and having children. I was their first child, born less than a year after they were married.

Mom missed him for the rest of her life. In 1970, divorce was still rare. I remember the weight of sadness as I walked through the house, trying to be invisible while doing my best to comfort my siblings. The house felt so hollow and heavy with sorrow. I felt abandoned and alone after he left. Mom had a hard time even looking at me, her resentment of the love that she knew I would always have with dad was evident. I couldn't fix it. Would life ever make sense again?

I was also scared. Who would take care of everything? There was only one person who could—me! It was around this time that I fully bought into the idea that it was my lot in life—my duty—to take care of others at my expense. The victim martyr pattern took hold in my life with a vengeance.

I never blamed my father for leaving. Not really. It didn't occur to me to ask him (or anyone else) for an explanation. I never really discussed what I felt because I was learning that what I felt didn't matter. As an adult with two teenage children and after years of therapy, I now know that Dad fully and truly abandoned us. You don't leave five small children with an emotionally broken mother incapable of even the most minimal of childcare, but he did. I also have to acknowledge that it was a different time. Mothers almost always kept the children in a divorce back then, and Dad desperately wanted a different life, a happier life. Divorce was the only way to get that.

It might have been a happier life for him, but for those he left behind, it was miserable. Once he left, there was no one to monitor what went on. Mom rarely got dressed, and most days perched herself on the couch, from which she kept up a steady stream of instructions and insults directed at whoever would listen, but mostly at me. The house grew dirtier, with no order, only children to care for and meals to be made, tasks that fell to me by default. It was almost as if Mom was saying to my father, "Okay, big shot. If you're done, so am I." The rest of us were caught in the crossfire.

When Dad left, he also took his side of the family with him, so to speak. It's not that we never saw Grandma and Grandpa again, but it wasn't the same. When Dad was home, we always went to his family's house for the holidays, especially Christmas, when we eagerly headed there after opening presents from Santa at our house. Mom came to miss the big Italian family gatherings and not just because she had been an only child and enjoyed the excitement, but also because everything had been taken care of before we arrived. All she had to do was show up with her kids in tow and loose them upon the family. It was a break for her. Having said that, she loved everyone on Dad's side of the family very much and would always continue relationships with them in the years that would follow. With Dad gone, it was up to her to provide the festivities, and she was rarely up to it. We only rarely had guests in our home at that time.

But when we did, it was quite a show. I assume that Mom was clinically depressed—she was never really diagnosed—but every so often she'd get a surge of manic energy and want to do something magnificent. I was the oldest, so I would be her second in command, in charge of most of the preparations except for cooking. It was always important to Mom to maintain an image of respectability to the outside world, and I learned early on it was my job to assist her

I hated those days. They started at seven in the morning. "Get up. You have a lot to do today. Start with the upstairs, then I want the downstairs cleaned and the kitchen scrubbed down! You have to be done by four, so get up and get busy." She yelled these instructions at me with a frantic anxiety. "And you better make sure everyone has a bath and is dressed properly. Do you understand me? Get out of bed now!"

I remember a dinner with the Zukowskis. I was in sixth grade, and my younger brothers and sisters were too young to help, while the sister next in line, just one and half years younger than me, simply refused. She never took Mom's tirades seriously, just let them slide off her back. I could never do that, and Mom knew it. I wanted to please Mom. I wanted her to be happy. So I took it all on, letting the rest of the kids go on about their business. To this day, I get overstressed putting on parties, as if possessed by the ghost of my mother's anxiety, on the verge of hyperventilating until I know everything is perfect and then some. I've gotten better, but it still takes me unawares, a kind of manic fury to put on the perfect party.

Mom did the grocery shopping and cooking, while I attacked the house, which was about four thousand square feet and a complete mess. It was a long, exhausting day, punctuated by Mom yelling at me to hurry up. Periodically, she'd also yell out, "Why the hell did I agree to this goddamn dinner!" It didn't occur to her that it had been her idea in the first place.

The fury and rage continued throughout the time she showered and dressed, but when the guests arrived, the curtain went up and she assumed her role like an old-time stage actress—the dignified, gracious hostess for whom putting on a party like this was but a trifle. It was the image she wanted to show the world. How we treated the guests and what they thought of us and the now spic-and-span house was always more important than the hell we went through to get there.

Mom had met the Zukowskis in our starter home in Farmington. It was important to her to show them she had survived the divorce and earn the admiration she desperately craved for how well she was holding up.

Joe and Carol brought their oldest daughter Linda, who was seventeen. They arrived at six on the dot, and the house was in perfect order, the table set in the main dining room with every plate and glass in place, the aroma of garlic and tomato sauce wafting from the kitchen. My brother and sisters and I were clean and dressed; Mom had transformed herself into the elegant hostess straight from the pages of *Ladies' Home Journal*.

I set up the kids' table in the kitchen, making sure they were on their best behavior. Mom rewarded me by letting me sit at the adult table.

The dinner went off without a hitch. Joe, Carol, Mom, Linda, and I enjoyed the food and company in a calm, civilized manner, as if we were in the movies. After they left, Mom beamed from her great success, and I cleared the table and did all the dishes.

I hated the torment and craziness the days before we entertained, but I loved the order that followed, at least for a few days. For that brief time, we pretended we were a normal family. But that wave of good feeling didn't last, and once it crested, Mom was back on the couch, the house grew dirty again, and we were back to living in chaos. I never mentioned what went on behind our doors to anyone. It was almost an unsaid law that you kept the family secrets. Most families have done this for generations, and I think that should change. If we are allowed the grace of learning from each generation's experiences, there will be less shame and more growth in society as a whole.

During these years, I learned the victim and martyr role to perfection, and Mom was the perfect teacher. Our soul selves had chosen each other for the lessons we needed to learn in this lifetime, but it seemed neither of us were learning our lessons very fast.

My father was mostly absent after he left, but he was sure to pick us up every other weekend, a customary arrangement set up by the court in those days. But in the early days of the divorce, after picking us up, he intervened by calling CPS at least twice after he saw the filth we lived in and how uncared for we all were with our dirty hands and faces, our ratty uncombed hair, and our stained and wrinkled clothes, some of which didn't fit us anymore. It was apparent to Dad on these visits that Mom never really helped us with homework or gave us the opportunity to participate in any other activities kids participated in, such as after school sports, clubs, or trips to the library.

CPS was not set up the way it is now, however, so whenever they arrived, they just asked Mom a few questions, and she was able to pull it together long enough to charm them with her answers. The secrets behind our doors continued for years. (Eventually, two of the younger kids went to live with Dad, but that's their story to tell.)

I was never angry with my father for leaving me with Mom. That's just the way it was. The pattern of repressing my feelings and creating relationships with unsafe boundaries had been thoroughly established by then. I figured Dad was doing the best he could, and many times his best was enough. But Dad was one of my teachers too, and my anger came later in life when I realized how dysfunctional my childhood had truly been.

In some ways, Dad's leaving was good for Mom. It may in fact have saved her life. It took a while, but once he left, she was forced to live a little at a time. She spent less time on the couch. She had to get a job and began working in the insurance industry, eventually becoming an insurance adjuster. She knew she eventually had to prepare to sell the house that she and Dad had bought together and downsize. What she thought was a terrible hardship created a new start, a new life for her. She began to grow.

This growth did not happen quickly. There were a few years of deeper darkness and always a great deal of fighting with my siblings before and after Dad left. As children, we didn't know how to behave respectfully, how to dress appropriately, or how to care for ourselves. We didn't even know how to behave in a restaurant or use utensils properly. We had to negotiate so much chaos that we took it out on each other. Because I was often in charge by default, I took on some of Mom's habits toward my brothers and sisters, particularly the yelling to try to get them to listen. After all, she was my role model for parenting, and I was angry and frustrated at having to babysit. I couldn't play with my friends after school or do anything else on my own.

There is one memory I regret. I was frustrated that day, and the pain spilled over to my brother and sisters. I'm sure this was not the only time, but it's one I remember. I was upset that I was stuck in the house and couldn't hang out with my friends. The kids were all screaming and playing. The house was a mess, and no one was helping me clean up. All four of them were on the stairwell of our home staring at me as I began to unravel.

"Why can't you guys help me?" I screamed in the same tone I was accustomed to hearing from my mother. "Why do I have to do everything?" I think I even shook one of them as I yelled with the rage I felt inside. My little sister Michele must have been about seven or eight at the time. She looked at me without reacting. She has always had that ability and still does. She didn't let my rage spill onto her, but she looked at me with such disappointment, as if she was an adult I had let down.

That look triggered something in me. I didn't like it when Mom treated me that way. Why would I do it to anyone else? I realized I had to make sure I didn't repeat the same patterns. I knew I had to get help, but that would be down the road.

Dad moved into a small apartment so the rest of us could remain in the house where we went to school and had friends. We would remain living there for a few years after Dad left. It was a nice neighborhood, but we all still found a way to hang out with the kids that came from a similar upbringing. When Dad would take us for the weekends, he began bringing us into his new world, a world we were not used to participating in with fancy people and fancy clothes. We were not the kind of kids you took to high-class events or places. We were pretty rough around the edges. Dad wanted more for us though. He tried to prepare us for a better life by teaching us how to take better care of ourselves, how to behave in nice places, to be ladies and gentlemen. When we visited Dad every other weekend, it was as if we were visiting an exotic foreign land of country clubs and nice restaurants.

Though Dad enjoyed his new life (I think he spent much of his time living large and making up for lost time), he still loved to spend time with us. I remember hanging out in his apartment before any stepmothers came into the picture. Dad was happy and fun. He had no furniture to speak of and had stacked bricks up against the wall for his TV and stereo. He was learning the guitar, and he liked to play and sing for us, especially James Taylor and Carole King. I snuggled up to him. As he looked into my eyes with affection, he played and sang "You've Got a Friend" in the flattest, most out-of-tune voice you could imagine. Yet he made my heart sing with joy. Those songs still echo in the memory of my dad. I always knew Dad loved me.

My father ended up marrying and divorcing three more times. With each wife, he had a similar dynamic as the one he had with my mother. They were all attractive, and I believe he had a lot of fun with each of them—until he didn't. He seemed to choose women he had to take care of and jump through hoops to keep happy—high-maintenance women.

None of the stepmothers seemed to like the fact that he had children with my mother. They made us feel unwelcome in their homes. He would pick us up for our visits every other weekend, or I drove me and my siblings after I had earned a driver's license. The moment we entered the house, we could feel the energy thick with resentment. I didn't know until I was much older that the resentment was directed mainly toward me. I was a daddy's girl, probably because I was the oldest and Dad and I shared more time together before he left.

This was made clear when I graduated from high school. My mother gave me a small graduation party in our condo's clubhouse, the condo we move into when I began high school. I had on a white and red striped dress, and I felt pretty and grateful to have such a lovely party with the people I loved there to celebrate with me. Mom was happy that day, proud that her first child was graduating. Dad was there too, along with Priscilla, my first stepmother.

"Hi, Honey, I am so proud of you!" Dad said, embracing me tightly.

"Congratulations," Priscilla added curtly. I was accustomed to Priscilla's resentment, so it didn't ruffle me. She seemed put out by all the people at a party for me. Priscilla never had many friends. I don't remember any of my stepmothers having many friends.

Mom had served the cake, and it was time to open presents. Priscilla was pressuring Dad to leave. Dad jumped up, holding in his hand a beautifully wrapped gift. "Honey, I am so proud of you. I wanted to get you something you would cherish forever and so you always know how much I love you." Dad nervously handed me the gift.

"Wow Dad, this looks fancy." I felt Priscilla's daggers from across the room. I ignored them and looked deeply into Dad's eyes. I could see his determination to share this moment with me. I had won, at least for the moment. I opened the box. "Oh My God! This is so beautiful, so gorgeous!" I gazed in gratitude at the diamond pendant laid out on the silky cushion. I shook as I removed it and let Dad put it around my neck. He was shaking too. On the day of my graduation party, he chose me.

I found out later just what Dad had to go through to give me that pendant. Though he had plenty of money, Priscilla was livid that he wanted to give me a diamond. They had several knock-down, drag-out fights about it. I'm not sure why. Priscilla had several nice diamonds of her own. But she never really liked me, saw me as a threat for my father's affection, and always tried to put me in my place. They fought about anything that took Dad's attention away from her. Finally, Dad just went out and bought the necklace, but the emotional cost must have been high because it was the only piece of jewelry he ever gave me. As a result, it's one of my most cherished pieces. I still wear it proudly today.

Their marriage lasted about six years. It unraveled when Dad restructured his will. He was doing well financially, and she wanted him to leave half the money to her and the other half split among her extended family of ten siblings and his five children (us). My father planned to leave half to her and all of the remaining half to us, which he thought more than generous. She saw this as disrespectful of her family and never forgave him. To Dad's credit, he stuck to his guns, but this led directly to their divorce. Once again, Dad had to walk through the pain of divorce, and I was there to witness his pain.

Priscilla and Dad lived in an English Tudor house built in the sixties in an upper middle-class neighborhood outside Detroit called Huntington Woods. It had a Japanese garden in the backyard and the charm of old-world elegance. Priscilla had put her heart and soul into the splendor of their home, having decorated each room to perfection.

During their separation but before the divorce, Dad flew in from Atlanta, where Priscilla was staying in their second home. I picked him up from the airport. Dad was disappointed and sad. He loved Priscilla, and he didn't want to divorce. We both looked forward to hanging out at the house for a few days.

When I entered the house, I couldn't believe what I saw. Every picture of Dad's side of the family had the faces cut out, every trace of us cut away. The pictures still hung on each wall, with all our faces removed. The rest of the house was still in perfect order.

"Oh Dad, I'm so sorry." I had no other words.

This was too much for him, and he fell onto the living room couch. I sat next to him and held him as we both wept. His heart was broken, and my heart was broken for him. Priscilla was an unkind and spoiled little girl, but Dad loved her more than anyone. (It must have been true. He told me so the week before he passed away, when I'm sure he had many things on his mind. She was his long-lost love.)

Dad was a sensitive man, and like many of us in the family, he had trouble establishing healthy boundaries. He chose women who wanted all of him, who wanted to be the sole focus of his attention. I would have two more stepmothers after Priscilla, all with the same objective: to be sure they were most important in Dad's life. Each was broken in her own way, with empty places they couldn't fill on their own. Each wanted someone— Dad—to fill the emptiness by making her his everything.

As long as I was alive, though, that wasn't going to happen, not as deeply and completely as they wanted it to. I'm not saying that as a threat or a boast, merely as a statement of fact. My father loved me very much. I was his cherished oldest daughter, and we were very close, which was apparent to anyone who saw us together or heard us talk about each other. Except Karen, the other women in his life—including my mother— weren't secure enough to let this father-daughter relationship take its course. They made me the enemy, the reason for their unhappiness, and attacked me whenever and however they could, in word and deed, by talking behind my back, by making visits to my father frosty and difficult, by pitching a fit when he tried to help me out or buy me presents. I didn't know how to respond, so I simply let them have their way. I didn't fight it, in part because I was always the peacemaker, but also because deep down, I knew they were in pain. I didn't want to make it worse for them.

I love both of my parents. We were all trying to do the best we could with the tools we were given in our human form. I have come to learn how important it was for both parents to play the role they played in my life. They were my teachers, and sometimes our teachers can only get through to us by accompanying us through painful experiences. In my soul state, I chose my parents to help me break my pattern as a victim and martyr. I am not sure how many lifetimes I have had to try to learn this lesson, but I have a feeling that in this lifetime it just might work out.

The worst kind of victim is one who creates other victims. Even in childhood, I knew I had to change the cycle, though I wouldn't have known to put it that way then.

Chapter 4
ADOLESCENT ESCAPE

Since my mother didn't really pay much attention to us, when I wasn't watching my brother and sisters, I was pretty much on my own. As a result, I had some experiences about which my adult self simply shakes her head.

When I was twelve, for example, we were still living at the house Dad had left. My girlfriend Yvonne's family was putting on a church function at their place on a school night. They were all members of a hip Christian church, and this was an event for teenagers to worship and sing upbeat Christian music. Yvonne had invited about five of us to hang out. Since she had two older sisters, we were the youngest ones there. It was winter, but Yvonne's house was close enough to walk the mile or so in the brisk February weather.

When I arrived, some of the older kids told us they had a surprise. I had never really drunk much alcohol, but I'd been smoking cigarettes in front of my parents for months, and I figured the surprise was either cigarettes or alcohol. It turned out to be a real surprise: acid. My twelve-year-old self thought, *Well, this could be fun.* I had heard acid was a cool thing to do, but I didn't really know, since none of us had taken it before.

Yvonne's house was full of people, so that made it easier for us to go unnoticed. As all the older teens sang their Christian music, we went outside. Our friend Nancy handed out a pill to each of us. Excited and full of anticipation, we all took it without hesitation and swallowed it together. We wanted to be cool like the older kids. It was 1971, and we were ready to party like all the other hippie teenagers living free and tripping through the sixties.

When the acid hit me, I rolled with it. My body instantly became an instrument of acute sensitivity to every particle of life within me and around me. We stayed outside, dancing in the snow and making snow angels in the front yard while through the living room window we watched the sober teens sing their Christian songs. Each time I moved my arms and legs, the snow felt like velvet against my body.

We wandered around for hours, noticing every tiny detail—the threads in our clothes, the sparkle in the snowflakes, every star in the sky moving in perfect harmony. I felt an intense euphoria, a sense of well-being and happiness I had never experienced before. Everything was alive—the rocks, the ground, the trees, the house. It was all moving, pulsing with life, but I wasn't afraid. Everything was lighter and brighter. Every sound was enhanced. The emotional melodies of the Christian songs coming from within the house—combined with the sounds of nature outside, the crunch of the snow, our heavy breaths—seemed to affect me in a profoundly spiritual way. It felt good, so peaceful, so tranquil.

Then I noticed the time. It was after ten, and I had to get home. It had snowed quite a bit that day. The neighborhood grew dark and silent. I couldn't keep my balance and kept falling in the snow piles lining the streets. Every time I fell, it was harder to get up. I grew scared. I knew I had to get home out of the cold, or I could freeze to death. I was twelve years old, all alone, on acid, and I didn't know what I would face when I got there.

It seemed like hours before I made it, and truly, I don't know how I did it. I don't remember much of the walk, having fallen into a state of suspension, where my body was moving but my mind was far away. The kicker is that no one at home even noticed. They didn't notice when I got home. They didn't notice I was on acid. I don't even think they noticed I was gone in the first place.

I headed to my room to crash, but the effects of acid can last a long time, making sleeping difficult if not impossible. I was up all night tripping, tossing and turning, my mind strobing with strange thoughts and visions. It was the worst case of insomnia in history. The more I told myself to get to sleep, the more impossible it became.

I must have fallen asleep eventually, because all of a sudden, my alarm went off. I went to school that day as if nothing had happened. Nobody ever asked about it. My guides had certainly been watching over me that night.

You would have thought I had learned my lesson, but I did acid a few more times after that. I didn't make a habit of it, but I didn't say no either.

Other times, my friends and I weren't so lucky.

We had moved three times by the time I was thirteen and were living in Farmington Hills, Michigan, where I attended sixth through eighth grade. Dad had moved out about a year and half earlier. Mom was working, so we had a lot of unsupervised time at home. The other young teenagers in the subdivision knew we were often home alone, especially the boys.

On a half day off from school in 1972, I was home alone. I was thirteen years old. My younger brothers and sisters must not have had a half day because they were still at school. I invited a sweet girl, Maureen, to come over and hang out. Maureen lived just up the street in a house on a hill that overlooked the whole neighborhood. Her mom loved to decorate, so their house looked like a model home, always ready for show with everything in place.

Maureen was also thirteen, a short girl with long black hair. She was new to the neighborhood and quite shy. She was an only child and seemed protected and pampered. She dressed much younger than our age. She was not as streetwise as some of my other friends. I liked her, though. She was easygoing and comfortable to be around.

We were setting up snacks when the doorbell rang.

I opened the door. Three boys I knew fairly well stood on the stoop. "Hey, why don't we all hang out," the one named Rick announced. "We haven't met your new friend." Rick was heavyset and lived next door. His parents were rarely home, and he had a lot of time on his hands. The boy from across the street, Mark, had red hair and freckles that covered his tall lean body. Tony, a good-looking boy with blond hair, had a hardness from years of living with an alcoholic single mother. Once when we were hanging out at Tony's house, his mom was so intoxicated she laid all over us, mumbling incoherently. I always felt sorry for Tony. I'd never seen that kind of behavior.

The three were part of a larger group that hung out in the neighborhood. By reputation, they were bad boys, but I knew them to hang out with in the park or someone else's house. I wasn't afraid of them, but I knew Mom wouldn't want them in the house when she wasn't there.

"Come on Lynn," Tony said in a flirtatious manner. "No one's here. It'll be fun!"

I wanted to be cool, and I thought Maureen might have fun meeting some new kids our age, so I let them in. We were all sitting in the living room when Rick and Mark tried to convince me to show them my room. They explained it by saying Tony wanted to get to know Maureen.

Before I knew it, they ran up the stairs to my room. I hadn't said it was okay, but I figured it wouldn't be cool for me to resist. I followed them into my room, where I found them sitting on my twin bed against the wall. I sat down with them. We were just hanging out and talking when I heard a scream downstairs. I jumped up to see what was happening, but the boys pulled me back on to the bed, then began feeling me up and kissing me. I pushed them away, but they pulled me back to them. We sparred like this until I heard a real shriek of terror from below. The sound startled all three of us, and we ran downstairs.

"Please let me go!" Maureen screamed as she ran across the foyer.

Tony ran after her like a wild animal, tearing at her clothes.

"You'll be fine. Just go with it," Tony laughed. "Quit being such a little girl."

This was too much for Rick and Mark, who ran out of the house. They were afraid of Tony.

I screamed myself and tried to get Tony off Maureen. "Why are you doing this? You are hurting her! STOP!" I pulled as hard as I could to release her.

He slammed his arm across my face and knocked me to the floor. I wasn't strong enough to stop him. I needed help.

I ran outside and yelled, "Help! Help! Help me!" But no one could hear. The houses were far apart and most everyone was at work or school. I ran back in. Tony had Maureen's pants off. Then he raped her in front of me. I watched frozen in disbelief. I couldn't help her. She was such a shy girl, so innocent. She was in shock, and I think I was too. I didn't really understand what was happening and how horrible it must have been for her. Tony finished, then ran to the door. He turned back to us and hissed, "If either one of you tells anyone, I'll come back for both of you." He slammed the door behind him.

I held Maureen as she cried. We were both in shock. I think I must have blocked everything out after that because I don't remember anything else, no matter how hard I try. I must have walked her home, but I don't know. I don't remember ever seeing her again, either, as unlikely as that sounds. It saddens me that I can't remember. I still pray for her.

Later that day, my mom came home, furious. A neighbor had called her at work and told her I had a bunch of boys over and that Rick was one of them. She called my dad and had him meet us at the house. When Dad got there, they went next door and got Rick. Dad was furious. Mom must have told him she was sick of trying to control me and my siblings on her own.

All four of us were standing in the living room. "Why do you behave this way? Why are you so irresponsible?" Mom yelled as she looked at my dad with such anger. She didn't have to say anything to him. He knew that was a look that meant: *This is what you have done to us.* Then she said aloud, "I can't take care of all of these goddamn kids! This is all your fault. You take care of it. I've had it!"

He grabbed me and put me over his knee in front of Rick. I think he reacted just to calm Mom down. I remember watching Rick for his reaction. He knew what had happened that day. Would he try to help? Would he tell them that I had been through enough?

Rick didn't say a word. We were both terrified.

"If you want to act like a baby, we'll treat you like one," my dad said, humiliating me while Rick watched. He had to show Mom he could get me under control so he could leave and get back to his new life.

My parents never learned what really happened that day. I never told anyone. I'm almost certain Maureen never told anyone either, as it was never talked about again. I felt as if I had to shut up and take it, like so many times before. In my immature state of mind and with my own past experience on the field trip, maybe I thought this was just life, that this is what happened with boys and girls.

When I ran into Rick in the neighborhood after that day, I went blank, pretending nothing had happened. I gave up my voice, and this time it hurt another girl. I buried it deep down, something I was used to doing in my family. I will have Maureen in my heart forever, though, and I beg her forgiveness. I feel awful that I wasn't able to do more, and I hope she was able to heal from that terrible day.

Mom had to downsize, and we moved to our little condo in Novi, Michigan, where I began high school. In 1973 Novi was not upscale, and the kids were a rougher lot. I tried to fit right in, and I did.

There were two main groups in our school, jocks and freaks. Jocks competed in sports, of course, and ran most of the student activities—student council, the newspaper, the yearbook, and so on. The jocks were the "good" kids. I was a freak, which meant I didn't do sports or other school activities. We were the "bad" kids. We partied a lot and put on a tough and cynical face to the world. No one really messed with the freaks.

Most of us didn't have good family environments. Our parents didn't have either the time or inclination to be involved in our lives, so we made our own. Outside my mother's house, I felt free. I enjoyed myself and had good friends. They might have been street kids, but I felt safer with them than I did at home.

When I did come home, I never knew whether I'd face rage or peace. I was anxious a lot of the time, always walking on eggshells, not knowing what would set Mom off on any given day. My room was in the basement, and most mornings I woke up to Mom screaming from the top of the stairs "Wake up!" I hated being startled awake like that, starting off my day nervous and jumpy. (As an adult, I cherish peaceful, quiet mornings, and work hard to make sure I get them. I also always made sure my own children wake to a loving and peaceful voice each morning.)

During this time, Mom was working hard as an insurance adjuster, so I had to take care of my siblings after school. She didn't pay much attention to us, so we ran pretty wild, beating each other up, crawling out the window at night, drinking, smoking pot, doing other drugs. It never occurred to Mom that any of this was happening. She had experienced such a different upbringing than we did, with two parents who did just about everything for her, and relatively sound emotional security. She had been a good kid and never got in trouble. She never really checked up on us when she came home exhausted from work. She didn't even know what questions to ask.

Here's an example of how strange things were. My boyfriend Bill lived with us. I was fourteen, and my boyfriend lived with us! His family was abusive, and before he met me, he couch-surfed most nights to stay safe, crashing at this or that friend's house until he wore out his welcome, then moving on to the next. Once we were exclusive, he stayed at our house a couple of nights as part of the regular rotation, then sort of never left. Mom didn't really mind. Bill made life easier by doing the maintenance the rest of us didn't know how to. He slept on the couch—until Mom went to bed. Then he took off his shoes and sneaked down into my basement room. It was a comfort to both of us.

The basement also gave us the privacy to grow pot. Bill was the school dealer. He even supplied some of the teachers. We set up seed planters in the closet and the lights they needed to grow. After the seedlings matured, we put them in the bay window in the living room so they could flourish in the sunlight. The window faced the lot where our neighbors parked their cars.

"What kind of plants are those?" my mother asked Bill once. She appreciated how green and healthy they were and how they spruced up our home.

"Aren't they great?" Bill said with pride. "They're called Sweet Williams." It was all I could do not to crack up laughing.

About a month or so later, one of the neighbors came over while Bill and I were out and asked Mom why she was growing marijuana in her front window.

"What, no, that can't be marijuana," Mom said.

"That's marijuana."

"I don't believe it!"

"Virginia, believe what you want. I'm just letting you know," the neighbor said. "They're not my kids."

"I'll talk to them," Mom said, turning shades of purple once she realized the neighbor must have been right.

Bill and I arrived home shortly after. Mom laid into us right away. "What the hell are you goddamn kids growing in my living room window?"

"It's Sweet William, Mom, just like I told you." Bill called my mother "Mom." He always knew how to play her.

"Get that shit out of my house now! I know what it is."

And that's the last we discussed it. She loved having Bill around and didn't want to chase him away.

I was still toying with drugs, and back then you could get anything you wanted at our party spot, the Hill in Hines Park. Hundreds of kids hung out at a time, so many the police had to bring a paddy wagon when they raided the place. In all the time I spent there, I always managed to avoid the round up, thank God. I was a good bad kid, and never had trouble with the police.

The Hill was a virtual drug store, where you could get pot and pills, acid, anything really. One day Bill and I decided to take Quaaludes, a popular drug in our crowd. I must have been about fifteen. Quaaludes are downers, not hallucinogens like acid. They mellow you out, put you in a relaxed, euphoric state. We took them at school, and it mellowed me out so much I fell asleep on my desk. Neither the teacher nor the principal could wake me up. Someone called Mom, but she couldn't leave work, so Bill took me somewhere to sleep it off—probably the Hill—then took me home. When I stumbled through the door, Mom was lying on the couch watching TV. "I'm going to take a shower," I slurred.

"Make sure she doesn't fall," she told my brother Donnie, her only acknowledgment that she knew what I had been up to. I don't know what she said to Bill, but Mom never talked about what happened. That was our MO. There were many such incidents with me and my siblings that she chose to ignore rather than address. It was easier to ignore it. That was the family way.

One thing Mom didn't ignore, though, was that sometime after this, she came home from work early and found Bill and me having sex in the living room. She kicked him out, slapped me across the face, and in general went a little berserk. She called Dad, which she always did when she didn't know what to do with me. Dad showed up with love and compassion. We sat in his car, and he told me how natural it all was. He calmed me down, helping me feel that I wasn't the worst person in the world. This was probably not the outcome Mom was hoping for, but Dad always understood me and knew what I needed.

Mom never let me see Bill again. He eventually found another girlfriend, and I was devastated. This was my first heartbreak. I didn't eat for weeks. I'm grateful that my first sexual experience was safe. We were both virgins and very much in love.

Though part of me enjoyed the escape of drugs, another part knew I was spiraling out of control. I was angry much of the time and taking it out on my brothers and sisters. I knew I had to reach out and get out. Through a high school friend and by the grace of God, I found a counselor when I was around fourteen. When the student is ready, the teacher appears, and I was ready.

Greg Young changed my life.

Greg worked at a state agency with no cost, so I could go on my own. Before I got my driver's license, I hitchhiked there. Back then, it was common to see hitchhikers on the side of the road, and I hitchhiked all over. Sometimes I crawled out my window late at night and hitchhiked to wherever the party was. I had no fear.

After Mom saw the impact Greg had on me, I persuaded her to get into counseling as well. We worked with Greg independently and together during my high school years. Mom stuck with him for several years afterward, about eight years in total. Greg helped my mother work hard at growing and healing her pain. I'm sure Mom's work with Greg made life better for my two younger sisters after the three older siblings left the house. He even worked with our whole family together, including my dad.

One session Mom and I attended together had a lasting impact. Greg asked us to stand up on either side of the room and walk slowly toward the other. We looked at each other in bewilderment. How in God's name could this be valuable? But we trusted him, so we shrugged and stood up awkwardly. The room was small and dingy, by no means a fancy counseling office.

As I walked toward Mom, one heavy foot in front of the other, I felt a surge of adrenaline. I had no idea what to expect.

"Lynn and Virginia, put out your arms," Greg said with encouragement.

"What are we supposed to do?" my mother asked, her voice quavering.

"Trust me," Greg said with compassion. "I'm here. When you get nearer to each other, I want you to reach out your arms and hug one another."

As we moved in closer, we both began to weep. We were so uncomfortable and emotional at the same time. Greg guided us with his hands closer and closer until we embraced in the most divine hug. I felt a deep love and warmth for my mother I had never felt before. For a moment, I saw her as the full human being she was, with all her strengths and weaknesses, her desires and disappointments. She wasn't just my mother. It was also the first time I remembered my mother hugging me. That alone was earthshaking. She wasn't a physically affectionate woman. She didn't like to touch—that's how she was raised. (My Dad always joked that they only had sex five times in twelve years, once for each kid. I always found that a very sad joke.) I can only guess what Mom was thinking, but she was crying too, and I hope it was something like this—that she missed being able to hug me, that part of her liked that physical closeness, and that she would try harder in the future. She actually did try harder, but physical affection was never easy for her, and she still doesn't like to touch all that much.

I worked with Greg for about four years. He helped me make better choices and learn to care for myself—learn that I was worth caring for, a lesson I've had to learn over and over again. I had been headed toward a life of drug abuse and relationships with damaged people, but Greg pulled back the curtain on a different way to live. Greg would also show up many years later in Scottsdale. He had moved there shortly after I did and was there with open arms after my assault. He was certainly a pivotal guardian angel in my life.

In elementary school, I received Cs and Ds since I had no academic guidance at home. By middle school I was old enough to manage my studies on my own, and I always received good grades throughout high school.

I never participated in activities other than school until I began working at fourteen years old. I landed my first job at a fast-food burger joint called Burger Chef during ninth grade. I loved being independent and away from the house. It wasn't work to me—it was a place of refuge. And they paid me! During school, I picked up a job helping the administrative staff in the front office. They thought I did such a good job that they recommended I work in the school board's offices after school as part of a co-op program. I worked at the school board for the next three years. I loved working there. It was another place of peace and refuge.

I know the board members sensed the turmoil I lived in, and they embraced me with love and guidance, opening many doors for me. I learned to type, to file, to answer phones and greet visitors, skills I used throughout my career no matter what job I held. They were wonderful examples to me, showing the difference people can make in the life of a child. (Later in life I paid it forward by reaching out to young people in the same manner.)

Other than classes, I didn't participate in school activities or programs. With Mom working full time, I had to be home to care for my brother and sisters whenever possible, and besides, freaks didn't do that sort of thing. It wasn't cool. I never went to a football game or an assembly.

This led to an embarrassing moment.

The school board wanted to acknowledge me for my work in the co-op program, and the school accepted their recommendation to give me an award. Awards like these were always kept as a surprise to the recipients. Without my knowledge, the board invited Mom to attend the awards assembly. She took the day off from work and took my four siblings out of school as well so they all could be there. It was the first time I was to be recognized for anything, and the first time Mom had a reason to attend anything I was involved in.

Novi High School had a large gymnasium that doubled as an auditorium. Hundreds of people attended the end-of-year awards ceremony, including the staff of the school board, who had taken time out of their day to see me get the award they recommended me for. My mom and siblings were excited to surprise me that day. They sat in the bleachers in anticipation, applauding each of the other students as they received their awards as they awaited my appearance.

"We will now honor the recipient of our award of achievement in Co-Op. She is being recognized for three years of outstanding service in support of the school board. Lynn Oliveto, can you please come and collect your award?" The speaker echoed loudly throughout the auditorium.

Then again. "Lynn Oliveto, please come to the stage."

My family and the staff who had guided me so lovingly over the last three years all stood clapping, eager to share my triumph at the award and my surprise that they were all there.

But I never went on stage to collect the award.

I didn't go onstage for a very simple reason.

I wasn't there.

I wasn't there because I always skipped assemblies and hung out with friends instead. That day I went to a park where we hung out, smoked cigarettes and pot, and drank beer. I always made sure to get back to school in time for my next class, but this time when I arrived, I saw that the assembly hadn't let out yet. I figured I'd wait outside the door, then mingle with the crowd when they came out, and no one would know I hadn't been there. My plan was blown though when I saw the jarring image of my mother and brother and sisters (what were they doing at school?) talking to the group from the school board. And suddenly, I put it all together—I must have gotten the co-op award. Shit, I said to myself. I stuffed a breath mint in my mouth to cover the smell of beer and cigarettes. Then I went in to face the jury.

They were all less angry than disappointed, and in many ways that was worse. I was mortified. I had let down all these people who cared for me and loved me. They wouldn't even let me explain, and rightfully so. There was no real explanation. So much for my first and only school award.

I never got punished. Although they were disappointed, my mom and the school board staff just laughed about it. They said things like, "Only Lynn" or "That's our girl!" They all knew very well that I didn't participate in the normal high school stuff. Even today, when it comes up, my mom and siblings just laugh and shake their heads.

At sixteen, I was already on my third serious boyfriend, Jimmy. The second had been Brian, a caring and loving boy. We were together about a year until I broke his heart. Brian was a few years older and had a full-time job. I remember spending a lot of time in hotel rooms. We checked in around 6:00, I went home at curfew, then I crawled out my window and spent the rest of the night with him until I crawled back in before everyone woke up in the morning.

Mom was married to Frank by this time. Jimmy and I had been together since I was fifteen. Frank had been living at our house before the wedding. She was sure to have him sleep on the couch, just like my boyfriend Bill had—well, at least until we went to bed, like mother like daughter. She was adamant about showing a good example in this regard. Mom dominated

Frank the way my grandmother dominated my grandfather. He was always gentle and kind to me, though, quiet and in the background. He didn't affect my life very much.

My boyfriend Jimmy was from Brightmoor, a rough area in Detroit, and had been homeless off and on since the age of ten. He was eighteen then, with long blonde hair and a muscular slim build. He lived in our basement for six months before anyone noticed, largely because the laundry room was in the basement, and no one in the house spent much time doing laundry except me. Jimmy climbed in and out of the basement window I had been using for years to sneak out at night.

Jimmy and I were in the basement, Jimmy brushing his teeth at the utility sink in the laundry room. I was doing something in the bedroom Frank had built for me. Frank was always great at building things. The condo was small, so the extra room was just what we needed to provide enough bedrooms for all of us. Our modest condo had three bedrooms upstairs. At that time, my two younger sisters lived with us, and Mom and Frank had just had a baby, Michael. My other brother and sister lived with Dad.

Frank came clomping down the stairs. "Lynn!" he called out. "Lynn! Where's your mother's white shirt? Did you wash it yet?"

He headed toward the laundry area. My heart did a triple loop when I heard his voice. I dashed out of my room, but it was too late.

"Oh, Hi Christine," Frank said to the back of the person standing at the sink. My friend Christine had spent the night, and she had long blonde hair like Jimmy, who was brushing his teeth with his back to Frank. But Jimmy was taller, and Frank quickly realized his mistake. "What the hell are you doing down here?" Frank yelled.

Jimmy must not have heard him come down the steps over the noise of the toothbrush. He startled like a rabbit, dropped the toothbrush, jumped into the laundry sink, scaled the wall, then went out the window as quickly as his limber young body could scamper.

I got kicked out of the house for that one. The family hated that I was seeing Jimmy, terrified that he'd steer me in the wrong direction. The fact that I had lied for so long and so blatantly enraged Mom more than ever. She had reached her limit of tolerance for the way I lived however I pleased. I stayed with other friends for a bit, then moved in with Jimmy in Brightmoor, a dangerous part of Detroit where he had grown up. There were motorcycle gangs everywhere, and the streets were lined with bars and pool halls. Most people were just a paycheck away from being on the streets if they weren't already living there. It was not uncommon to find people over dosing on the street from heroin or other drugs.

My father and mother were shocked that I moved there of all places, but Jimmy adored me. We moved into a small, beat-up home in his old neighborhood. I cleaned it up the best I could to make it comfortable. I had finished high school by then and got work as a secretary for a small company called General Binding. Jimmy worked as a janitor at Novi High School, the high school that I had attended. We made enough to get by.

Despite that rough Detroit neighborhood full of crime and tough realities, we were happy there. I don't ever remember having an argument with Jimmy. It was the first time in a long time I didn't have to wonder what would greet me as I walked through the door. I could care for myself without the distractions of a needy family. I felt safe. My counselor Greg had even encouraged the move. I controlled my life there and how it would unfold each day. I was on my own, independent, learning how to navigate the world as a young adult, and it was glorious.

Living in Brightmoor was lifechanging in another important way because I saw real hardship there firsthand. Despite my personal pain, I realized just how much I had to be grateful for, that I was blessed with much that others didn't have. In our family, for example, we didn't have to worry about the necessities of life—money, food, or shelter. I had had a warm bed to sleep in every night, food in my stomach (even if I had to prepare it myself), and a family who loved me, however dysfunctional we may have been.

Jimmy, on the other hand, had been more or less homeless since the age of ten. His mother had died when he was young, and his father was a late-stage alcoholic whose wife was just as broken, so broken she peed on herself when she was drunk. Shortly after she gave birth to their baby, I walked into the baby's room to check in and saw a huge rat in the crib, which I chased away by stomping and waving my hands. I comforted and fed the baby as often as I could, but there was only so much I could do, since he wasn't mine.

To this day, my family remembers Jimmy as messed-up, but in his family, he was the normal one, the best of them. Child Protective Services found a foster home for Jimmy during part of his childhood, which helped him to overcome some of his hardships. Jimmy was one of the dearest and kindest men I've ever known in my life. He had had a tough road, but he was a gentle and loving person. He adored me and showed me in so many ways—by listening to me talk about my day, by holding me safe in his arms, and by taking care of things around the house. I felt easy with him. I didn't have to be on my guard all the time. It was a revelation.

When I still worked at the school board, Jimmy picked me up there every now and then, so the folks in the office got to know him. It didn't take them long to learn he was an abused and neglected young man. They had compassion for him and helped him get the janitor job at the high school.

The people of Brightmoor lived in constant crisis and most didn't know any different. Teenage pregnancies and drug addiction were common. Many never graduated from high school. The home that Jimmy and I created together became a kind of waystation for the lost and damaged. People stayed with us when they were evicted or lost their jobs. Teenaged moms arrived at our door when they couldn't afford diapers or food for their children. Those who came to us shared many sad stories of abuse, addiction, and incarceration. They may have been broken, but they still had life to live. They were funny, smart, vital people brought down by the pain of their circumstances. Without even thinking about it, we created a community of everybody helping everybody else. I wanted to share what I could with those who had grown up with so much less than I had.

This experience opened me to the idea of service, of helping those less fortunate than I, of reaching out to heal others in pain. This has always been a strong purpose in my life, but at the time, I didn't consciously know what I was doing, nor could I have articulated it clearly if you had asked me. All I knew was that my soul recognized the pain and suffering in the souls of others, and I wanted to do what I could to help them heal. It was the first time I felt as if I was in service to those more vulnerable than myself, and it felt good. I will be forever grateful for my experiences in Brightmoor. They took me out of my own pain and taught me to reach out to the pain in others.

I had moved to Detroit to start a new life, my life, and a life with Jimmy, who asked me to marry him on a summer day in 1978 in front of his whole family. I was nineteen years old and newly graduated from high school. We had been dating for about two years. Jimmy and I were visiting his father, who had abandoned him years before. The living room reeked of urine and stale whiskey, the aura of poverty and addiction thick in the air. His father was a thin man with the lines of alcoholism etched deeply in in face. His stepmother was anything but a mother, heavyset and unkempt to such a degree it was difficult to look at her for long. Jimmy's brother Gordie was a heroin addict, thin and broken, but he had a kindness within him. Gordie's wife was also an addict and had one child after another they could not afford. It broke my heart to see the pain she was in and the pain she inflicted on her beautiful children as a result.

In front of his father, his stepmother, his brother, and his brother's wife, Jimmy surprised me by going down on his knees. "Lynn. I love you so dearly. Will you marry me?" he said with excitement and anticipation, and perhaps a little fear that I might say no.

I hesitated, caught off guard. "Ye-es," I responded. "Yes, of course." I had to say yes, though I hadn't pictured my wedding proposal this way, and though I loved living with Jimmy, I wasn't quite ready to make it permanent. I knew how desperately he loved me, though, and I didn't want to break his heart, especially in front of his family. Deep down, I knew marriage to Jimmy wasn't for me, even as I gave him a big hug and accepted his family's congratulations.

When I worked up the courage to tell him I couldn't go through with it, he was heartbroken, with the air of someone who saw the best thing in his life fading away before his eyes. He said he understood, and that deep in his heart he knew I couldn't stay in that life, that I would go in a different direction, that it had just been a matter of time. He knew I wanted more than Brightmoor—that's part of what he loved in me—as did I myself. I knew I was capable of more. There was a wide world out there, and I was strong enough and smart enough to make something of it. I just didn't quite know what that was yet.

My father thought so too, and on a pivotal day in July 1978, he came to the rescue. This was the time he still lived in the Tudor house in Huntington Woods with Priscilla. He had seen the ring before I had a chance to give it back to Jimmy. It broke his heart to see the direction my life was going. He knew there was no time to waste.

Dad was so determined, he visited me in Brightmoor, though he really didn't like to. He walked into our tiny beaten down living room with some old furniture my sister's boyfriend's parents had given us. A lime-green velvet couch laid up against the cracked and battered walls, but I made sure the house was always clean and orderly. He hugged me tightly with a look of nervous anticipation, then carefully found a place to sit on the couch. He held himself erect, as if he had something important to say but wasn't sure how I would take it.

"Lynn, I have a proposition for you," he said.

I looked at him with my I'm-listening face.

He cleared his throat and went on. "What if I bought you a whole new wardrobe of clothes?"

"Why would you do that?" I said doubtfully. I knew he was up to something.

"Well, there *is* one tiny catch. I'll buy you the new clothes..." he said drawing out the suspense, "... if you go to college."

I looked at him wide-eyed.

"I'll pay for it, since it's my idea." Dad was doing quite well at the time, and he was determined to get me out of Brightmoor. "Well, one other tiny catch. I want you to visit Cousin Donnie in Atlanta for a while. I'll pay for that, too."

An all-expenses paid trip to visit Donnie, whom I adored and who lived in a style to which I could grow accustomed? I could go for that. I loved hanging out with Donnie (actually my second cousin, since he was my father's first cousin). He was always one of my favorite people.

Out of pride, I held out for a bit, but soon agreed to Dad's proposal.

Donnie was a gorgeous man and had a personality to match. He drove the hottest cars and looked perfect driving them. Donnie respected those who worked hard and became successful as a result. He surrounded himself with those who shared the same values. Some of his closest friends had tremendous success, such as the founder of Pier One and Home Depot.

In Atlanta, Donnie took me shopping at all the high-end stores and to the nicest hotels and restaurants, all the while saying things like, "You'll never have any of this if you don't make a serious shift in your life. College is the first step."

Dad and Donnie had ganged up on me, but they didn't have to twist my arm too hard. I was ready for a change. Living in Brightmoor had given me a taste of freedom, but it was a constricted kind of freedom that came at a cost. After living in Brightmoor for over a year, I said goodbye to Jimmy and his family, and left for Western Michigan University in Kalamazoo. It was about three hours west of Detroit, but as far as I was concerned, it was on the other side of the world.

One of my favorite songs growing up was, "Ooh, Child," by the Five Stairsteps. I listened to the lyrics all the time, like a mantra: "Ooh child / Things are going to get easier / Ooh child / Things will get brighter // Someday, yeah / We'll put it together and we'll get it undone / ...Someday, yeah / We'll walk in the rays of a beautiful sun / Someday when the world is much brighter..."

Someday had come. The world was much brighter. I was going to college, and it probably wouldn't have happened if I hadn't set out on my own to live in Brightmoor with Jimmy.

Jimmy came to see me years later in Phoenix, 1985 I think. He just showed up at one of my properties. A friend from high school had told him where I was. He was still sweet, but I had already made a life with a boyfriend and a career. I told him he could stay in one of our furnished units for a week or so. I had to leave that week for a business conference in Atlanta, so I only saw him a day or so. I think he hitchhiked back to Detroit after that. It had been his last-ditch attempt to win me back. I felt bad, but my life had changed so much by then that I was embarrassed about him a bit. Many of my employees and residents at the property were surprised by his rough and uneducated nature.

Chapter 5
LIFE INTERRUPTED

My time in Brightmoor had turned me into more of a street kid. When I first arrived in Kalamazoo for college, the other students seemed like dainty little princes and princesses, while I was more independent and self-reliant. I felt as if I had gone back in time to a childhood that had passed me by long ago. Most of the other students had never lived on their own, and though I was the same age as they were, I felt much older and found it difficult to relate to their "immaturity."

Then one day I woke up and looked around. What did I see? Disneyland for young adults. More than 20,000 kids my age lived within a two-mile radius, and all we had to do was play and go to classes! Compared to Brightmoor, this was paradise, and once I saw it for the gift it was, my attitude and life did a one-eighty.

College was a blast. My friends called me Mary Tyler Moore I walked around so happy, as if I was throwing my hat in air and dancing on the sidewalk. In college I was free. I loved school and I loved being away from home. For the first time in my life, it was all about me. My family lived over three hours away. I didn't have to clean the house. I didn't have to watch my brothers and sisters. I didn't have to prepare meals. I didn't have to make sure my mother was happy. I didn't have to do anyone's laundry but my own. I went to class, studied, and got great grades, I picked up some waitressing jobs for cash, and I still had plenty of time to play. I was so happy there.

If Brightmoor had shown me how to be independent, college showed me how to be independent and happy. I had a whole new beginning, and

I swore I wasn't going back to the way it had been with the unhealthy family dysfunction. No way! I loved them all dearly, but I knew that to take care of myself, I had to be on my own.

I graduated with a Bachelor of Business Administration with a minor in Marketing and kept that promise of independence to myself by moving directly to Arizona after graduation, with no job, no car, and no money to speak of. Why Arizona? I just knew I had to move to there. I was drawn to Arizona. My soul knew. And as a bonus, it was sunny all year round and two thousand miles away from family expectations.

In no rush to start a career, I got a job waiting tables at a fine restaurant in Phoenix, the Hungry Hunter, with a great live band, many regulars, and a staff that replaced my family. I rented a furnished studio apartment across the street, and since I had no car, it was perfect. For work I wore a spandex leotard and a tight skirt. We were expected to flaunt it, and I did. I didn't mind. I was young and attractive, and I made great money and had a lot of fun. We worked hard and played hard, meeting up after work and on our days off for drinks and dancing. I had had enough of the drug life in high school, so I stayed away from drugs and didn't drink much either. I had fun being on my own, in charge of my own life. I was high on freedom.

After about a year in Phoenix, I figured it was time to put my business degree to work. I had thought about what I wanted and concluded that corporate America wasn't for me. After years of servitude to my mother and father (as it seemed to me in my twenty-something state of mind), I knew I wanted to work at my own pace, as if I ran my own business. At the same time, I didn't have enough capital or experience to invest in my own business yet. I settled on property management, which had several benefits: I could always live on site, which gave me free rent and an easy commute, and if I took positions at properties with out-of-state owners, I could work at my own pace without someone always looking over my shoulder.

I started at the bottom as a leasing agent and quickly moved up to general manager of apartment communities. I obtained my real estate license and was excited about networking my skills in the community and moving up the property management ladder. I have always been good at reading what others need; working with employers had always come easy. I have never been fired, written up, or involved in controversy. I was the perfect employee and people pleaser, a role for which my family had prepared me well. But now I was using those traits for my own good. And it was good. I was riding high, managing my own apartment complex, ready to conquer the universe. But the universe had other ideas.

That's when I was dragged into the desert by a masked stalker and raped, the fallout from which took me years to recover.

When I reached my apartment after the assault, I was virtually catatonic for I don't know how long. Then I shook myself out of it. I had to report the rape; I knew that much. But I couldn't call the police. He told me not to, that he would know if I did, and he would come back and kill me. I called a close friend, Chris, and she called the police. My roommate, Judith, arrived shortly after, and I told her what happened in my state of hysteria. Then the police, my friend and her family, and my boyfriend Tom followed.

I don't remember much about those conversations and how much I was able to tell the police. I do remember one question. "How was he able to get in young lady?" one of the police officers asked.

"There is no evidence of forced entry," another officer said in an accusatory tone.

"We leave the sliding door open when we're leaving just for a few minutes. I was coming right back," my roommate explained. Then she shook in horror when she realized she might have been responsible.

It was clear from the officers' tone they thought we had been irresponsible, that we could have avoided this. I grew angry at their implication.

So many victims over the years have been blamed for their rapes, blamed for what they were wearing, what area of town they were in, what they did or did not do. I hope we, as a nation, have come farther since the day of my rape. Rape is never the fault of the victim. No one has the right to violate anyone for *any* reason.

While the police asked their questions, I realized the rapist had stolen my purse with my ID and all my keys, including the master key to the 500-unit apartment community I managed in a tough part of Phoenix. I grew even more frightened when I realized he knew where I worked, and now he had a key to the apartments of I didn't know how many other women he could stalk and make his next victims.

"He'll hurt other women," I said, my voice rising in pitch as I spoke. "He knows where I work. He has the master key. He has the master key!" I repeated, hoping to get through to them.

I don't recall their response, only that they tried to calm me down so they could get on with their job.

To my surprise, the officers had no trouble finding where he had taken me. To me, the desert had been so vast and dark, I didn't think anyone would find it. They also found the ankle bracelet that had broken off in the desert. They looked closely for other clues. I thought if they could find the bracelet, they could find him, right? They could stop him from hurting other women. He had gloves on and a mask, though. How much could they do to find him? Did I tell them enough? Could they identify him?

These kinds of questions bounced around my head like a ping pong ball.

I'm not sure who took me to the hospital, but once there, I became another rape victim who experienced the humiliation of a rape kit. Everything seemed a further violation—the medicinal smell of the hospital, the rattle of gurneys, the glare of the bright lights. My exposed body trembled in the stark, cold examination room where the speculum entered my body to pry me apart and collect "the specimen," as they called it. The specimen? To me it was pure evil, the rapist's mark, and it left me feeling dirty, empty, and achingly alone. *Will I ever be Lynn again?* I thought to myself more than once. There was no one to talk to, no counselors to comfort me, no one who understood what I was going through, how I was feeling, to tell me I'd be okay. Everyone who attended to me was very professional, but they all had their jobs to do, and those jobs didn't include comforting me, though that's what I needed most right then.

I never heard from the police again after that one interview. I'm guessing the rape kit remained on a shelf with the thousands of others like it, never to be investigated. (According to some sources, there are more than 200,000 untested rape kits in storage around the country today.)

I had been the victim of a rapist who had complete control of me, and though the rape was an extreme case, it was also a familiar dynamic in my relationships that I unconsciously understood very well: I didn't matter; I was here for the benefit of everyone else. As a result, I didn't pursue vindication. I didn't go back to the police myself. It didn't occur to me or anyone else in my life to do so. I'm sure part of me believed I didn't deserve such vindication. I had survived, hadn't I? I was still alive. That, supposedly, should have been enough.

I had been beaten during the ordeal and badly banged up, but the injuries weren't enough to keep me in the hospital, so they released me even though I was still in shock—maybe not the technical definition of shock, but I really wasn't thinking straight. I was virtually catatonic. I didn't call anyone in my family, not that night. I'd become accustomed to handling everything on my own. Besides, they all lived in Michigan. What were they going to do? I didn't have the capacity to think about even the simplest of next steps. I had lost the ability to make decisions.

One thing I knew, or rather felt down to the marrow, was that I was never going back to that apartment. My friend must have told Tom and me we could stay at her place, because hours later we found ourselves lying in an empty room with two pillows and a blanket for sleeping, not even an air mattress or futon. The floor was hard and uncomfortable, given my bruises and abrasions. I wore the same clothes I had on when the rapist accosted me, and I couldn't sleep. Everything about that night went around and around in my head. Was it my fault? What could I have done differently? Should I have screamed louder, fought harder, tried to wrestle the knife away from him? It all started with the nap. Maybe I shouldn't have taken a nap, how lazy can you be? Then I would have known that my roommate was out, and I could have locked the door behind her. But would I have locked the door? If only I had worked late that night....

These and a million other thoughts and questions whirled in my head as Tom slept easily beside me.

When I think about it today, I wonder how we ended up on my friend's floor. Why didn't we just go to a motel or hotel with a huge queen bed and clean sheets? It wasn't the money. We both had full time jobs. Why didn't I insist? Or more to the point, why didn't Tom insist, since my decision-making was not at its sharpest? Why didn't my friend suggest it? Why didn't Tom and my friend take care of me?

Here's the answer I've come to, one of the lessons I've had to learn over and over in this lifetime. They didn't take care of me because I taught them not to. Neither of them had the empathy or ability to see what others needed and make it happen. In both relationships, I had been the one taking care of them. As with many of my family members, the caretaking was never mutual, and when the time came that I needed them—and when would I need someone more than they needed me, after a vicious assault—they didn't know what to do.

And I didn't tell them in even the smallest of ways what I needed, because again, deep down, I felt my needs were not important. I didn't even know how to take care of myself. I knew I needed to be taken care of, but I couldn't ask for it. I wanted them to do it on their own. I remember thinking, *How odd is it that they can't understand what I've been through and how I need to be taken care of?* But when they didn't understand, I mentally shrugged my shoulders and said Oh well and went along with whatever came my way. I never knew how to care for myself, so I unconsciously taught others not to take care of me either.

In the following days, life remained chaotic, and I kept my vow not to go back to the apartment. *He*—there was only one *he* at this point—invaded every thought of my waking hours as well as many of my nightmares. Was he watching me? He told me not to call the police. Had he seen them arrive? Was he angry because I broke our agreement? Was he coming back to finish the job? He knew everything about me. He could find me anywhere, anytime. This was true terror.

As a stopgap, Tom moved us into his sister's place, but that was like moving back home with my family. His sister's house was as chaotic and filthy as Mom's was. She and her husband had three small children and barely made ends meet to care for them and each other. It was a household of depression and sadness, but Tom had been raised that way and thought nothing of it. For me it was the chaos I had been running from all my life, but given the circumstances, I knew I could put up with it.

I must not have been putting up with it as well as I thought, though, because a few days later, Tom called my mother. I still hadn't told anyone in Michigan. She was devastated, Tom told me, and was getting on a plane as soon as she could. You can say this about Mom. She wasn't very good with the day to day, but she always came through in a crisis. What I knew and still know for sure is that she loves all her children very much, and when something serious happened, she was always there. I have always been grateful that I could count on that.

While we waited for Mom to arrive, I couldn't find it in myself to shower and dress—to function at any level, really. I couldn't eat. I couldn't work. I couldn't carry on a coherent conversation. I was an empty shell. Would I ever be whole again? The management company where I worked was great, saying to take as much time as I needed. But they wouldn't spend the money to change all the locks when I asked them to. I was appalled that the police didn't provide a court order to make them change all the locks. I felt a deep burden of guilt and anger that I let the rapist take the master key, that other women could be subjected to the same horror I had been, and it would be my fault. No one listened. "It'll cost too much," they said. "We never change those locks. Besides, the guy's probably long gone by now. Why would he come back?"

To do it again, I feared. Or worse. I couldn't get that out of my head.

Though I had left Michigan in part to get away from my mother, I needed her now. I got myself to the airport to pick her up wearing the sweat suit I had worn for days. I'm sure I hadn't showered for some time either, but at least I had gotten out of that dress. Part of me never wanted to care for myself again—never wanted to be attractive again. Look where it had gotten me. I wanted to be safe. When Mom walked off the ramp from the gate area, I fell into her arms like a five-year-old.

We were still at Tom's sister's house, but Mom was accustomed to chaos and fit right in.

The day after she arrived, she took me to my one-week follow-up at the doctor's office connected to the hospital. Mom was in the room with me just as she had been when I was a teenager at my first gynecological exam. My reaction this time was not nearly as calm. I trembled as I took off my clothes. I wanted to stay covered, to stay hidden. I wasn't ready to be naked to the world, literally or figuratively. I could barely touch myself, let alone have another person do so, a man no less.

Mom must have noticed how much I was shaking. "Honey, the doctor has to examine you. I'll be right here." Those words didn't have the same calming effect as when I was a teenager.

The door opened slowly, and the doctor squeezed into the room. As he approached, I felt the helplessness and humiliation of the rape all over again.

"No! No! Don't touch me," I screamed. "You can't touch me." I jumped up and pushed by the doctor as though he were the Devil himself and hid behind the door, curling into a fetal position on the floor, too terrified to look up. I rocked back and forth, sobbing, clutching my legs.

"Honey, I am so sorry this happened to you. I promise I will be very careful. You'll be safe," he said in the most gentle, loving manner. His name was Dr. Foltz. "Your Mom's right here. We just need to make sure you're okay."

"No, No," I yelled. "Not again. No one will ever touch me again!"

My mother came to me and reached in behind the door with her hand. "No one is going to hurt you again. I will hold your hand until it is over, and we'll get through it together." She said this with a deep compassion. That day, she was the mother I needed. She took care of me and did it well. I will always cherish that memory of her.

Mom slowly brought me to the other side of the door. I lifted my head and looked into the eyes of one of the most caring and loving people I've known. He had a strong, nurturing energy. He knew just what to do. He remained calm and empathetic. He helped me feel safe and got me through that examination, the first step toward taking my life back. Dr. Foltz made such an impression that day that he is still my doctor and became a dear family friend as well. He has seen me grow and handle many of life's challenges. Dr. Foltz still cares for our extended family and delivers our babies to this day.

After the appointment with Dr. Foltz, it wasn't long before Mom convinced me to return with her to Michigan. I was still in shock, needing to be cared for, and she knew it. I had nowhere else to go, really, since I couldn't go back to either the apartment or the company as long as that animal still had the master key. As an apartment manager, I had to walk many strangers—many of them men—through vacant units before they signed a lease. I wasn't ready for that. Too many women had been assaulted that way. Tom and my roommate moved my personal stuff out of the apartment, I resigned from my job, and Mom and I went back to Michigan together.

Mom wanted to take me home to heal, yes, and to protect me. She was heartbroken about what I had gone through. But she was Mom, so she had another motive for getting me back to Michigan as well. She had never wanted me to move away in the first place. She loved me, she said, and I knew that was true, but she also needed me to help her, to fix things, to keep her life on track. "You're the only one I can truly count on," she told me time and again. What she meant was, she always knew I'd put her first. This was her chance to get me home.

My father had the same reaction to this rape as he did to the childhood assault when I was ten. He was never able to call me or discuss what had happened. I do know, because my stepmother told me, that he was completely devastated. My grief and his remained unspoken between us.

For these reasons, I had mixed feelings about returning home. I had tried very hard to get away from the codependence and dysfunction of my childhood and create my own life—a life that would be free of the control and demands of others, including my mother. Mom was so happy I was back under her roof! By then, she and Frank had had Michael, who was three years old, and my two younger sisters had already moved out. Even though I found a job waiting tables while I was there, the old patterns emerged, and much of the childcare, housecleaning, and errands fell to me. How could I say no since they were so generous in letting me stay with them? This is how they hooked me, and I wasn't strong enough to resist.

After a few months home, I realized that in many ways I was as unsafe at home as I had been in that dark vast desert with the predator. I had spent my life until then trying to escape the role of servant victim, and clearly hadn't succeeded. To do so, I had to get away from the demands of my family—again.

I wasn't healed from the assault—that would take many years—but I was healing, and soon the drawbacks of living in Michigan outweighed the fears I had to face in Phoenix. I had left Michigan the first time to have the freedom to live my own life, a life I had embraced and lived fully until the rapist took it away from me. It was time I took it back. I had to find my way back to my life in Phoenix, back to myself, to my way of living there, independent and apart from the demands of my family. I left a second time. This was 1985.

I was quite broken for some time after returning to Phoenix and will always be grateful for the support I was blessed to receive in the coming months. I returned to work at the same property, after deciding that the monster had taken enough from me. I even found another apartment to share with the same roommate in a community I didn't manage. We were both ready to move forward. It felt good to do it together.

At the hospital after the assault, I had been given a pamphlet for an organization called the Center Against Sexual Assault (CASA). Once I returned to Phoenix, I looked them up and began using their services. I know for sure that without them it would have taken me a great deal longer to recover. All the counselors had been assaulted themselves, and I found it important to get help from those who could understand what I had gone through. I found it hopeful to see how they came out of it whole and helping others.

I wanted to be the same girl I was before that night, but I knew that she was gone now, forever. I had to grieve the loss of that innocent young girl, while at the same time growing into a stronger, more powerful woman. The counselors helped me do that by explaining more about rape and rapists. They explained that rape is really about power, not sex, the power to control. Over the course of many sessions, they helped me get my power back and learn to take control of my life again. That is why it would have been dangerous for me to stay in Michigan where I would have further lost my power.

At the center I also attended what they called "rape groups" at the time, but which today are more often named something more positive like "strength in support." We all became very close in those group sessions. Some of the stories I heard were heartbreaking and will haunt me forever. We were there to help one another to heal.

My work with this group also helped me acknowledge and heal from the childhood assault. I had never really talked about it at any depth with anyone and had sort of forgotten about it—repressed it. But it was always there, deep within me, one of the destructive patterns I was trying to break away from, and these individual and group sessions helped me connect the dots and see the larger patterns.

I continued to work with CASA and the rape group until I had gotten through the worst of the post-traumatic stress disorder (PTSD) that rape survivors often experience. For some years after the assault, I had more panic attacks than I could count. I looked behind every shower curtain and inside every closet. The crack of a twig or the scrape of a shoe on a dirt path could set me off. A certain event, time of year, or even the weather gave me severe flashbacks, which were often as terrifying as the event itself.

One night after a few years had passed, when I thought I was on my way to putting the assault behind me, I had a flashback. I was living in a big, beautiful house with my boyfriend Eric. I had taken a nap around the same time of day as the night of the assault. It was the same month and the same type of weather. The front door blew open. I awoke abruptly and freaked out. There's no other way to put it. The sounds were the same, the smells were the same, and I was positive that he had found me again and was coming to murder me. I was hysterical, my heart thumping, my breath coming in gasps that were close to sobs. I hid behind an easy chair for what seemed like an eternity before I realized no one else was in the house. I sprinted to the door to close it and called my sister Darline.

After these frightening experiences, I have always found it amazing that soldiers endure what they do for weeks and years on end, seeing what they see, doing what they do, and still have any capacity to function again. My heart and respect go out to them.

I lived in a state of extreme fear for the next four years or so, terrified that my attacker knew my name and would try to find me again. I got married briefly at twenty-nine, and I remember being ecstatically relieved that my last name had changed. After the divorce, I kept my ex-husband's name until I married again.

After receiving support and guidance from CASA for a number of months, I started working with CASA as a volunteer, and a deeper level of healing began. For the next five years, I answered the CASA hotline for those who had been assaulted and for children being sexually abused. I also volunteered at hospitals to meet rape victims, to help calm them and hold their hand through the rape kit exam—something I knew would have made a difference for me during that awful experience. I became a spokesperson for rape survivors, speaking at events and doing news segments about how to be aware of your surroundings and what the experts advise when you're attacked.

What I discovered from my volunteer experiences is that those who have gone through a tragedy—once they have walked through it and healed, at least in part—can be of immense help to others going through the same experience. Reaching out your heart and your hand to those who have just been through a similar ordeal gives purpose to your pain. It helps you heal, and it helps others heal, too.

Toward the end of that five years volunteering for CASA, I was ready to move on. When children called the hotline, their young voices describing their awful experience became too painful for me. Too many times the person abusing them lived in the house or visited frequently. Most times the children were too afraid to tell me who they were because I had to inform them by law that I had to call CPS. Once I said that, many of them hung up, terrified of the trouble they would get in if they told the secret.

In the years after volunteering at CASA, I continued informally to help other assault survivors referred to me by friends and organizations, and I will continue to do so for the rest of my life. Working with others who have been sexually assaulted transforms what was painful to me into something positive. Each time I see someone begin to heal as I did, their healing comforts me and I grow just a little bit stronger. Being of service to those beautiful individuals at CASA and beyond has healed me.

Since that time, we have learned a lot about sexual assault as a culture, but there's a long way to go to provide the necessary services and support for rape survivors. It broke my heart to hear that CASA lost its funding recently. Social services like these are always the first to be axed in tight financial times, and that just shows how much farther we have to go create stronger laws that focus on the storerooms of rape kits that continue to remain unsolved. If organizations like CASA had more funding, our victims would receive more of the much-needed support that can be crucial in survivors' healing process.

For many years, I was sad and angry that I hadn't been vindicated, that my attacker had never been punished for what he had done to me.

Fast forward to more than twenty years after the assault. I was working out at a gym on a machine with a TV. *America's Most Wanted,* or a crime show like it, was playing on the screen. I never really watched shows like that, but this one got my attention. It told the story of three men who had broken out of a jail in New Mexico many years before and gone on a spree of murder and rape. They had finally been recaptured several years before this program, and all three were now in prison.

I just knew that one of those three was my attacker.

Now I was grateful he had told me so much about himself the night of the rape. I was supposed to hear his story so that when I watched this television program twenty years later, I would recognize him and learn of his rearrest. Knowing he was in prison gave me closure and a sense of peace. He was finally being held accountable for what he had done to me and many other women. He would never hurt me or anyone else again.

I now understand that my soul had to evolve to learn the lesson intended for me in this part of my journey, this painful walk through surviving and thriving after being brutally raped: to stop being a victim, to be able to forgive those who have hurt me, to find my own sense of safety and worth within.

I'm no longer angry about the assault, and now, thirty-five years later, I rarely think about it at all.

Chapter 6
LIFE LESSONS FOLLOW YOU EVERYWHERE

Once I returned to Arizona, I vowed not to let the assault take over my life. As a result of my work with CASA, I was able to move on. That work turned something bad into something good as I paid it forward and continued to volunteer with the organization. And though I certainly had some bad days of flashbacks and PTSD, in general I worked and played hard for the next few years. I got to the point where I loved my life again, and I could say that I was happy. One reason I was happy was that I was on my own and no one had any expectations of me. I was free. The distance from my responsibilities at home allowed me to be stronger, with healthier boundaries.

That all changed in 1987, when Mom, Frank, and Michael moved to Phoenix. The lessons began again, and I was not happy about it, a feeling I couldn't keep to myself. My mother scolded me many times for not being happier when they moved to Arizona. I couldn't hide it. Phoenix was my town. I feared that my life as I knew it—free and independent—was over, that I'd fall back into the family pattern of people pleasing, keeping the peace, and fixing everyone's problems.

A few years later, my brother Donnie and my younger sister Darline and her little girl, Ashley, moved to Phoenix as well. Both of my siblings had suffered from the dysfunction we had been raised in and had gone through a lot in their own lives, but their stories are not mine to tell. Although I loved them and love them more than words can say, their presence, however, added another layer to the complicated family dynamics.

With much of my family in Arizona, the chaos returned. It was confusing for me because I appreciated them being close and spending time with them, but I knew that it came at a cost. I knew even then, in the early stages of my spiritual journey, that the family dysfunction was not any one person's fault, that we were all living our lives according to our natures, that we all had wounds that needed healing. My problem was buried deep within me: I believed that I was responsible for saving every one of them, for making their lives better, so every time there was trouble, I mounted my white horse and came to the rescue. They looked to me for direction and comfort, and I let them. I taught them how to treat me. I focused on caring for others at the expense of the life I was trying to create for myself. And at some level, I thought this kind of martyrdom made me a better person. I don't believe they thought it was a hardship for me, just my role in the family.

I carried these dynamics into my romantic relationships. All my life until I met Neil, I went from relationship to relationship, never sticking around for long. Some men I took care of and some men tried to control and take advantage of me. Some boyfriends had characteristics of my mother and some of my father. When a relationship became too much work, I was out of there. When a relationship was too easy, I was out of there. I hurt a lot of kind, wonderful men over the years. The emotionally balanced men who adored me never seemed to be a good fit. Maybe they were too easy. Maybe my soul, my true self, knew I needed different kinds of teachers to overcome my shortcomings and learn the lessons of this lifetime.

I played all kinds of mind games with myself, trying to escape what I saw as the chains of my family's dynamics without doing the hard work of growth. As I approached the age of thirty, I had what I thought was a brilliant idea. The best way to get away from the demands of the family I was born into was to get married and have a family of my own!

So I did. I got married on May 27, 1989, when I was twenty-nine years old. Mike was an ex-marine and part owner of his family's carpet cleaning company. That's how we met. We used his company at the property I managed, and I saw him often. He was good looking and worked hard. We started dating. He fell in love with me and proposed. I accepted, though I don't think I was truly in love with him. But I did want to get married, and in my craziness, I thought we'd have cute kids, and that was enough.

Once we married, he stopped working at the family business, informing me early on that he was an alcoholic and good at hiding it, but now that I was his wife, I had to accept it. I think he always felt insecure about us being together. In his heart, he didn't think he was good enough for me. He spent his time drinking in local bars. Periodically, when he was stumbling and incoherent, bartenders called me to pick him up and take him home. It turns out he had severe anger issues toward women from a painful upbringing with his mother, who eventually deserted him and his brothers. He threw me against the wall once, and that was it. I may have been broken in some ways, but I had that much self-respect. Six months later we were divorced.

Instead of escaping the dynamics of my family by marrying Mike, I had replicated them. I had unconsciously married someone I had to take care of, someone else to fix, even though I needed fixing myself.

Though I certainly had some issues with my family's unhealthy dynamics, sometimes a family just has to rally together. We all learned that the hard way in 1991.

A group of us were holding a baby shower for another one of my employees in the clubhouse of the large luxury apartment community where we all worked. I was the property manager. The community was like a little town with its own movie theater, beauty salon, gym, and even convenience store. We were all young and just starting our careers. We were a tight-knit group that had begun working there during planning a nd construction, excited about what we had accomplish ed. To this day, they are some of my dearest friends.

On this beautiful day in the perfect place, we were surrounded by so much camaraderie and love, sampling the appetizers, and talking in groups of twos and threes. The shower's main events had yet to begin. Suddenly Travis, who was covering the office that Sunday so the rest of us could go to the party, ran into the clubhouse out of breath, obviously upset. We jumped up from our seats.

"Lynn, there's been an accident. I'm so sorry to have to tell you this, but you have to go to the hospital right away. Your little brother Michael's been hit by a truck. It's serious. They had to air evac him to the hospital."

"What, me? No. No! What brother? What are you talking about?" I said, flustered and confused.

Travis walked toward me with his hands open and put them around my face.

"Lynn, it's your little brother, Michael." He gently laid my head on his shoulder.

Each of my friends gathered around me. They all embraced me, crying in disbelief, heavy with that feeling of unreality you have when you hear truly bad news.

I don't remember anything until I arrived at the hospital. Some or all of my friends must have driven me there. I was in no condition to drive myself.

Michael is my youngest brother, Mom's and Frank's son, their only child together, and eleven years old at the time of the accident. He had been born when I was twenty-two and just graduating from college. I moved to Arizona directly from college, so I never had a lot of time with Michael when he was young. Even after they moved to Arizona when he was seven, I was busy developing my career and living my own life, so I never really spent much time with him. He was a smart child but kept to himself. He was very easy to be around, never seemed to need much, and rarely complained.

I must have had the wherewithal to call Ced, my boyfriend at the time, who was a doctor, a general practitioner, to meet us at the hospital. As I pushed through the stark hospital doors and ran down the cold white hallway, I could see that Ced had already arrived, along with Mom, and Frank, and my youngest sister and her husband.

Their eyes told me how serious it was. I couldn't run fast enough to reach my mother and hold her as close as my body would allow. We all embraced and looked at each other in disbelief and shock. There was nothing to do other than hold each other, waiting and praying, each of us trying to contain the storm of fear and worry in our hearts.

I looked up and saw a doctor coming toward us in his lab coat. His grim demeanor said a thousand words. We braced ourselves.

"Are you the family of Michael Goodrich?" he asked in a professionally neutral tone.

Some of us nodded.

"I'm so sorry to tell you this. Michael is in serious condition. Very serious. We're not sure he'll make it. He is in intensive care now, but we have to perform surgery right away to eliminate the swelling in his head. His legs are in bad shape, too, broken in many places, but we are more concerned about the head trauma at this point. I have to run to surgery. We'll update you as often as possible. We will do our very best to take care of Michael." Then he ran off to save my brother's life.

A medical team wheeled out a gurney from intensive care, headed toward the surgery ward. We didn't recognize the patient on the gurney at first. Then we realized it was Michael. His head was enlarged and face swollen, his features hidden. None of us moved. We were numb, filled with anguish.

Just then a man ran toward us.

"Oh My God, is that Michael Goodrich?" the man said with a look of mortification.

"Yes, who are you?" I asked as the tears rolled down my face.

"He was in the middle of the street when I saw him. Oh My God, I am so sorry." His body shook with despair.

Mom went to him and opened her arms, her severely injured child just behind her. This man fell into her embrace without the slightest hesitation, and they wept, melting into each other with deep grief and commiseration. Mom was always concerned about what image she showed to the world, but here she let her guard down. She truly felt pain for this man and what he must have been going through and was able to comfort him while herself experiencing the agony of not knowing if her child would live or die. By reaching out with love, she used her pain to begin the healing process for herself and our family. I have never been prouder of her.

Michael was Mom's sixth child. She and Frank had him shortly after they were married. As with all Mom's children, Michael never really had much supervision. We had always been able to go out and about doing our own thing, just as Michael had been doing that day. He was returning a video tape and planned to pick up a new one. Helmets weren't as prevalent then as they are now, and he often rode his bike on busy cross streets without one. He didn't cross at the intersection but rode directly across the street. We learned much of this from the police report. He doesn't remember anything from that day.

We spent the next weeks living at the hospital. I slept in the waiting room on the hard chairs and benches, never thinking to bring a blanket or a pillow. Self-care has never come naturally to me. The intense lighting buzzed just enough to keep me awake and creep me out at the same time. Thank God for McDonald's House, where my mother and stepfather stayed for the next few weeks. I stayed each night at the hospital alone, falling naturally into the roles of family sentinel and family caretaker. I wanted badly to make it better, and barring that, to take away as much of the pain as I could from Mom and Frank.

After we knew Michael survived the surgery, I returned to work. Michael was in a coma for over six weeks. I worked each day and went directly to the hospital each night. My mother and stepfather had to return to work as well and find a way to be at the hospital as much as possible. My sister was quite pregnant and had a small child at home, so there was little she could do to help.

My other sisters and brother took turns flying in from Michigan. They had their own lives and jobs at home, and they did what they could. Our friends pitched in too. There were always plenty of homecooked meals arriving at the hospital waiting room each day. Once we went back to work, our friends created a sign-up sheet to make sure someone was at the hospital when family couldn't be there.

As tragic as Michael's accident was, it brought out the best in friends and family. I learned at the deepest level the importance of service, both for the giver and the receiver. On many days, the waiting room was packed with friends, each one doing anything they could to help. Each one of those wonderful people taught me the healing that comes from the compassion of reaching out to one another in times of need. When we are in service to one another, we can endure even the most painful of circumstances. The love and compassion we received during those days will fill my heart forever. It kept us from despair, helped us face our pain with renewed faith. It was a lesson I remembered all my life and try to exemplify to this day.

Michael had a significant brain injury and remained in the hospital for the next nine months. He has and will suffer from traumatic brain injury (TBI) the rest of his life. His doctor put it this way: "It is likely that Michael won't mature past the age of eleven, his age at the time of the accident. As an adult, he'll act much like a child. It'll be difficult for him to see his own limitations or have the ability to monitor his temper and other emotions. He won't have a filter and will likely blurt out whatever pops into his head. He won't be able to anticipate the consequences of what he says or does."

Michael also had severe physical injuries. His spine was intact, but his arms and legs had been broken in many places, and he would spend months in rehab to recover even the most basic functions. He has had difficulty walking since then.

For the next several months, all I did was go to work and the hospital, and spent every weekend taking care of Michael. The nurses were often too busy to attend to the basic nonmedical needs of their patients in a timely manner. It fell largely to us. Thank God for Ced. He came in and took over, changing diapers and making sure all the equipment was working. He evaluated Michael's progress for us when we were concerned and interpreted the medical language we couldn't understand.

While he was still in the hospital in a coma, we all read and talked to Michael to let him know he wasn't alone, to try to get through to him and stimulate his brain. When he first began to wake up, it was much like any of us feel and behave after coming out of deep sleep. He muttered in low, inaudible grunts with an empty confused look in his eyes.

One day, the nurses had him at their station in his wheelchair to get him out of bed and give him as much stimulation as possible. We were at work. I had been reading a book to him by Magic Johnson, called *Safe Sex in the Age of Aids*.[5] God knows why I was reading an eleven-year-old that book. I think I read anything the hospital had on hand. Out of the blue he looked up and announced to the nurses, "Practice safe sex." His voice was hoarse from disuse, but what he said was perfectly clear. I don't think he knew what sex was at eleven, but he remembered *that* part of the book! And so does every nurse at that station who heard his first words. They giggled as they told us the story later. Finally, some good news.

We soon realized that Michael would have to learn every basic skill all over again, all the ones we normally take for granted: talking, walking, eating. It was an exhausting process for all of us, let alone for Michael. For that year and more, just about all our free time was spent at the hospital supporting Michael through the sometimes very painful therapy.

We soon realized the doctor was accurate in his assessment of Michael's future. Michael has remained eleven years old and without a filter or the ability to understand his own limitations. Since then, he has found it difficult to navigate the demands of growing older and living a healthy and productive life.

The day Michael came home from the hospital was a day of great celebration at Mom and Frank's house, with balloons and signs welcoming him home, all kinds of snacks and drinks, a buffet of food and appetizers. We invited everyone we could think of—friends, family, neighbors everyone who had helped us through this ordeal. It was a thank you to them too. Michael's expression fluctuated between pride and bewilderment. Was all this fuss for him? But he was finally home.

From that point on, Mom and Frank took on Michael's care for many years, and the rest of us returned to our lives. My dance with Michael wasn't finished, however. It was merely on hiatus.

Chapter 7
FAMILY AND BUSINESS DON'T MIX

When one dance ends, another begins. This one would be with my father.

I continued to develop my career in property management, running a property called Crown Court, but I was getting restless working for someone else. With my father as an example, I had always intended to own and run my own business. Now that Michael's condition was more or less stable, and Mom and Frank were in charge of his care, it seemed like as good a time as any.

Around then I met a man named Thaine, who became a great friend and a profound influence on my life. About six feet tall, with light brown hair, an athletic build with the face and eyes of a cover model, Thaine was hot, charming, smart, and driven. He partied hard and worked hard and had every intention of making it big. He had charisma and style. Women fell at his feet, but I wasn't one of them. We never had anything other than a close friendship and deep admiration for one another. Our souls were meant to go on this journey together, and what a journey it has been. From that time on, Thaine has been involved in just about every major milestone of my life. He even introduced me to my husband Neil, and today his wife Tahna is one of my dearest friends.

While I was running Crown Court, Thaine pitched me an idea for a vacation rental company using some of my units. He would take out a long-term lease on a number of units at the going rate. Then he'd lease them out by the week or month at a much higher rate to winter visitors ("snowbirds") or companies in need of corporate housing. I didn't see any reason his idea wouldn't work. Even if Thaine's units stayed empty, he'd be paying us rent. With permission from my bosses, I agreed.

We had plenty of office space at Crown Court, so I had Thaine move his staff in with us, which gave me the opportunity to see how the vacation rental business worked from the inside. I liked what I saw, figured I could do something like that, and decided to go for it once I asked Thaine's blessing to begin another vacation rental company on the other side of town. I didn't want him to think I was poaching his territory. He supported the idea; I gave my notice as property manager at Crown Court and began my life as an entrepreneur.

In 1992, I met Eric at a hockey game. He was from London, about fourteen years older than me, and we became friends immediately. I mentioned that someday I was going to start up a vacation rental company. He had invested in many companies over the years, and thought it was a great idea. We joined forces as business partners and set up a vacation rental company called Desert Deluxe with the same structure of Thaine's company. Eric had the cash, and I had the experience and contacts within the community. Eric was a 70 percent partner and, of course, I retained 30 percent. We began the business shortly after we met in 1992. The business worked great from the start. We ran about fifty vacation rentals in luxury communities from the perfect location in downtown Scottsdale and had very few vacancies from the start.

I always checked in with my father to let him know what was going on in my life, especially with work, which was common ground for us. He had hit another rocky patch in his life, being on his fourth divorce and third bankruptcy. God love him, he was a brilliant automotive engineer and at one time driven, but now he spent too much time on a golf course, drinking often and early each day. He needed a new direction, and he headed straight for me.

I have always been proud that my father owned his own companies and worked very hard when we were young. By the time I was a teenager, he had established five successful companies with many employees and a great deal of success. While in college, I worked at his offices in the summers, hustling twice as hard as anyone else so I wouldn't be seen as the boss's princess of a daughter.

Although I was proud of my father, the success became hard for him to manage as golf and martini lunches became more of a priority. After every bankruptcy and divorce—they were usually connected somehow—I helped my father pick up the pieces, attending each court hearing, whether it was bankruptcy by divorce or by a business collapsing.

Dad was approaching retirement age, but between the bankruptcies and divorces, his savings were nonexistent. At the rate he was going, he'd never be able to retire. He desperately needed a plan. That's where I came in. He saw how well I was doing with Desert Deluxe and thought that could be the answer—a vacation rental company of his own. Well, not of his own, exactly. He wanted to partner with me because I already knew what I was doing … and I was his cherished oldest daughter … and he had helped me through college … and how could I say "No." He dialed up the dad guilt.

My intuition told me it was not a good idea, but of course I wanted to please him. He was my father, and maybe I could help him out of a jam. That was my role after all, wasn't it, fixing other people's problems? The danger was that I'd get sucked into old family patterns and lose the independence I had worked so hard for. I guess my soul wasn't ready to lay claim to that hard-won freedom by saying "no." Dad was my soft spot. I gave in to the family pathology once again and said "yes." My life would not be my own for a long time.

I didn't say no, but I felt the heaviness of the responsibility from the moment I agreed. Our business goals didn't really align. At that age, I never felt the need to make a lot of money. I just wanted to have fun and be comfortable. Dad wanted to make as much money as possible to ensure a comfortable retirement. More accurately, he wanted *me* to make as much money as possible to ensure a comfortable retirement for him.

Even before I went into business with Dad, my partner with Desert Deluxe and I were looking to go our separate ways. I had made the mistake of getting romantically involved with Eric, but I wasn't in love, and I wanted out of both the romantic and business partnership. He was in the process of buying me out, and this gave Dad the opening to push for us to create a business together. So we did. In 1994, my father and I started up a company called Sunsational Suites, and I hired a friend, Carol who had wonderful marketing and decorating talents, to help us out. Each of our vacation rentals were in high-end communities, and each had a different desert theme: the Coyote Suite, the Cactus Suite, the Kokopelli Suite, and so on, every southwestern theme you could think of.

As it turns out, my father didn't really want to work the business; he wanted me to do it. He wanted to be the silent partner, to play golf and drink, and that's what he did. Actually, it was more like he wanted to be the silent CEO, because, well, he had run many more businesses than I had, and besides, I was the daughter. I was expected to be at his beck and call and jump to attention. There were many drunken calls at midnight or whatever time he was sober enough to read a spreadsheet and have a conversation. And the calls were always on his timetable.

I had given myself away once again. The success of the business was all on me, and I was in hell! I worked crazy hours just to make ends meet. Dad was taking money he didn't have from his company in Michigan to feed our company in Phoenix. The pressure on me to succeed financially was immense. I was Dad's retirement package and the burden of that consumed me. I was no longer working only for myself. Every decision I made affected him as well. In his mind, that meant he had a right to question everything I did. It wore me out. I began to lose my spirit, trying hard to climb the mountain, only to slide down before I could reach the next level.

Of course, I couldn't directly say no to my father, so I had to escape through the back door again. I met a sweet and kind man, another Mike, who lived in Kentucky and wanted to marry me. We met through the good friend of the husband of one of my good friends. It seemed like the perfect plan: get married, get my own life back. If I lived in Kentucky, I'd be free to live my own life again. This Mike was a calm, tall, confident man with a hint of insecurity, not a player at all. He preferred a quiet, uncomplicated life. He had been married once before to his longtime sweetheart, Claire, but I found out later even though they'd been together for many years, she had left because of his drinking.

Mike was a partner in a successful pre-need funeral business for people who want to invest in a funeral package ahead of time, so their family didn't have to deal with it later. He lived in a world unfamiliar to me with the kind of wealth few people ever experience. Claire's father was the founder of Batesville Caskets and Hill-Rom hospital beds. Mike had been brought into their family business, which led to his career in the pre-need side of the industry. He lived in a beautiful home in Newport, Kentucky overlooking the Ohio River and the city of Cincinnati.

Although Mike and Claire were still close, I always felt loved by him. He worked for Batesville Casket for many years and used his knowledge of the industry to pave the way to his success in the pre-need funeral business. I enjoyed being around him, he was kind, considerate and fun. I thought Mike was wonderful, that we might have a future. The timing was also great for my escape from my own family responsibilities. I was now thirty-five years old and looking for any exit available. I had had enough of the pressure and chaos of working with my father and living near my mother.

We dated from a distance for a few years before we decided to get married. Mike had lots of airline miles, so I flew to Kentucky two or three times a month, then back to Phoenix. While I worked the business, I was also trying to sell it, so I could move to Kentucky full time. In my convoluted thinking, if I could just sell the business and get to Kentucky with Mike, life would be good. All my problems would miraculously disappear.

I couldn't really wait, though, so we married before we found a buyer. We had a beautiful wedding on October 27, 1994, at L'Auberge in Sedona, Arizona, on the hilltops of the majestic red rocks overlooking Oak Creek below, but our honeymoon was cut short. I had to get back to the business. We were hemorrhaging money, and my father was busy on the golf course.

The pressure of the business affected our marriage from the start. I was gone a lot of the time trying to save or sell the company. I even had to borrow large sums of money from Mike to keep things afloat (though

I always paid him back). This put even more pressure on the marriage. What's more, Mike was a drinker, and when I was gone, he drank more and more to fill the time.

I didn't understand alcoholism then, but his behavior became very destructive. The summer after our October wedding, I had invited a beautiful teenage girl that was very special to me, Frei, to stay with us in Kentucky. She was fourteen and with her family's blessing, I was a Big Sister-type mentor to her, which I'll write more about later in my story. That summer Frei and I flew to Detroit and spent time with my family. Then we rented a car and made our way to Kentucky. Mike had already been frustrated at my time away, so the fact that I brought Frei home with me, someone who took more attention from him, only infuriated him more.

One night Mike and I had gone to dinner, and he had been drinking. When we arrived home, Frei was in the living room and ready for my attention. Mike had other plans for us that night, and they did not involve hanging out with Frei. Mike went off on her, a full-blown alcohol-fueled rage. She was so terrified she ran off into a neighborhood she didn't even know. By this time, it was almost midnight. I was frantically running through the neighborhood and by some miracle I heard her through the window of a neighbor's home. Thank God someone safe had taken her in. I can put up with a lot for myself, but when you go after someone in my protection, look out. I packed us in the car the next morning, drove to Phoenix, and never went back.

The divorce had no hiccups. I left all the wedding presents there, and since we had never commingled money or property, there was nothing to dispute. Except when he was on a bender, Mike was basically a decent guy and felt terrible about what happened.

After treatment, Mike never drank again. He spent much of his time and money opening halfway houses for others trying to get and stay sober. He knew he had lost a lot to his addiction and healed himself in part through service to others. He inspired me to find ways to be of service too.

Once he was sober and knew it would stick, he approached me about getting back together, but I turned him down. I knew I had married him for the wrong reasons in the first place and that my life was in Scottsdale. We remained friends until I married again, after which it became too painful for him to stay in touch. I found out that in May 2020 that Mike had had a stroke and passed away. He was only sixty-five years old.

My escape plan through marriage to reboot my life hadn't worked—again—and I had to go back and face the music. The business had still not sold, and my father and I were just barely treading water. Dad had a new plan, though, now that I wasn't distracted by marriage. Not only were we not going to sell the business, we were going to expand it by signing a huge lease with a gorgeous brand-new property being built in the middle of the prestigious Arcadia neighborhood in Phoenix. I knew that our company was too new and underfunded to take on such a risky venture, but I still couldn't say "no" to my father. I already felt guilty about trying to escape and make it all go away. This was my way of making it up to him.

So by stretching our limited funds to the breaking point, we went ahead with it, signing the lease and buying the desert-themed furnishings for all our units. The property was to be completed in October 1995 and by working the phones, we filled up every single one of our units for most of the winter. Since our renters weren't due to begin their stays until December, we had plenty of cushion for the developer to finish the property.

And then we got the news. The builder had run up against some major obstacles, and the property wouldn't be ready until after February 1996. We were left holding the bag, with over $500,000 in deposits and nowhere to put our guests. I looked into suing the developer for breach of contract, but the parent company was huge and had expensive corporate lawyers on retainer. I didn't have the resources to fight.

Dad played golf and drank while I dealt with the business, the creditors, payroll, and returning the deposits to our guests. Since we were already running thin, we were in big trouble with a panic-attack inducing debt of $300,000. It was my job to take care of it, of course.

During that time, my friend Thaine introduced me to an organization called the Young Entrepreneurs Organization (YEO), which is now called the Entrepreneurs Organization (EO), an international networking and support company that helps young entrepreneurs learn and grow. Thaine had started the Phoenix chapter and thought it would be a good opportunity for me. To qualify then, you had to be the founder of your organization and have a minimum of one million dollars in gross revenue. Your success was not determined by your net earnings—thank God for me! I was there to learn. Each member belonged to a forum: a group of entrepreneurs that would meet monthly to discuss each other's business challenges. It was like having your own board of directors.

A street girl from Detroit, I was terrified when I first joined. Who was I to think I'd fit in with successful people like that? At the time, the organization was about 95 percent men. But I pushed myself to walk through those doors trembling with fear and insecurity.

That organization and the people in it saved my life. I was able to keep my head up and push myself forward. Because I was one of the few female members in YEO and because my friend Thaine looked out for me, many of the other members looked out for me, too. Their encouragement and support gave me the confidence to continue to learn and grow. Many are still my dearest friends today, and I met my husband and the father of my children through YEO and Thaine, but more on that later.

Many of the spiritual writers I study observe that there are times in life when we give, and others when we receive. This was definitely a time for me to receive. My forum consisted of many successful men and a few women over the years. If I was working on a deal, they helped me with the negotiation. They guided me through financial decisions, operational decisions, decisions about employees. The women, in particular, helped me navigate a largely men's world. Some men I did business with tried to barrel over me, thinking I wouldn't stick up for myself. My women mentors gave me the tools and confidence to push back. I made many mistakes along the way, but with the help of YEO and my forum, I was able to keep the business going—sometimes just barely. To this day EO is a big part of my life.

After Sunsational Suites lost our winter season, we had to find a way to stay afloat. We still had three other properties where we leased units, but the Arcadia loss was taking us over the falls. We needed cash to keep going or we would have to sell the business.

My father met some men on the golf course (of course) who said they might be interested in our company during the fall of 1996. They were new to the area and had just started a vacation rental operation themselves, Scottsdale Resort Accommodations (SRA). Through my connections in YEO, I also learned of another company that was interested.

The company my father found wanted to merge with Sunsational Suites, pay off a good portion of the creditors, and take me on as an owner-partner with only a very small salary. The other company wanted to buy Sunsational Suites outright, pay off the debt in full, and hire me as an employee, since they needed my expertise and contacts. The salary would have been a great deal more, but I would not have an ownership interest.

I took a leap of faith and chose the first deal, the harder route. I didn't want to give up being an entrepreneur and took the arrangement where I'd remain partner. Our new partners had been in the industry for quite some time in Telluride, so partnering with us gave them an entrance into the Scottsdale market. They didn't waste any time as the winter season was fast approaching and by December 1996, we had a deal.

As a result, for the next two years, I worked three jobs to stay on top of things: running the company with my two new partners (while obtaining my broker license); cleaning houses on the week-ends; and babysitting for a childcare network at night. Not only that, but I also had to move in with Mom because I couldn't afford rent. I was thirty-six years old, both defeated and determined to work my way out. I knew things had to get messy before I could put my life back together. I had to keep pushing; I had to keep climbing the mountain.

The time was such a blur. I could barely fit it all in, with no time for fun. My mother would have let me stay there no matter what, but I insisted on earning my keep by cleaning her cupboards and closets whenever I could fit it in. I had a big client with several condos in Scottsdale. After I lived at Mom's for six months, he let me move into one of his condos for low rent until I was on my feet. Paying off my personal debt and the company debt was all I could keep up with, but by the grace of God, that wonderful client stepped up to help, and I will be forever grateful.

Dad had moved back to Michigan and had been out of the picture once we merged with SRA. I was beginning to see the light at the end of the tunnel. Exhausted and needing to take better care of myself, I was determined to learn from this experience, to say "no," and to detach from the family pathology. I continued to work hard each day to make my life my own.

And then, the miracle happened. After two years of hard work, our senior partner made a deal to sell our business to a public company. Just when I was about to collapse from fatigue, I was free! God always knows how much we can take, and I was at my limit. It was Friday, February 12, 1999, the best Valentines gift a girl could ever want!

After the sale, I continued to run the company for a salary we had agreed on. The other partners had done well from the sale and went on to other adventures. With the smallest percentage of the company, I had still done well from the sale but was in no position to stop working. I really loved running the company anyway and was able to pay off my personal debt as well as that of Sunsational Suites. At almost thirty-nine years old, I could afford my own condo. I had always had a job, always been responsible, but it was the first time in my life that I wasn't in debt and living paycheck to paycheck.

I learned another valuable lesson during this time—or rather relearned it. When I left SRA in the spring of 2001, years later (Neil and I were married by then, and I was expecting the twins), Thaine took over for me. While I helped him settle in, I came across his salary in the paperwork—it was *40 percent more* than what I had been paid! I was livid, but of course there was nothing I could do about it. I had been paid a lot less than men for the same job all my life, but to have it shoved in my face like that was eye-opening. I didn't blame Thaine. It's an ingrained part of our culture, but this was the twenty-first century for crying out loud. I was not, and I am not, going to be quiet about it any longer.

Nor am I going to be quiet about another dirty little secret for women in business. (Well, it's not a secret to us!) Sexual harassment is real and rampant. I can't count the number of times I had to put up with the innuendo, and sexually laced barbs of male colleagues, and do the businesswoman's cha-cha-cha to evade their wandering hands or keep my pants on and keep my job at the same time—all while having to do my work twice as well for half the recognition and compensation and the "privilege" of working with these fine citizens. (Don't get me wrong. I was also blessed to have partners, YEO forum members, and many clients who were nothing but respectful.)

Today with the Me-Too movement, women are making progress, but that progress is grindingly slow. I hope that my college-age daughter and every other young woman will have a better experience than our generation (which had a better experience than the previous generation). I hope they will be able to prove their value proudly with hard work, rather than with the way they look. And I hope the world will be ready to recognize them equally and give them the same opportunities and financial security as anyone else. It is up to us parents to raise healthy confident girls to go out in the world and to raise our boys to see nothing unusual about that and treat everyone equitably and fairly.

Selling SRA saved me financially, but it came with a huge downside. Dad stopped talking to me.

Dad had never worked at all with SRA and very little with Sunsational Suites, though he invested a significant amount of money and spent a lot of time watching it. In the initial deal, we merged Sunsational Suites with SRA, and in return for paying enough of our debt to maintain good standing in the industry, SRA acquired me, my contacts and abilities, and our client base. When we sold SRA, I gave Dad about 30 percent of what I earned from the sale, which paid back most of his investment. He didn't get it all back, but that's the risk you take when you start a business. I used about 30 percent to pay off Sunsational Suites' remaining debts (which he had helped incur, of course), and kept the last 40 percent for myself. This seemed like a fair distribution, considering he had left it up to me to work three jobs to service the debt while he was off playing golf. Legally, I didn't have to give him anything, but he needed the money, and he was my father.

He didn't see it that way, though. He thought he was being cheated in some way. He demanded to see the paperwork, but he was not a partner and really had no right to do so. Because he was my father and I craved his approval, I showed him anyway. He found nothing suspicious in the papers, but that didn't change his mind. He saw the deal as a failure and a betrayal—my failure and his betrayal. Dad always thirsted for the acceptance of successful people and strove to appear successful himself, to be seen as living the good life. This is how he proved his value to the world, and to himself. What I offered him, as far as he was concerned, was an attack on his self-worth, a grave insult.

But for my own good, I had to say "no" this time—and he ghosted me. I was heartbroken. I had worked so hard. He should have been proud of me! We should have been celebrating our accomplishment—my accomplishment. I was devastated by his silence. He was broken by his own insecurity, and he unfairly projected that burden on me. He was acting selfishly without regard for how hard I had worked, and I was tired of it. His rejection hurt, nonetheless.

The silence lasted about two years. One night I had a vivid dream in which my grandmother, Dad's mom, who had passed a few years before, came to me with my grandfather. We were all at a party my father was attending. Together they brought Dad to me and made us embrace. When he held me, everything fell into place; I had Dad back. Then I woke up.

The very next day I went to a party celebrating my sister's wedding, and my father was there too, the first time I had seen him in years. I told him about the dream, and we embraced as we had in the dream, and just like that, everything was okay, never to be discussed again. I have been told by some very spiritual people that I have the gift of dreams, which means that I receive spiritual revelations and blessings through my dreams. I believe that this was one of those times.

Dad and I continued to heal. He started coming to Scottsdale more often, staying at my condo and golfing at the course next door. He hung out with me and my friends, just like we'd done over many years earlier. We had a lot of fun. In fact, Dad and I had always been more like friends than father and daughter. I had missed him, and he was back. I had taken care of myself by finally saying no, and it turned out okay. I was learning my lessons a little at a time.

Dad passed away in 2005. By then I was married for the third time and our twins were almost three years old. It was a very difficult time when I lost dad. I miss him desperately.

My Dad was very spiritual, always seeking a path to God. His favorite book was *The Prophet* by Kahlil Gibran. He always wanted me to read it and gave me a copy when I was thirty-something. Every now and then, he asked me, "Did you read it yet?" and I always had to answer, "Not yet, but I will, I promise." This went on for a few years, and after a while he stopped asking.

About two years after he died, I was sorting through a storage bin full of books. My husband Neil and I had put an addition on the house with a new office. I love books and always have. I was finally able to move all my books into one place in my new office.

As I arranged the books on the shelves, I stumbled on *The Prophet*. I opened it up, thinking I would scan a few pages. What I found was a gift from heaven. Throughout the book, my father had written notes to me. My name was everywhere, showing me with each angelic thought and word how much Dad had learned and how much he loved me. He had glued a note on one of the first pages that began "Dearest Lynn, May this book begin a lifelong journey in an attempt to understand God & Love." Throughout the rest of the book, he had underlined and commented on many passages. For example, on Page 11, he had underlined, "For even as love crowns you so shall he crucify you, even so he is for your growth, he is for your pruning."[6] I immediately thought of the phrase I use all the time: the pain is the medicine. In this case, the pruning is the medicine. We had been on the same track all along.

My children had never gotten to know their wonderful grandfather. One day I will be able to share this with them, their grandfather's beautiful wisdom and love. I got my father back again for a little while on that miraculous morning. That book is one of my most cherished possessions.

After I sold the company and received the payout, my father wasn't the only one who wanted to share the bounty. It certainly wasn't a fortune, but I was able to put a down payment on a condo, furnish it, and even have some savings for myself.

Once my mother learned of my good fortune, though, she asked me to lend her a substantial amount for an at-home business $25,000. Since she promised to pay me back, I agreed. I had a savings account for the first time and felt secure, but it did make a significant difference. I had done it again, feeling obligated to fix everyone's problems.

Just after we signed on the dotted line and sent in the money, I found out the company was fraudulent (thank God for my YEO forum). I had to hire an attorney, which cost about $2,500, but I got the money back. Another lesson learned. Do your due diligence before signing a contract.

But here's the kicker. Mom expected the check to go to her, even though it had been my money we invested, and I was out the $2,500 for the lawyer. Not only did she refuse to go in on the $2,500, but she also expected the rest of the money for herself. She said she would be happy to take *only* the $22,500 they were returning, as if she was doing me a big favor.

I was stunned. I told her we had had a close call and were lucky to get the money back—my money—and now that I thought about it, I wanted to put it back in savings. You would have thought I drained her retirement fund to buy a sports car, repossessed her house, and put her out in the street in her housedress by the way she reacted. She blew up, that full blown rage I remembered all too well from childhood. She screamed and yelled, wept and pouted, saying things like *You owe me; I'm your mother; You have to; After all I've done for you; You ingrate.* I think everyone in the office heard her, and we weren't on speakerphone.

She worked the mom guilt on this call and many others that followed, and though her barbs still hurt, and I shook with anxiety, I didn't back down. I couldn't. It was my money and my future, and there was really no gray area. By this time, I had learned a little something about setting boundaries.

I'm not sure how long that fight lasted, but we got through it. There was no dramatic moment of reconciliation like hugging my father at the party. She eventually lost interest and let it go. Since I was used to being treated that way, I guess I just let it go too. An apology was too much to expect.

Just after selling the Scottsdale Resort Accommodations in 1999, I had found security in my career, some money in the bank and no one to answer to. I was searching for the freedom to be myself, to find my voice and use it. I had to learn to heal my wounds on my own. I had to keep moving forward, to keep learning, to keep standing up for myself. Every time I was rewarded—with a good healthy outlook on life, with business success, with financial security, with healthy relationships—I knew I was doing the right thing and was inspired to keep going.

By saying no to both Mom and Dad, I was learning to stand up for myself. I'm convinced that with a little self-reflection, we all realize what our lesson is for this lifetime, the character defect we need to overcome. My main lesson is to stop being a people-pleasing victim and martyr, to learn the difference between being a servant and being of service. Being a servant means being an enabler of unhealthy behavior in others; it means owning other people's choices as your own, trying to fix things for them that they should fix on their own, trying to make life's challenges go away for them. Being of service means helping people in a healthy way with strong boundaries, accompanying them on their journey for a while, not conducting the journey for them.

When my father asked to go into business together, it would have been healthier for both of us if I had said, "I love you Dad, and I understand your concern about retirement, but going into business together crosses too many boundaries, so I'm going to have to say 'no.'" And when Mom asked me to put up money for her business, it would have been healthier to say something similar and weather the storm of her disapproval then. Because here's the thing. I had to weather the storm of her disapproval anyway when I didn't give her the refund, and by then, it was much worse. Doesn't it make more sense to weather the storm when it might be a minor squall and not a full-blown hurricane?

Hindsight is twenty-twenty, of course, but sometimes it's healthier to simply say *no* sooner than later, as hard as that may be.

Chapter 8
MY HUSBAND, MY TEACHER

I drove to Lake Havasu from Phoenix with a sweet woman, Anna, whom I had never met before. We chatted about the usual get-to-know-you stuff—where we lived, what we did, anyone we might know in common—and passed the time pleasantly enough. It was a beautiful sunny day in September 1995, and still quite hot in Arizona, perfect for boating. Lake Havasu was formed by the Parker Dam on the Colorado River between Arizona and California. It's famous for its floating parties during spring break, kind of an Arizona Fort Lauderdale.

When we arrived, we drove directly to the boat launch. I walked up to the fence separating the ramp from the parking lot. Neil, the man I was meeting for a three-day blind date, stood on the other side with surfer blonde hair and a tanned body glistening with water splashed from the lake. I was bowled over, feeling an immediate connection, as if I already knew him. He reached out his hand to introduce himself. When I took his hand in mine, Neil's confidence radiated through me. Then after he looked at me with his ocean blue eyes, I was a goner, love at first sight for the first time in my thirty-seven years.

"You're much prettier than Thaine told me," he said with a smile. He woke a part of me that had been in hibernation, waiting just for him. I knew immediately he was The One. I had dated many wonderful men in my life over the years, but never had I been so drawn to someone as I was to Neil.

"Well, thank you, I think," I responded, trying to come across as confident as he did.

He introduced me to his entourage of friends (something I would learn that Neil was normally surrounded by), and we were off on a weekend of getting to know each other by way of fun, adventure, and a fair amount of partying.

Thaine had set us up for the initial phone conversation, and Neil, with his natural charm, had persuaded me, sight unseen, to meet him for a weekend in Lake Havasu with a group of his friends for our first date. He had even convinced me to drive there with a friend of his I had never met. I would soon learn how well Neil could persuade just about anyone to do just about anything and put a smile on their face while doing it. That's his super-power.

There were many signs of our connection that weekend. After the first few minutes, I told him he reminded me of my two biggest clients, whose personalities and energy were very much like Neil's. "Oh yeah? Who are they?" he asked.

"I'm sure you don't know them. They're from Canada."

"What are their names?"

"Dave Steele and Phil Carroll."

Neil started laughing and told me they were his best friends. I cracked up along with him. The universe had surely been trying to connect us.

That Neil knew Dave and Phil posed a dilemma for me. They were great to work with, but I wasn't in their league. They were wealthy, successful men with energy, confidence, and a lifestyle I could only dream about. Because they were my biggest clients and Sunsational Suites was vulnerable, I knew I had to watch my p's and q's and tread softly with Neil. There was more at stake for me. I wasn't sure getting involved with Neil was such a good idea, no matter how much I had fallen for him.

Nonetheless, Neil was hard to resist. He was very much the gentleman that weekend. He set me up in my own room at the Nautical Inn, an infamous party spot I knew well. We had fun, but he let me guide the pace. It's such a special time when you meet The One. With no preconceived notions, there's a purity about it, and instant, electric connection. You accept each other without judgment, allowing each other simply to be.

The author Joe Bailey puts it this way: "We fall in love with each other's natural self and in time begin to cast shadows on one another."[7] These magical new relationships exist outside of time and history, without built-up frustrations or expectations, often false, about how the other will act. The businesswoman in me may have been nervous about starting anything with Neil, but after the first day, I was already in love with him. I knew he was who I was waiting for. I didn't know exactly why consciously. It was a powerful energy that pulled me to him, perfectly aligned to help me evolve into my higher self. A soul connection.

But the relationship was complicated, as the saying goes. When I first met Neil, I was trying to keep Sunsational Suites afloat without much help from my father. It felt stressful. I had also just joined YEO, terrified I didn't fit into that high-powered world of movers and shakers (95 percent of whom were men). I'd entered a world I wasn't familiar with but wanted so much to be part of. Neil likely felt my anxiety about both, but I was too proud and insecure to share any of that with him—that I felt lost and terrified much of the time.

The first big trip Neil and I took together after Lake Havasu was a Caribbean cruise sponsored by YEO. It was March 1996. We had meet in September of 1995 and began an intimate relationship in October, so I felt comfortable accepting his exciting offer. I had never been on a cruise and was so excited. I hadn't been a member of YEO for long, having only attended local events. This trip opened a whole new world to me. Money was no object for anyone, with the Dom Perignon flowing, many fancy events to attend, and much partying. Many of the people I met on that cruise are still good friends today. It was on this trip that I developed a more personal friendship with Dave and Phil.

That trip was the beginning of a whole new life for me, but I was terrified. Was I worthy? Did I belong? I was barely holding on to the business, secretly feeling an immense amount of insecurity about the tangled imprisonment of the pressures at home. The last thing I should have been doing, both emotionally and financially, was taking a vacation. Neil paid for the entire trip, though, so I didn't have to worry about the expense. I felt no qualms about that. He certainly could afford it and was accustomed to paying for women he invited on trips. The emotional cost was something else.

One day Neil and I decided to take an excursion on a smaller boat with a group of YEO members. The cocktails were flowing, and many beautiful people in bikinis and swim trunks strutted their stuff. Once the dancing began, the people became more physical with each other. Before I knew it, Neil was on the boat deck with another woman. She wore the most amazing pink bikini and filled it perfectly. They seemed mesmerized by each other. I did everything in my power to behave as if it wasn't happening, despite side-eyed glances from the crowd to see how I was taking it. Who was I to say anything? We weren't married. We weren't even a serious couple. Neil was a YEO celebrity, one of the initial founding members. He captured the interest of many pretty women.

"Wow, Lynn, looks like Shelly and Neil are hitting it off," Mike said, pulling his beautiful wife Kara a little closer to him.

"Hey, we're all just having a good time, right?" I responded, stinging with embarrassment. I wanted to fit in badly, to be part of this world of success and adventure, but Neil's flirting with another woman didn't do much for my confidence.

I couldn't get off the ship, and Neil and I were sharing a suite. I had to get through it somehow, and I did. We spent a lot of time apart, so instead of moping in the cabin, I made a point to meet as many other people as possible. After all, this was a business networking and learning event with many talented speakers to benefit the young entrepreneurs that were enjoying the cruise. Neil and I were still sharing a bed, but he had moved on to a different woman and had no interest in being intimate with me. I'm certain Neil could feel the deep worry and insecurity that had been swallowing me whole. He didn't want to be bothered with my feelings. He wanted to party. I would learn later that Neil shies away from people that seem like work to him or people that don't naturally enjoy themselves. He sensed my insecurities, my awkwardness about a world that I wasn't accustomed to, and that I wasn't in a good place in my life. He didn't want to save anyone, and frankly, it was not his responsibility.

Two days after the cruise, Neil "broke up with me," but by then, it was somewhat of a moot point. He had met yet another woman on the cruise, and "left me" for her, not the woman in the pink bathing suit. His new infatuation, his new girl crush, happened in front of me, night after night, as she sat with us at dinner. I had had no idea they were beginning their romance in front of my eyes and planning a romantic getaway the moment the ship docked at the end of the cruise.

I was heartbroken, humiliated, and devastated, but I had learned growing up to keep my feelings at bay, to make things easy for other people even when they were hard for me, and I did just that. This was not the crowd to lose it in front of. My biggest clients and other YEO members from Arizona were on that trip. I had to stay emotionless and professional. My future depended on it.

The encounters that took place during our first round of dating would become defining moments in our relationship, though I didn't know it at the time. I unconsciously laid the groundwork for the patterns Neil and I established later as a married couple and as a result of my past, a past that I was now recreating in the present. As I always had, I ignored what was happening in front of my eyes and pretended it was okay. Neil's gaslighting began then as well. We began dating in September of 1995, the infamous cruise took place in March 1996, but I saw him with other women in situations I knew were provocative and seductive encounters, all in the guise of having fun at a party. When I brought them to his attention, he told me I was imagining things, that what I saw happening wasn't really happening. He was the perfect teacher to show me how I was repeating the patterns I had set up with my parents and many others: to question my own needs and my own feelings, my own intuition, and to remain silently stoic.

After Neil broke up with me, I was devastated. I felt a despair I had never experienced before. I sobbed uncontrollably throughout the night. The next morning, I had a meeting with Dave and some of his investors. Dave was Neil's best friend, and I was determined not to show Dave just how devastated I was. I iced my swollen eyes and put on as much make up as I could to hide the depth of my heartbreak and survived the meeting. When I arrived at the office that day, everyone knew something was terribly wrong. After many hugs got me through the day, I went home and cried some more.

Looking back, I'm grateful I had so much to do. This was about the time I merged Sunsational Suites with SRA and began the regimented schedule of working with my new business partners and holding down two other jobs to pay off debt, my own and the company's. I had little time for anything else. I had to pick myself up, and I did.

Three years or so later when we sold the company, I was a new woman, free from debt and from my father, independent and financially flush for the first time in forever. I had climbed a mountain and come down the other side. Having to work only one job, I took better care of myself. I was hiking again. I had a social life, having a blast with my girlfriends and dating some exciting men. I was in my late thirties and had become quite comfortable in my own skin. I worked out all the time and felt and looked better than I ever had. We took lots of girl trips, and if you make yourself available, you can find lots of men to play with.

When I was a younger woman, I was so worried about behaving "like a lady," the way society teaches us a lady should behave. Once I was older and more comfortable with myself, I had the confidence to live as I chose, in many ways acting more like a man, happily working, traveling, and playing. I still ran the company for the public corporation that bought us out, but now I was free of the worry of ownership. That's when I bought the condo. Life was good. I was free. I was my own boss, enjoying life on my own terms and living my true self. I had everything I wanted. Well, almost everything.

I didn't have Neil.

Neil and I had remained friends and saw each other quite often socially because of YEO and my clients, Dave and Phil, who had now become my friends as well. Somewhere in my heart I always knew Neil and I would get back together. I know now that I manifested a reunion. I always envisioned our life together, and in my mind, I replayed such a life over and over. I was not consciously aware of why I did this, but my soul knew what I was doing.

Not long after I got back on my feet, Neil saw how happy and self-sufficient I was, no longer the terrified train wreck he had dated a few years earlier. That's when he knocked on my door again in October 2000. Neil doesn't do needy or broken, and I was repaired, or at least it seemed so. At the time, I was dating the founder of Go Daddy, and we were having a great time together. I was enjoying all my friends, traveling and living large. I loved my beautiful condo set within the giant granite boulders of Troon North, which I had decorated perfectly to my taste. I had money in the bank. I was secure and happy. When Neil came knocking, I answered the door. It was a leap of faith; one I didn't hesitate to take for a second.

Just a quick reminder that I am telling *my* story, not Neil's. We all live in our own separate realities and see life from our past experiences, which are largely unconscious. Dr. Bruce Lipton, who has done research on how our conscious and unconscious minds work, explains it this way. We only consciously use about 5 percent of our brain and the other 95 percent represents unconscious behavior. In other words, 95 percent of our behavior results from unconscious past experiences.[8] We don't even notice the behavior because it's what we always do—it's unconscious. It's easier to see the behavior patterns of other people better than our own.

That's why my perception of my marriage will not mirror Neil's. I believe we all come into this earth school with certain lessons we are meant to learn. Neil's lessons are not my lessons and vice versa. In fact, I think in our case our lessons are from the opposite ends of the spectrum. Neil and I have different weaknesses and gifts we have struggled with and benefitted from all our lives. "Soulmates" are souls who make agreements with one another to help each other to grow into their True Selves. That's why I knew Neil from the second I met him. He is my soulmate.

Soulmates help each other attain what our souls are lacking. Author Harville Hendricks, who wrote *Getting the Love You Want*, states that when we are attracted to another person and have the kind of passion that I immediately felt for Neil, for example, there is a reason for it, and the reason is always linked to the parts of ourselves that are wounded and need to be healed.[9] This all occurs at an unconscious level, but our souls are very aware of the purpose of our attraction. If we can get through the pain and the power struggles of the relationship, we can get to the purpose and heal the wounds.

Real soulmates help us grow, but we each come at it from our own perspectives. I'm telling my story from my perspective. It's not my place to tell—or to judge—Neil's story. My intention is to show Neil's role in my journey to finding my true self and purpose, not to criticize, complain, point fingers, or try to interpret what lessons are intended for him.

It has been quite the adventure, full of fun and travel and a very busy, fast-paced, exciting life. Neil has had a life that would seem like a fairy tale to most people. In fact, his story has been published in many news articles and magazines. He has been on over three hundred talk shows (Oprah three times); he has written a book; he has spoken all over the world about his success story that began when he was seventeen years old.

Neil grew up in a middle-class family in a tougher part of California, the San Fernando Valley, no silver spoon in his mouth. He had to earn every penny. Neil and I both find it easy to relate to people up and down the socioeconomic spectrum, given the way we both grew up.

Neil started his first business, California Closets, at seventeen. Yes, that company. It was the first closet organization company in the world. He started out of his garage and the idea took off. His company grew very quickly and at a very young age, he was regarded with a tremendous amount of awe and respect.

Neil has always been a leader and a force in accomplishing whatever he sets his mind to. When he walks into a room, you can't help but know he's there. His charisma radiates with an energy that both astounds you and exhausts you at the same time. A master of words, he can negotiate just about anything his way, big or small, from multi-million-dollar contracts to the best table in a restaurant. He loves to negotiate. He loves the contest and the conquest—he loves to win, and he won't stop until he does. He has two modes: on fire and asleep. There's no in between. When you're with Neil, you're moving and doing, a pace I would learn well in the years to come.

Neil was raised in a different environment than I was, knowing he was special. His parents and his brother adored him. He had a rough start, though. He was born with club feet, which were corrected with surgery and physical therapy. He couldn't speak until he was four years old, but he certainly makes up for that now! Though he was never formally diagnosed, he likely has ADHD. With determination and the love of his family, however, he overcame these challenges and learned that he could accomplish anything. He was the youngest child and his family let him be a kid. He was well taken care of and not expected to take on responsibilities that weren't his own. As a result, he has always taken good care of himself and has very strong boundaries. The relationship we have with ourselves determines the relationship we have with others. Neil has been a clear example of that.

The biggest challenge Neil ever told me about regarding his family, besides the fact that his mother never cooked (not terribly destructive to a child), was that his parents waged a constant power struggle. Neil's mother and father were both strong willed. They fought a lot, with yelling and threats of breakups, but no physical violence. His father, Jack, had affairs, which were often the source of the fights, and his father constantly criticized his mother, Roberta. She was on the heavy side, and he would tell her how fat she was by calling her Chunky Chunky, Moo Moo, and the like. He criticized what she bought, how she dressed, how she cooked or didn't cook, how she acted and on and on. Neil and his brother learned not to respect her, although they loved her dearly.

Neil saw the power struggle between them as a painful part of their otherwise happy family rather than as his mother rightfully sticking up for herself. I believe watching this power struggle created a need in Neil to always be in control, to always have the upper hand, to always win. Whether consciously or not, to avoid the struggles his parents endured, he chose a partner (me) who was more submissive than his mother, more of a people-pleasing conflict avoider. For Neil, conflicts like these were not to be resolved but to be won. Neil's family dynamic may seem difficult to many, but he insists that he was always able to block that energy from his experience. He has shown me over the years that he is a master at self-protection, and I believe he is. His parents treated him with tremendous respect, and it stuck.

This time around dating Neil, we decided our relationship would be different. I knew, even though we hadn't been together for over three years, how deeply I loved him and told him I would rather we simply remained friends unless he was ready to make a commitment.

He agreed, and we had a quick transition to a serious relationship. In January of 2001, we went skiing at Lake Tahoe, the first time he told me he loved me. I was beyond elated. In February, we took a trip to China and Hong Kong with YEO, my first international trip with Neil. I was a YEO member myself at the time, so I insisted on paying my own way. Neil was astounded.

It was a wonderful trip, the first of many just as fabulous to follow. In Neil's style, we flew first class with every comfort provided. We arrived in Hong Kong for the conference, where we stayed at the Mandarin Oriental Hotel in a romantic room overlooking Victoria Harbour, with its magnificent skyline and city light views. Each night after partying, we sat in front of our window and watched the ships pass in and out of the harbor. When we made love, we felt as if we were soaring over the still water.

On that trip, we reintroduced ourselves as a couple to YEO and our friends, Dave and Sherry, Phil and Jen, Max and Lisa, and many others who would travel the world with us for years.

Each time we attend a YEO (now EO) University event like this, we took a separate excursion with this core group of friends. On this trip we went to Beijing, Shanghai, and Xi'an. Each day we had our own private tour buses and historians, as we did with every trip. Traveling with Neil meant private yachts, sometimes private jets, first-class seats, private chefs, fancy restaurants, and five-star hotels.

I moved in with Neil by June 2001. We were in our early forties, loved each other, and Neil confided in me that he wanted a family before he got much older, so we took a leap of faith. I sold the condo, but Neil didn't propose to me until we were on our way to Lake Powell for his annual Fourth of July houseboat trip in 2001 with friends. In a way, it wasn't even his idea. Cathy and I hit it off from the moment we met. She was very close to Neil and saw how much I loved him from the moment she met me.

We were in Neil's suburban, with Neil driving, Cathy's husband Steve in the passenger seat, and Cathy and I in the back. "Lynn, it has been so great getting to know you. Seems like you and Neil are getting kind of serious. Is there marriage in the picture?" Cathy asked, raising an eyebrow.

"We really haven't made any plans," I replied nervously.

"Neil, what do you think?" Cathy said, not giving up.

"I guess that's a good idea. We're not getting any younger," Neil said without the least bit of emotion.

"Did I just get engaged?" I looked for reassurance that this was really happening. I couldn't see the expression on Neil's face.

"When should we have it?" Cathy persisted. "Let's pick a date! I want to be sure Steve and I can be there."

Thank you, Cathy, for closing the deal.

Neil and I had a lovely engagement party at a Seattle YEO University event that summer. After champagne and chocolates, Neil got down on one knee and put a gorgeous diamond ring on my finger. Everyone drank a toast, and I was officially engaged.

We married four months later on October 27, 2001, in an elaborate, elegant wedding with over 300 people, a fairy-tale event, the wedding of a lifetime.

Life with Neil has been dazzling—traveling the world, attending fancy events, meeting many wonderful new friends. I always thought I had a lot of friends until I met Neil. It was hard to keep up his pace while still taking care of my own work responsibilities and the other relationships in my life that were important to me. In Neil's world, he's a celebrity, and I'm the celebrity wife. It's my job to help him shine, but he doesn't really need my help. He loves the spotlight, and with his charisma, he shines all on his own.

A typical event goes like this: We're in California. The grand ballroom of the five-star hotel is filled with hundreds of franchisees in the closet industry gathered to honor Neil's many achievements as the first closet entrepreneur in the world. A video is shown reflecting Neil's life and the success of California Closets and his new business venture with Organizers Direct. Neil is the main speaker, with many of his original franchisees in the room to honor him.

"What is it like living with Neil?" Carol asks me in a quiet moment. She has the googly look of a fangirl.

"It's busy, but lots of fun," I say, taking a deep breath and recalling my week of effort and exhaustion just to be there.

We all watch Neil perform his magic, and I glow with pride. This is what he loves. This is who he is. The man who by the power of will, persuasion, and charisma has inspired these hundreds of people in the room and thousands more worldwide to share in a small part of his success. And they love him for it. And he loves them. And like any celebrity wife, I've had to share my husband with his adoring fans.

Neil has been my teacher in many ways. I am still learning from his example when it comes to caring for myself and creating healthy boundaries with those inclined to take advantage of me. Because of his accomplishments and the force of his personality, people respect Neil. I have never seen anyone take advantage of him or treat him disrespectfully. He wouldn't stand for it. He was raised to know that not only did he not have to put up with disrespect, but that he should not. What a blessing it is when children are well cared for and taught that they're special. I had a very different childhood.

My mother-in-law, with whom I had a blessed relationship and learned so much, always said, "The only job a parent has is to make sure their kids are able go out into the world and accomplish anything they set their mind to, so they can become happy, independent and successful adults." She and Neil's dad sure did that for Neil. My father-in-law passed away before I was able to meet him, but I feel I know him well through the many wonderful family stories. My parents, on the other hand, gave me many gifts, but confidence and security were not among them.

In many ways, Neil and I are also the same, which must be part of our attraction. We both play hard and work hard. We both have an underlying curiosity and the courage to take a leap of faith into wonderful adventures. Neither one of us has ever lacked for friends or exciting opportunities. We never get bored. We generate our own excitement. We have the same spirit and zest for life. We both had plenty of fun dating before we married and didn't lack for companionship. My grandmother used to say, "Lynn is like Jesus. She just loves them all!" At first, I was insulted. Then I said what the heck and embraced it. Neil had a reputation as a player himself and was rather proud of it.

Both of us are also able to connect with a wide range of people, from the janitor to the CEO. The difference between me and Neil is that he knows whether a person is worthy of his friendship or attention. Neil has never had time for needy or high maintenance people, not because he has a cold heart but because he has strong and healthy boundaries. I'm more of a people pleaser who doesn't want to hurt anyone's feelings even when they don't deserve my consideration. My boundaries aren't always as healthy as they should be.

We all have our beautiful sides that reflect our true selves, but we all also have our shadow selves. Debbie Ford describes the shadow as the part of ourselves we'd rather not show to the world, the part we are ashamed of.[10] We don't even know the extent of the shadow because we'd rather not think about it. We push it aside.

But the outside world mirrors our shadow. By using so much of our energy to hide the shadow, we give it great power to affect our lives, usually for the negative. If we are willing to face the shadow, however, if we are aware and willing to address it, we can acknowledge our true selves and uncover our greatest lessons for this lifetime. Addressing our shadows helps us to see the unconscious 95 percent Dr. Bruce Lipton refers to. When we are open to being more conscious of the unconscious, we grow.

Neil and I have run up against each other's shadows in our marriage, exposing our shadow selves to the world. All the patterns and roles quietly unfolded from day one, and they challenge us to this day. For one thing, Neil takes care of Neil first and foremost, and I take care of others and try to please them at the expense of myself. One of the most difficult things we've had to overcome in our marriage is that I don't always know how to create healthy boundaries even with Neil. Neil is a born leader and a highly successful entrepreneur. He's used to getting his way.

He expected that to carry into our marriage as well, not because he's a bad or overbearing person, but because that's how it's always been. That's how he lives his life. And because I'm a people pleaser, and he's the love of my life, I want to please him most of all. Neil is used to people jumping to attention when he needs something, and I'm used to asking how high. It isn't always a healthy combination, especially for me.

We always moved at his pace, for example, though I had other responsibilities, especially once the kids were born. And since he had always been the boss, the CEO, he fell into the role of critiquing me about just about everything in my life: my opinions, the clothes I wore, the way I decorated the house, how I treated the children. If I pushed back, he'd start the gaslighting. "Why are you so sensitive? I'm just trying to help." His way was the best way. He couldn't conceive that every single one of his "observations" weren't incredibly valuable to me. In fact, they were hurtful, often destructive, and made me feel like I was going crazy, which is what gaslighters do by trying to manipulate or control other people into believing that they don't know what they're talking about and can't trust themselves.

Neil's gaslighting bled into our social interactions as well. He was an avid flirter, which didn't change once we were married. Sometimes that hit me wrong. If I called him on it, he'd say, "What? I'm just being friendly. You're too insecure. Do you want to turn me into someone I'm not?" And so on. Sometimes it seemed that no matter what I did, from his perspective, I was wrong.

Now, don't mistake me. Neil is the love of my life—a sexy, vibrant, warm, inspirational man, and a great husband and father. But that doesn't mean that these shadows of his haven't caused very painful and transformative lessons for me, and ultimately, for him, too. I'm just now learning to take care of myself, to stand up for myself, to set better, healthier boundaries. It's been the work of a lifetime, but at this point in my story with Neil, I had only just begun my journey with him, and he'd only just begun his journey with me.

Chapter 9
TWINS R US

Because I was forty-two and Neil forty-one when we married, we had to get to work on having children right away. We decided to try on our own, and if unsuccessful, then we'd adopt.

I wanted to tell everyone, starting with Mom.

"Mom, I'm so excited. We want to get pregnant right away. I can't believe it. It's all happening so fast, like a wonderful dream." I was practically jumping up and down while I told her.

"You really think that's a good idea?" Mom said. "Your life will never be the same. I would think about it very carefully before you can't change your mind."

"It's really not so great." As her voiced echoed that belief, my heart hurt.

I should have expected this response to something that didn't benefit her directly, but I was stunned anyway. What she meant was, *her* life would never be the same. Couldn't she be happy for me? She hadn't been crazy about the wedding, either. I'm sure she thought Neil was stealing me away from her, that Neil was her rival and with his strong personality, she'd never be able to win.

Many of my friends and other family members felt the same way, telling me in no uncertain terms that I was somehow responsible for their happiness and was abandoning them by marrying Neil, daring to try for a family of my own. It was a reality check. I was learning who loved me for me and who loved me for what I could do for them.

Despite my mother's and friends' objections, Neil and I began our journey with fertility directly after the wedding. We made several visits to Dr. Nemiro, one of the best fertility doctors in the city, to determine what direction to take.

On one occasion, Dr. Nemiro told us he needed a semen sample. He left the room abruptly to attend to another patient, leaving a container behind.

"Well, let's go, Lady," Neil said in an I-am-man-hear-me-roar tone.

"Batter up, baby." I jumped up on the examination table and removed my panties. Sex was never something we had to work at, and before we knew it, we had our sample.

Dr. Nemiro entered the room still in a hurry, the practice quite busy that morning. "Neil, you can go in the room down the hall next to the restroom to collect your sample. We have plenty of material to help you along if you need it. Be sure to bring the container," he said.

"Here you go." I handed him the container, already full.

"What? How? The room just opened up."

"You told us to get the sample, and we got the sample," Neil replied with pride.

"Where?" Dr. Nemiro was confused.

"Right here," Neil replied, gesturing at the exam table.

"You did what?"

"We had sex. That's what you told us to do, right?" We both looked at him confident that we had followed directions and accomplished our task.

"You had full-on sex right here?" He looked at us in astonishment.

"Yes," Neil replied. "Isn't that right?"

Dr. Nemiro laughed hard and long, and when he stopped, he had no words. He simply shook his head. I'm sure he's told that story more than once since that day.

We surprised him again in the next step. After one unsuccessful attempt, we determined that using my eggs likely wouldn't work, so we decided to go with donor eggs. When you use donor eggs, you have to choose a donor. Dr. Nemiro gave us a book with the pictures and bios of the young women who had signed on as donors. "Sometimes it takes a while," he said. "Don't get discouraged."

The doctor left to see another patient. When he returned, we pointed to the page of the person we'd chosen. He was astounded. "What do you mean? It takes people weeks, months, to decide. Don't you want to put more thought into it?"

"We're good, Doc. Gotta take that leap of faith, right?" Neil said with confidence.

I nodded.

"You two never cease to amaze me," the doctor said.

At least we made his life interesting.

I have always known in my soul that we are all one, that all children are our children, and that everything happens as it should. It wasn't difficult for me to decide to use donor eggs or to choose the wonderful donor angel we did. I wanted to do this for Neil, so he could share genes with our children. Yes, sometimes I did get a little jealous that the children would look like Neil and not me, but I was much more grateful we'd get to have a baby.

The very good news was that, after many fertility shots, three surgeries through my belly button, and more doctors' appointments than we could count, we got pregnant the first try! It was April 2002, six months after our wedding. We were relieved and crazy nervous at the same time.

Like any newly pregnant couple, we were excited to see our little baby growing within me. I lay on the examination table for the first ultrasound after we found out. The tech squirted the probe with cold gel and rubbed it on my still perfectly flat belly.

"Well, you two, I see a perfect little baby right here," she said, watching the screen as she swirled the wand around. "Oh, wait, there's another one. Twinsies." She continued her exploration. "Okay, oh my, there's a third baby." Now she was downright giddy. "You're going to have triplets!"

Neil and I looked at each other in astonishment, neither of us breathing. *Holy Shit*, I thought, *is this really happening?*

"Oh boy, Neil and Lynn, look right here on the screen. There's one, there's two, there's three," she pointed with a blue capped pen. "You're having triplets!" She searched our faces for our response.

Still holding his breath, Neil had turned a shade of purple. I grabbed his hand and clutched it firmly, hoping to bring him back into his body. He finally gasped for air.

We left the office in shock, trembling with excitement and fear at the same time. I reassured him it would all be okay, but I'm not sure I believed it myself.

Once home, I could see that Neil wasn't happy. He was not prepared to have three children all at once at forty-two years old. Frankly I didn't know how I could pull it off either at forty-three.

We contacted Dr. Foltz. He told us that it would be way out of his comfort zone to handle a triplet pregnancy for a woman my age, that trying to carry all three put them all—and me—at risk. He encouraged selective pregnancy reduction.

I was devastated and very emotional, given the hormones I was receiving. I didn't know what to do. Neil was scared, both for me and our future children. We had many heated discussions trying to figure out what to do. I wanted to leave it to God and not terminate any of the embryos. Neil took a more practical, risk-mitigation approach, as he called it, and insisted we listen to Dr. Foltz.

At eight weeks, God made the decision for us, though, when we lost one of the babies. God made sure our twins would be safe.

The next months were difficult for me with the mood swings from the fertility drugs and the anxiety of a difficult, high-risk pregnancy. Pregnancy brought me back to the vulnerability of childhood, when I felt helpless and unprotected in the face of my mother's erratic behavior.

The fertility drugs were hard on me physically and emotionally. They triggered feelings of insecurity and self-doubts I had long tried to stuff down. My behavior became volatile. One night Neil and I were in the living room watching *Monster's Ball* with Halle Berry. We came to a sex scene with Berry and Billy Bob Thornton, and Neil was fully engaged.

"You never look at me like that!" I yelled out. "You'd rather have sex with Halle Berry than me!" I burst into tears rubbing my bloated, pregnant belly.

"Have you lost your damn mind? It's a movie." Neil was a little raw from anxiety as well. He stormed out of the room to escape my craziness.

But it wasn't just the hormones. It hadn't been long since I had moved into the house and Neil still had pictures of his old girlfriends on the walls and desks, even the girl he had the affair with on the boat that led to our breakup. Neil had been single his whole life. He just didn't know how to be married, but he loved me. I was sure of it. Still, he wouldn't take the pictures down, saying I was trying to control him. Every time I saw one of them, I felt vulnerable in my precarious condition and wept or threw a tantrum or both. I had no filter with the fertility drugs. But he wouldn't budge. I finally took the pictures down myself, and he must have decided it wasn't worth further fighting, because he let it alone after that.

During my pregnancy, all the lessons intended for me unfolded with greater intensity. I was terrified that I was losing my independence, that I was losing myself, that I would never be in control of myself and my choices again. The fertility drugs only enhanced my dance of dependence with Neil. I had lost the ability, once again, to care for myself properly and to ask for what I needed. I regressed to that scared little five-year-old girl who wanted to be taken care of but didn't know how to ask for it. To Neil, I was hysterical and needy, and Neil doesn't do needy. He mostly ignored me.

About six months into the pregnancy, I could no longer work and gave notice. Neil and I had always intended for me to stay home with the children. It was just happening a little earlier than we had planned. I was ready to nest and prepare the nursery.

We lived in a smallish but nice home in the Arcadia area of Scottsdale, which Neil had shared with his friend Gary until I moved in and booted Gary out. Gary still teases me about that. Because two bachelors had been living there, the house needed a woman's touch. Now that I wasn't working, I had my chance. I pictured leisurely days of decorating and daydreaming about the babies: What would they be like? What color eyes and hair would they have? Would they be chubby? All the things mothers-to-be think about.

The first day of my maternity leave, Neil was just about ready to leave for work. "Honey, I have to go, but I left you a list on the kitchen counter of what needs to be done while I'm gone." He stuffed a few things in his briefcase. "I should be back around six. I'll let you know what sounds good for dinner."

I was stunned, so taken aback I didn't say a word, just gave him a hug and said, "Love you. Have a good day." After Neil left, I did my morning cleanup, then went to the kitchen and reviewed the list.

The list wasn't at all the dreamy nesting I had in my mind. It included errands, paperwork, and housekeeping chores. Did he think I worked for him? Later that morning I went into the office of my new home and noticed a sticky note on some paperwork he wanted me to review. It said *See Me* in thick black letters. "What the *fuck*?" I said out loud. Was this a joke?

That night I made a wonderful dinner. As we lingered over chit chat and I cleared the dessert dishes, I brought the list and sticky note back to the table, holding them prominently in my hand. In a jokey tone, I said, "You know how hard I worked to get my business degree and then my broker's license, right? And how I managed huge properties for years and owned three of my own companies. You know why I did that? I did that so I could be my own boss. I like being my own boss, and I didn't get married to get a new one."

He looked at me blank-faced and shrugged. "What's the big deal?" he said, clearly not seeing the humor I was going for. "It's stuff that needs to get done. I'm at work. You're home. It just makes sense."

He truly didn't get it. He was used to telling people what to do without question. It's what he always did. He was smart enough to stop leaving lists for me, but he still had expectations of my responsibilities, and look out if I didn't fulfill them the way he wanted me to. Once I left work, the distribution of labor fell along old-school gender lines, with Neil as the head of the household. He made the decisions and gave directions, and I followed them. I didn't get to express *my* expectations for *him*.

At one point, he took the pile of bills I had forwarded to the house—my bills—and sorted through them, deciding which were worthy and which weren't. Some were pet charities of mine. I had a monthly payment for a little girl in Africa with whom I had actually built up a relationship—that was out. I had also been paying a monthly amount to a Christian radio station—that was out. And I didn't even push back! I had reverted to the parent-child relationship my parents had taught me so well. The patterns of my life.

Why did I put up with it? Oh, all the usual reasons. I was a peace-maker, and was it really worth the fight? Maybe I was being too sensitive. If I was at home, it made sense for me to take care of the house stuff, didn't it? Someone had to keep things organized, and why shouldn't it be Neil? He was good at it. He also made a shit ton of money, and maybe I should be grateful. He loved me, even if he didn't show it in ways I always appreciated. And I loved Neil more than anything in the world and didn't want to lose him.

None of these made for much of an equal partnership. The choreography of our dance was established from the start, and it was clear who took the lead.

On November 19, 2002, our beautiful twins, Jack and Brianna, were born after I had been on bed rest for two months and in intensive care for two weeks. Dr. Foltz had put a belt on me to trigger the nursing station if I went into labor and didn't realize it. The twins were born at thirty-four weeks and stayed in the neonatal intensive care unit (NICU) for two weeks to make sure they were thriving and could breathe on their own. When we took them home, Brianna weighed three pounds and Jack four.

On the way home, the twins were in the back seat of the car in their little pink and blue outfits swaddled and strapped into the huge car seats that made them seem even tinier and more fragile. Neil looked over at me in the passenger seat and said, "Now what?" I think he was trying to make a joke, but he was wide-eyed and dead serious.

Now what, indeed.

Chapter 10
AUTISM IS A FAMILY JOURNEY

After enduring the long and emotional process of fertility treatments and a difficult, high-risk pregnancy, we had done it. We had our perfect boy and girl. Life was wonderful and crazy at the same time.

Like many mothers, I vowed to give Brianna and Jack everything I thought I had been lacking as a kid. I would engage with them and put their needs first. I would never yell (I very rarely ever have). I would keep a clean house. I would give them regular meals and keep their clothes clean. I would not subject them to the indignity of stepparents. I would not give them responsibilities beyond their years. I would give them the security of structure.

Because of the chaos of caring for twins amid our very busy lives, I can't say that I remember much from when the twins were babies. Thank God for photographs. Having twins at forty-three was a huge adjustment for Neil and me, but we were very grateful, and the twins were adorable. Their personalities were established from the moment of conception. Brianna was always the easy one, even in utero. Calm and content, she barely moved. That may be because Jack didn't give her much choice. Jack felt like a circus tumbler high energy, always moving, using the womb as his very own bouncy house.

Everything was busy times two. Neil was still working hard, so we hired a nanny during the day and one at night for the first two months. When the night nanny left after the two months, Neil took one of the feedings at night while I took the others. We charted all their feedings, bowel movements, sleep times, and so on, so we wouldn't miss anything and could share the information with the pediatrician. Neil has always been an involved father, but because he worked full-time (more than fulltime, really), the bulk of the childcare fell to me and the nanny, especially when they were sick. Neil always had time for the kids when he was home, though, and loved playing with them. If Neil got to be the "fun" parent, at least he wasn't an absent one.

When Jack began to walk (correction, when Jack began to run—he has never really walked anywhere), life got even more hectic. Jack was an energizer bunny, and we spent a good deal of the day chasing him down and keeping him safe and out of trouble. He was a climber and an escape artist, every chair, dresser, or set of shelves his Mt. Everest, every door a portal to a great new adventure. Whoever had Jack duty couldn't let him out of their sight for a nanosecond. Getting him into his car seat or a highchair was always a relief, giving us a few seconds to catch our breaths.

Brianna, on the other hand, had an even temperament and rarely got in trouble or was cause for worry. She was an easy child to raise, but she was no wallflower. She is naturally daring and athletic, and as she grew up, she came to love hiking, skiing, snowboarding, and water sports. Even when she was quite young, she had no fear of jumping off high dives, climbing to the highest point on rock walls, zip lining, parasailing, and paragliding, to name just a few of her favorite activities. From an early age, Brianna has also been a wonderful sister to her brother, willing to help him at any time.

With Jack, things got so out of hand sometimes that Neil and I argued about whether to use a toddler leash for our son. We'd always traveled a lot and having twins didn't change that. I remember racing through airports, amusement parks, and children's events to catch Jack and save him from getting lost or hurting himself. I wanted the leash for my sanity. Neil said no because it was treating Jack like a pet. So, we didn't use a leash no matter how many times I tried to explain that sometimes I just needed a break.

After visiting Disneyland for the first time when the kids were three, I was devastated. Hundreds of families were sharing this wondrous place with their children, who seemed perfectly capable of waiting patiently in line for the rides and exhibits, eating at tables with no more than the usual mess and noise, standing off to the side without doing a runner while the parents checked in with each other, not screeching at every tiny setback or irritation.

Because Jack did all those things, and since Neil didn't have the patience to watch over him, I spent the whole time we were at Disneyland chasing Jack, cajoling Jack, comforting Jack, placating Jack, encouraging Jack, guiding Jack, trying to keep Jack from screaming. I was exhausted after the first half hour, angry and resentful that all these other perfect families were having such a great time. And Neil was angry at me. He and Brianna were having a blast. He didn't understand why Jack and I were so miserable. He thought I must be doing something wrong, that I was making it too hard on myself, and in the process was ruining his and Brianna's time there. It's a wonder the marriage survived that trip.

I soon realized that something was off with Jack, but I didn't know what.

After the trip, I had a spousal retreat for YEO. (Now that I wasn't working, I had moved from the business forum to the wives' forum.) I went right from the airport to the retreat in a beautiful house in Scottsdale. These retreats were the time to bring up any concerns about the family, business, or life in general and get support and feedback in a safe environment. All of us were married to type-A, high-energy entrepreneurs, and we all understood better than anyone what we were all going through.

Exhausted, I had to push myself to have dinner with the group before they went out to celebrate. I had decided not to go with them that night. I was too tired. During dinner, the tradition was for each of us to update the group. When my turn came, I couldn't help it. I let it all out. "I hate Disneyland! I hate it. It's an awful, horrible, nasty place, and I never want to go there again! Ever." I all but stamped my feet while the tears poured down my face.

"Lynn, what happened? It's Disneyland. How could it be that bad?" one of my friends said.

"I don't know what's wrong with me. Jack wouldn't stop running and screaming. I lost him three different times running into a crowd. He wouldn't sit still. He wouldn't stay in line without screaming. I couldn't control him. Neil and I fought the whole time. All the other families were having so much fun. I'm a terrible mother. I'm awful. What's wrong with my baby? Something's wrong with my baby. I can't take it! I can't take it anymore."

I blamed myself. Why couldn't I be a better mother? What was wrong with me? I wondered if Jack was hyperactive, since Neil had been considered ADHD as a child and likely still was. But I should be able to handle that, shouldn't I? I had learned early on it was my fault if something went wrong and that it was my job to fix it.

My friends looked at me with astonishment and compassion, all of them coming to me, letting me collapse in their loving arms. My body released all my pent-up fury. I felt like Michael Clarke Duncan in *The Green Mile* when the bugs flew out of his mouth. Those special friends gave me the freedom to release it all as they held me through my pain. When it was time for them to go out, they were afraid to leave me alone, but I convinced them I would be asleep in minutes, and I was.

I hate Disneyland to this day.

I was running on empty and quite thin at 103 pounds. Brianna hit her milestones before Jack did, but I always attributed that to the fact that girls learn quicker. I never had any real concerns about Jack. I remember thinking it was odd he was always obsessed with anything round. He would stare at the tires of a car and scream if you took him away from them. I just figured he was a boy who liked things that went vroom. He often flapped his hands and stood on his tiptoes, but I didn't know enough to be concerned about that. He was always running and jumping and could never sit still. Because his father had many of those same qualities, I thought Jack suffered from hyperactivity if anything.

In September of 2005, before their third birthday in November, I decided to enter the twins in preschool so they could socialize with other children. I put them both in the same class for a few hours a day. I knew Jack was a handful. One of the reasons I entered him in pre-school was to get feedback from teachers who worked with children that age.

It wasn't even a week before the director of the school asked me to see her in her office. Debbie had wonderful curly black hair and large deep brown eyes. She handled our meeting with grace, gently leading me through her concerns about Jack's disruptive behavior. She suggested we have Jack evaluated. I gave my permission for a woman they worked with to observe Jack in the classroom. In my heart, I knew he was likely to be diagnosed with ADHD. The next day I took Jack into school for the evaluation and waited in the parking lot for the kids to get out of school. The expert who had done the evaluation called me on my cell.

"Mrs. Balter, my name is Shayna. I have just spent the day evaluating Jack, and I would like to discuss my observations with you," she said in a dry, professional tone.

"Yes, hi Shayna, I'm here in the parking lot. Would you like me to come in?" I said nervously.

"No, no need. I had to leave, but I do believe you have some serious issues to address with Jack. I think you had better prepare yourself for the 'A' word. I've worked with children for years in this field, and I'm sure I can be of assistance," she said.

"Excuse me, what is the 'A' word?" I said "A word" more loudly than I intended. I had no idea what she was talking about. When she explained that the A word was autism, I discounted what she said. I had heard of autism, but knew nothing about it other than from the movie Rain Man. What I did know was that Jack didn't have it. His pediatrician had said Jack was fine. Who did she think she was? She wasn't a doctor. What were her credentials? How could she have the audacity to tell a parent something so serious without a physician present? "Right. Right. Got it. Okay." I told her whatever I had to get off the phone.

Then I threw the phone across the car.

Then near to tears, I gathered up the phone and called our pediatrician, hysterical.

"Don't worry, Lynn," he reassured me. "I'm sure Jack doesn't have autism." That was all I needed to hear. That young woman didn't know what she was talking about.

Later that same afternoon, the doorbell rang. I was in no mood to see anyone. I opened the door and saw a young brown-haired woman in her late thirties. I didn't recognize her and had no patience for a sales call just then.

"Hi, can I help you?" I said shortly.

"My name is Shayna. I spoke to you on the phone today about your son Jack?" she said, looking at me with the most sympathetic eyes. "I'm here to help you understand what I saw in Jack today."

In my flustered state, I must have told Shayna she could come by our house to evaluate Jack further. "Look, I don't know who you are, but what you said today caused us a great deal of pain," I said angrily. "Who do you think you are to tell me something like that on the phone? I've never heard of anything so unprofessional and irresponsible. And what do you know about it? Do you have a medical license? Jack's doctor said he's fine. We've got this from here!"

I practically slammed the door on that poor young woman. I had talked to Jack's doctor and my little boy was okay as far as I was concerned. Cynically, I thought Shayna was trying to scam us into treatments Jack didn't need.

All the signs suggested something was up with Jack, though, so to find out for sure, we made an appointment with a behavioral and developmental specialist at one of the most prominent centers in Phoenix. I thought the doctor would confirm Jack had ADHD, we'd get some tips for how to help him and maybe some meds, and that would be that.

The appointment was November 4, 2005, a few weeks shy of Jack and Brianna's third birthday. It was the only appointment available and just happened to fall on the same day that I was leaving for a trip I had been looking forward to for months. My father had recently passed in August. We were taking a girls' trip to Miami, my sisters and one of my dearest friends, Bette, were all going to be there. My flight was leaving directly after the appointment. They were all from out of town, except for my sister Darline, I missed them all so much and had been counting the days to see them. We were all grieving the loss of my dad. We needed some R&R and some time together. I had scheduled a driver to pick me up at the doctor's office to take me to the airport.

Neil and I had sent over paperwork that described our concerns and those of the preschool: that Jack disrupted class by climbing on anything and everything; that he ran out of the classroom every chance he got; that he didn't make eye contact with students or teachers; that he never played with other children or engaged with them in other ways; and that he had screaming fits when there was too much noise.

Neil, Jack, and I arrived at the doctor's office early that morning. While we waited nervously for them to call our name, Jack cycloned his way through the waiting room, pulling magazines onto the floor while ripping some of their covers, climbing on unoccupied chairs, emptying the box of toys set aside for children, spinning around in circles, and kicking the legs of furniture and some of the other patients as he did so. I had my hands full keeping him out of the way and making sure he didn't break anything.

The door opened and a professionally dressed, serious-looking nurse called our name. As she led us through the narrow hallway, I heard the scream of a child in distress. I peeked into the room and saw a child flapping his hands and spinning in a circle. Jack does that, I said to myself, not knowing whether that was a comfort or not. We entered a room with a play area and lots of toys. The doctor told us she had gone through our paperwork and wanted to play with Jack for a bit to get to know him.

Filling out the paperwork had been painful, particularly the survey of Jack's behaviors, many of which we had to rate on a range from Very Serious to Not an Issue. Neil and I quarreled over many of them. Does Jack stand on his tippy toes? for example. I had seen Jack repeatedly standing on his toes, so I called it Very Serious. Neil was at work much of the day and hadn't noticed, so he called it Not an Issue. (Why Neil didn't simply take my word for it is a question for another chapter.) We argued like this about several of the questions, because each one seemed a scathing judgment of our parenting. We were over-sensitive and terrified.

The doctor played with Jack while we clutched our hands and squirmed in our seats, wincing every time Jack threw a toy, made a noise, or flapped his hands, watching every flicker of expression on the doctor's face.

After about twenty minutes, the doctor left Jack on the floor with the toys and returned to her desk. She made her notes in the file, then said, "Do either of you have any concerns for Jack?" Her tone was perfunctory, as if she was working her way through a script.

"No, not really," Neil said in his usual confident manner, as if he could negotiate a favorable diagnosis. "I had ADHD as a kid. I'm sure I still do. We think it might be that."

She looked over her notes, then raised her eyes to us. "Have either of you had any family members with special needs?"

Growing agitated in the small room, Jack was pulling at the door handle to get out. I tried to redirect and comfort him, but he was having none of it. I couldn't calm him and was growing agitated myself. All I wanted to do was get on that plane for a trip I desperately needed.

She asked again.

"No, not me," I said. "We used donor eggs, so my history isn't really relevant, and I don't know much about the donor." I felt a pang of guilt. Maybe we should have done more research on the donor.

At his turn, Neil said, "Nope, just the ADHD, Doc. So what's the bottom line? What can we do to help? Drugs? Therapy? What?"

The doctor looked at both of us without emotion and took off her glasses.

"Your son has autism," she informed us. "I have a book you can read. It's called 1-2-3 Magic, about children and discipline.[11] It doesn't address autism specifically, but many parents with autistic children have found it useful. Call me in six months, and we'll go from there."

She announced this as if she'd already told twenty other families the same thing that week. There was no emotion in her voice or body language. I felt like a stranger had just punched me in the stomach and walked away.

"No way!" we both said loudly, talking over each other. "Impossible. That doesn't make sense. Jack's pediatrician said he was fine."

"This book will help you understand more," she said, opening the door to get to her next appointment. "We'll talk in six months." She left us with Jack.

The world spun out of control. I was dizzy and disoriented, as if walking through a funhouse. I held Jack in my arms. He kept squirming, as always, to get away. Neil and I looked at each other, not knowing what to say. Maybe if we didn't say anything it wouldn't be real.

We made our way outside where my driver waited. I didn't know what to do.

"Get in the car," Neil said. "We'll be okay."

I was conflicted. My little boy had autism. Shouldn't I stay behind to be with him? But Neil said to go. That they'd be okay. Shouldn't I take him at his word? I so wanted to go on the trip. I so needed to go on this trip. I let myself be persuaded. I was in shock. I got in the car and went to Miami.

It was not the best decision I've ever made. It's not like I had fun. I was numb the whole trip. I know now Neil cried much of the time I was gone. I should have been there for him and Jack. We would have gotten through that terrible weekend together. But I did what I was supposed to do that morning. That was the plan, going to Miami. If I stuck to the plan, it would be all right. We could pretend none of it was happening.

But it was happening. Jack had autism and ADHD.

When you are first diagnosed with autism (and when I say "you," I mean the whole family), it's life changing for everyone. I went through Elisabeth Kübler-Ross's Five Stages of Grief: Denial, Anger, Bargaining, Depression, Acceptance.[12] I grieved the loss of the child I thought I had and the life I had expected for him and our family. I was also still grieving the loss of my father who had passed away two months before, and the griefs overlapped and intertwined. People go through these stages in different ways at different times and I cycled through the first four stages for about two years before getting to acceptance. As Neil and I watched our friends and family with neurotypical children navigate their very different lives, we cycled back to denial, anger, bargaining, and especially depression. In the years ahead, Brianna and her friends were a constant reminder of the different lives of neurotypical children, and we worked hard to make sure we didn't overlook her needs, given the time and effort we devoted to Jack. We valued and celebrated Brianna's every birthday party, every holiday, every activity. We have raised a confident daughter who has had a happy, adventurous, and action-packed childhood.

When you have children, you have all these plans, all the ideas for what you dream their lives might be. You want to make sure they are safe, kind, and happy. You want to provide them with all the experiences that will serve them in life. When your child is diagnosed with autism, all those dreams change. The new dreams aren't bad, but they sure are different. You learn to let go of how you thought your child's life would go, and your own life as a parent. It wasn't always easy.

Believe it or not, after he passed away, Dad helped me through the early stages of Jack's diagnosis, when my gift of dreams came in to play. The first time he came to me was not long after the diagnosis. I was exhausted, broken, and overwhelmed by what lay ahead. In the middle of the day, I took a nap. Before falling asleep, I said out loud, "Daddy, I need you so much right now. I wish you were here."

He heard me. In my dream, I was sleeping. He came up next to me and held me in his arms. I could see his reflection in a mirror, full of peace and love. As he held me, he took away my pain, absorbing it into his own body, and passing on to me a divine peace and wisdom. I woke up refreshed and clear headed, ready to take on our challenges. Dad had comforted me in a way I will cherish forever.

Jack, too, has the gift of dreams, and Dad came to Jack as well shortly after he passed. After his death, I worried about Dad—his soul—because he had been so lost during his lifetime. Had he learned enough? Was he at peace?

Just after he was diagnosed, Jack sat in his booster in the back seat of the car on the way to preschool. Jack didn't use a lot of words then, but he did that morning. "Mommy, Grandpa came to see me last night," Jack said in his sweet toddler voice.

"Grandpa Frank?" I was confused. I knew that Grandpa Frank, my stepfather, Jack's only living grandfather, hadn't been to the house recently. "Was Grandpa Frank at the house?" I looked at Jack's reflection in the rearview mirror.

"No, Mommy. Grandpa Don. He told me to tell you that he is just fine and has many more lives to live."

Jack has always been in tune with the spirit and has many special gifts. There is a thin veil between this earth school and our loved ones on the other side. I believe that veil is much thinner for younger children who have more recently come from spirit and for those with disorders such as autism. Sometimes I wonder if they are really disorders at all but special and misunderstood gifts that give such children a deeper insight into Spirit.

The years to come were filled with many classes on autism and many therapeutic approaches. Two weeks after the diagnosis, I apologized to Shayna and brought her back to our house to help Jack. It turns out she was the daughter of the women who ran the Jewish Community Center, and she spearheaded the Jewish Community Center, autism initiative.

Shayna was the first in a long line of therapists to spend many hours at our home and take over many of the roles that I, as Jack's mother, thought should be mine—another lesson I had to learn about letting go, trusting, and believing. In essence, I had to hand over my precious child to those who understood autism and the need for intense and aggressive early intervention. As a result, they decided when he could play and when he couldn't; how long he should scream when he wouldn't cooperate; when he could eat and drink; what rewards he received when he did cooperate, and how he would be punished when he didn't. Some days I felt like an intruder in my own home rather than Jack's mother.

I remember when Jack began applied behavior analysis (ABA), a treatment to teach him skills that neurotypical children learn naturally from the environment. When Shayna introduced the therapy, Jack screamed for what seemed like hours, unable to do what she asked of him. I sat in the hallway listening to him scream, paralyzed, while someone I hardly knew had taken charge of my son. I cried for hours that day and many days to follow. Despite Jack's many tantrums while adjusting to his numerous therapists, I knew they all had his best interests at heart. Many of these experts be came part of our family. I will always be grateful to the talented and beautiful people who are patient and kind enough to work with special needs children and adults. They are truly a gift from God.

Jack began a life of sixty hours a week of therapy: occupational therapy, physical therapy, speech, ABA, social skills, and school. When we weren't driving around town to take Jack to therapy, we had a house full of therapists working with him at home. Life with our family was always hectic, and it didn't slow down because Jack had autism; it just got crazier. We did have a nanny, Taula, and thank God she was able to help manage Jack's schedule and that of our household in general.

Nothing was ever entirely easy with Jack, and sometimes we had to rely on the "it takes a village" concept to get through it.

In the summer of 2007, when the twins were four-and-a-half, we were going on our annual summer trip to Kelowna at Wood Lake in Canada. That year we were hitching a ride on a private plane owned by a family we were friendly with. One of the family members would be on the plane with us, and we were taking off from the Scottsdale airport. At the entrance to the airport was a sparkling red Ferrari surrounded by barriers with large signs reading, "Do Not Touch" in large print. Because it's a private airport, there are very few people there.

Once we settled in the waiting area, I got on the phone with Jennifer, one of our friends in Canada, to arrange to have groceries waiting for us at our condo. As I looked up, I called out, "Oh My God! Jack," then dropped the phone on the seat next to me and ran as quickly as I could to Jack, who had climbed onto the Ferrari and was now jumping on the spoiler. I grabbed him as quickly as I could before anyone could notice and carried him back to my seat, where Jennifer's voice blared from the phone asking if everything was okay. Jennifer was familiar with this airport, and when I told her I had just pulled Jack off the Ferrari, we had a good laugh.

Once we were seated in the plane and settling in for takeoff, the door to the plane began to close. "Wait, open the door please," an airport employee commanded. Then he climbed the steps and entered the plane. "We have a bit of a situation," he said, looking at Neil and me.

We looked back at him as if to say, Yes?

"The spoiler is cracked on the Ferrari with little foot prints all over it that look just like the little feet right over there." He pointed at Jack who was already trying to break free from his seat belt.

"Are you sure?" Neil said. I'm certain he was calculating the thousands of dollars it would cost to replace the spoiler of a Ferrari.

The employee gestured as if to say, Who else could it be?

"Yeah, I guess you're right. That sounds like our boy. Let us know how much it costs, and we'll take care of it."

Tim, the owner of the plane, didn't even react.

"Tim, we are so sorry," I said, abashed that I hadn't seen the damage when I swept Jack away from the scene of the crime.

Neil gave our contact information to the attendant, and eventually we took off.

Tim made no mention of the incident the rest of the flight, even as Jack ran around the plane in his normal hyper manner. It was much easier to contain Jack on a private plane than it was on a commercial one, so we let him out of his seat when it was safe to do so.

We never did get a bill or hear a thing from anyone about paying for the spoiler. In his graciousness, I'm sure Tim and his family took care of it, perhaps out of sympathy for our trials and tribulations with Jack.

We had many crazy, fun, and unpredictable experiences traveling with our sweet Jack over the years. Some were innocent, some embarrassing, some expensive, but all have been part of our blessed journey.

Autism requires many therapies. When a child's brain is forming up until about ten years old, their brains are like sponges. This is the most important time to engage the child with as much therapy as possible. These essential services make all the difference in the quality of life as they grow and mature.

As soon as a family member is diagnosed, the state provides paid respite care and ABA therapy, but there's much more to it. When we first began our journey with autism in 2005, it was difficult to get insurance to cover the other therapies. As the numbers of children diagnosed with autism have risen around the world due in part to greater awareness, the laws have changed significantly. Neil and I have had the opportunity to play a part in that change, as I'll describe in the "Healing Through Service" chapter.

Because of the many therapies and therapists required, I had to learn humility. Remember, I had been self-reliant from early childhood, and my role with friends and family had always been to take care of everyone and everything—to fix things, to make things happen. Now I had to give that all up and rely on a team of people who knew way more than I did. I was usually the one giving, but only gradually did I learn that this was a time of receiving. The autism community put their arms around us to help us understand the impact autism would have on our lives.

Many of the therapists are young adults just out of school, and though they have more experienced supervisors overseeing their work, these twenty-somethings (more women than men) do the bulk of the hands-on care. I had to learn to put my son and my house in their hands, and this wasn't always easy. (Our neighbors used to laugh. They saw all these young women coming and going from the house and wondered what the heck we were running.)

As a forty-something mother with what I thought were fairly significant life experiences and wisdom, initially I had trouble accepting the younger women's expertise in caring for my child. That was my ego talking and, of course, my heart, too, because to me, some of their methods seemed harsh. Their goal was to help Jack get along in the world, and sometimes that meant he had to face consequences in the form of schedules, discipline, diet, and even punishments. He often grew frustrated, and when he was frustrated, he shrieked. As the mom, I just wanted to take him in my arms and comfort him, but that wasn't always the best way.

I've come a long way since then, and today the experts are just part of our extended family. They've helped Jack and the rest of the family so much I really couldn't imagine it any other way. That's acceptance. I knew I had to embrace the changes autism brought to our lives. I had to put Jack first and let go of the need to do it my way. I had to learn to put my trust in the team.

The team meets every two weeks even now that Jack is eighteen (at the time my book was completed) to discuss his progress and next steps. Everything is decided by the team: the way Jack is disciplined, his schedule, what he can and can't do that day (games, electronics, and so on), what he should eat. Forget about privacy. Our family life is an open book.

From the beginning, our goal was to help Jack function in the world and live his best possible life. For us, that meant public schools. By mainstreaming Jack in the public school system, he would learn to navigate life in the neurotypical world. But having a special needs child in the public school system is difficult, although it has gotten better since we began.

We were stuck in the middle with Jack. Autism is on a spectrum, with Jack being on the higher functioning end of that spectrum. But that doesn't mean he requires any less therapy. The special needs classes are for the more severely affected students with more physical and verbal challenges. Jack wouldn't get the academic stimulation he needed from them. At the same time, because he is impulsive and easily frustrated, the typical classroom is difficult for Jack to navigate. Our solution was to put in place an Individualized Education Plan (IEP), which sets up specialized instruction for those with autism and ADHD, and a 504 plan, which is slightly different and gives assurance that a child with special needs will receive access to the education and services they need. We would revisit both these plans every year.

Most teachers want to do the right thing. They try their best to embrace all their students, but I don't envy them their jobs. They have large classrooms and don't necessarily have the training to educate all students with special needs. I understand that when the needs of the few are given precedence in the classroom, this can affect the quality of education for everyone. But this is my son we're talking about, and we wanted to give him the best education possible. We fought the school district for the right to have an aide from a professional autism program shadow Jack through each school day, and we finally won.

Even with the aide, I was in and out of the principal's office every week.

I'd get a call from Mr. Sweeney, our principal, the sweetest man. He directed traffic with a smile every morning and afternoon. "Mrs. Balter, we are going to need you to come and pick up Jack again. His behavior is not acceptable. He is affecting the learning of the other children." These phone calls were as painful to him as they were to me. Jack was in the third grade.

I was in the middle of my workout at the gym, but I always had my phone next to me. "I'll be right there, Mr. Sweeney. I'm so sorry." I grabbed my gym bag and left. At school, I rushed into the lobby still wearing my damp workout clothes. Sweat ran down my face. I didn't want to think about how I smelled.

"What happened?" I asked Mr. Sweeney when he came out of his office. I was still catching my breath from the workout and the rush over.

"Jack kept walking around the classroom, distracting the other students. We asked him to sit down, but he wouldn't. When we pushed the issue, the tantrum began. We couldn't get him to settle down. Mrs. Cunningham couldn't really teach the class."

"I'll discuss options with his aide and our team. Please give us another chance. We think it's important for Jack to be educated with his neurotypical peers. We'll figure it out. I promise." I looked at Mr. Sweeney for compassion.

"Alright, Mrs. Balter, but we have to get a handle on this. I'd like to see you and your husband in the next few days to discuss what to do about it." Mr. Sweeney liked Jack and was on our side. But he had the rest of the class to think about as well.

From kindergarten through fourth grade, I spent a great deal of time at Sonoran Sky, the public school, putting out fires like this one. To earn good will, I volunteered for everything possible, made sure that we often donated classroom supplies, and brought in lots of little gifts for the teachers and administrative staff. I also developed relationships with the special-needs administrators in the district so that I could educate them about autism and the growing need for professional aides who understood autism in the classrooms. I did anything and everything I could think of. Once I even had a carnival at our house with a hundred kids, so Jack had some friends to hang out with. But no matter what we did, I was called in for meeting after meeting with the administration. Jack was always in trouble, even with a full-time aide.

After my talk with Mr. Sweeney, we hired a new aide, which smoothed things over for a little while. We had gone through many different aides, and what we learned was that aides and special assistants weren't enough. The simple fact was that no matter how hard Neil and I—not to mention Jack—tried, mainstreaming Jack in the public school wasn't working, and Jack's self-esteem was plummeting as a result. Jack could not accomplish what was expected of neurotypical students. It became too stressful for him, and it achieved the opposite of what we aimed for. Maybe it was time to consider a school for special needs students.

Many autism experts believe that you should mainstream autistic students so they are better equipped to live in the real world, that children with autism must learn how to adjust to the way the world is, not the other way around. Others believe that neurodiversity should be addressed in the way that other forms of diversity are addressed, and that the world should be made more accommodating for the neurodiverse population. Neil and I have fought long and hard about these issues and have tried our best to do what is right for Jack—and not just what's easier for us or other adults caring for and teaching him.

Moving Jack out of public school was a big decision, but we were running out of other options. Neil was against it.

"Lynn, I'm not putting Jack in that school just to make your life easier. He's got to learn how to function in the real world."

"His self-esteem has been battered to pieces!" I countered. "What good is keeping him where he's miserable—and so are we! Honey, I'm worried about him. He's a human being. He can only take so much. Doesn't he deserve a break like anyone would from the stress of getting into trouble all the time? It's too much for any child to live like that."

We visited the small number of private schools in our community that specialized in children with autism, but we didn't think they'd be the best fit for Jack. We continued to think Jack would be better off learning from the example of neurotypical children, so we compromised and enrolled Jack in Lexis Preparatory Academy, a private school that specialized in ADHD, which he attended for fifth and sixth grade. We knew both of the owners well.

To create an accepting atmosphere, I involved myself in many of the same ways I had at Sonoran Sky. I joined the PTA, volunteered for anything and everything, and donated time, money, and supplies when requested. I even did a presentation in which I introduced Bigsbee, a character in a book by my friend Jennifer Carroll called *Cool 2 Bee Me: Bigsbee's Unbee-lievable Journey to Fly*.[13] The book told the story of a bee who taught children to be the best they could be and accept each other's differences. As part of the act, Neil dressed up in an adorable Bigsbee costume that Jennifer had created.

The kids loved the presentation, but it didn't really help Jack's disruptive behavior. At one point, Neil had a camera installed in the classroom to monitor Jack, but that backfired on us. Neil grew obsessed with watching Jack and punishing him after school each day for his infractions. That just made things worse, as you can imagine, with much arguing and hurt feelings. Neil wanted so desperately to keep Jack in the public school system, but he knew that we had to take a different direction. Jack needed a school where the teachers and administrators understood both ADHD and autism.

Neil begrudgingly agreed, so we moved Jack to a more specialized school called Gateway Academy, which was designed for students just like Jack. The teachers and administrators understood Jack's needs there, and life was calmer for us all. Jack attended that school for the seventh and eighth grades and did quite well.

After another round of debate, we decided to try public school again for high school. This way Jack could have a more typical experience with all the extras a large school offers, and he could attend the same school his twin sister Brianna did.

Jack's high school experience has been amazing. Since we were diagnosed in 2005, awareness in our schools about how to educate students with autism has grown tremendously and Jack has benefitted from that. We've had a thorough IEP done every year, and the staff has responded with compassion, knowledge, and skill. It has never been easy, but Jack was managing there, enjoying social situations more than ever, especially those involving girls. Brianna and her pack of friends always had Jack's back. Then COVID hit, but we are managing through that as well. By the time this book is published, Jack will have graduated and with a high-grade point as well!

As autism awareness becomes more prevalent, better services have become available for those affected. Since graduating from high school in 2021, Jack is now attending First Place AZ, one of the first transitional academies for people with special needs, located right here in Phoenix. First Place specializes in helping people with autism like Jack step into the real world. They offer a two-year program that will help Jack independently navigate social situations, develop healthy life skills, learn about basic finance, train him for employment, cooking skills, and so on. It's a fairly new program that has already changed the lives of the many individuals with special needs and their families that have had the opportunity to benefit from its valuable life changing steps toward independence and freedom. A miraculous community of warriors within the autism community have created an environment for growth and support, providing the skills for a happy, productive and independent life for those with special needs. Neil and I have had the opportunity to be a part of this groundbreaking advance in housing through our work in autism over the years and will be forever grateful to the heroes that have made it possible. My hope is that programs like these will spread across the country so that all families who have members with special needs will have access to them.

We are very blessed that we have had the means to provide Jack with the best therapies, aides, and schools available—not every family does. We are grateful that no matter where Jack lands, we will be able to provide Jack whatever he needs to ensure he has a happy and productive life. But resources aren't only financial. Families undergoing the journey of autism must look in two directions for the resources to get them through: they must dig deep inside themselves for the strength, love, patience, and wisdom to embrace the ups and downs of lives affected by autism, and they must let go and open themselves to outside help, not only from the world of experts but also the wider community, the village we all need to raise our children.

I will be forever grateful to all the wonderful people in the autism world who embraced us along the way. We needed them, and they were there. When a family begins their journey with autism, they face a tremendous learning curve. It is critical that parents who have been through the autism journey be able to offer their support and experience to families who are new to the journey.

I learned that from Maya Angelou, "When you learn, teach. When you get, give."[14] When our turn came, we served the autism community in return, which I write more about in my chapter, "Healing Through Service," and we will continue to do so. This service has taught Neil and me how to turn something difficult and painful into something miraculous by giving us purpose. The work we have done over the years has made our family happier and healthier as a result. Through it, we have received much more than we have given. I know that God has given us these lessons for our best good, to help us to evolve in this lifetime. We will continue to support Jack in whatever capacity necessary throughout his lifetime.

What else I know for sure is that Jack is absolutely perfect the way he is, and he will be just as perfect as his life unfolds. The best gift I can give Jack for his growth is to let him experience natural consequences whenever possible. Those could be the natural consequences of a bad grade, of not trying to form his own friendships, of not being independent, or of getting in trouble for a temper tantrum. I don't do Jack any favors when I enable him. I need to be strong enough to give Jack the opportunity to fail so he sees how important it is to try harder. It has been a struggle to find the balance between supporting Jack by clearing the way for him and giving him the tools to navigate his own life in his own way. He is an important part of my journey toward healing and acceptance. This was all supposed to happen this way so I could learn to be of service to others while continuing to heal myself.

Chapter 11
THE NANNY WARS AND OTHER BATTLES

In addition to the challenges unique to a family with autism, Neil and I faced all the usual parenting and marriage challenges as well.

Parenting is the most rewarding and exhausting experience all wrapped into one. I remember hearing this joke once: If parenthood came with a GPS, it would repeat "Recalculating" over and over again. That goes double in a family with autism. The twins have always been adorable, and throughout their lives I've had to pinch myself many times with gratitude that God entrusted such wonderful children to me. God has his hand everywhere. Without fertility science, they wouldn't be here.

I am blessed to have a successful husband in Neil who can provide us all a good home and a lifestyle that wants for very little. Since the twins were six months old, we've lived in a beautiful house in an affluent neighborhood in North Scottsdale. The house is of a Spanish old-world design with five bedrooms, five baths, and a spectacular backyard that captures the essence of Spain and Tuscany. We gutted the house before we moved in and added wonderful features to the old-world décor that brought it up to date and enhanced its warmth. Inside we added terrariums and stained glass, outside sculpted fountains, an Italian Renaissance garden and other gardens throughout.

But all that came with a price, at least for me. Neil has a very traditional idea of home and family, with him as the head of the household making all the major decisions and me as his helpmate making sure it all happens to his satisfaction. For example, when we were decorating the house, Neil wanted to be involved in every decision, no matter how small, and everything turned into a huge negotiation. For every single thing I wanted to do, I had to present him a sales pitch justifying every aspect of my idea—cost, color, quantity, quality, vendor, and so on. Sometimes it was exhausting. Do not misunderstand, I realize that each partner should have a say in the décor of their home. In our case, from my perspective, it was just part of our dance in who had the final say and more control.

I never formally agreed to this arrangement, but fell into it naturally, given the patterns of unhealthy codependence I learned in my family and my fundamental nature as a people-pleasing enabler. After all, I loved Neil and wanted to please him. Isn't that what a good wife and partner is supposed to do? Marriage requires compromise, right? It took me a while to realize the compromise was mostly on my side. As I began this new life as a mother and homemaker, I gave up further independence and control, becoming more of an extension of Neil and the children than an autonomous human being with the agency to make her own decisions.

I still hadn't learned to ask for what I needed. Worse, I didn't really feel that what I needed mattered—or *should* matter. I was married to a tremendously successful man who was accustomed to jetting off whenever he wanted to for work and pleasure. Once we were married, Neil lived as he always had, on his terms. A new wife and children weren't going to slow him down! I don't think it ever occurred to him to consider any other way. And because I wanted his approval at any cost, I bent to his will. If I wanted to spend time with Neil, I had to keep up with him. I had to be available to travel often and at the drop of a hat, as well as meet all his other expectations. A traditional job with a few weeks off a year could never be an option for me given these expectations. I became a stay-at-home mother, with a twist. Because we traveled so much, we also needed a nanny for the kids when we were gone.

Through the Nanny Exchange, we found Taula, a large, powerful Tongan woman five years younger than me. In Tongan, her name meant "Priestess," and the name suited her. Taula soon became one of my soul teachers, often bringing more chaos into my world than peace. I had a difficult time sharing my house and children with another woman. Also, as hard as it is to admit, because of her size and don't-mess-with-me attitude, I was often afraid of her. She seemed to be one of those women who doesn't like some women, especially those she sees as privileged. From the day she arrived, she and I struggled for power—in *my* house! She did whatever she pleased and how she pleased, no matter what I told her, and she was an expert at manipulating men. Neil was not immune, often siding with her in our "domestic" disputes. As time went by, Taula became more clever in her manipulation. Her saving grace was that the kids loved her, and I was too scared to upset that apple cart, especially since it helped me keep up with Neil's expectations.

With my lack of boundaries, I didn't really know how to take charge of a nanny. I had managed many employees over the years without a problem, but there was not nearly that much at stake. I didn't know how to establish and maintain authority in my own household. I rarely said "no" because I didn't want to be seen as *that* wife. For example, whenever we went on a trip without the children, not only would Taula stay at our house, but I agreed to let her whole family stay there as well.

We always left the twins home for our annual Fourth of July Lake Powell trip. We owned a timeshare on a houseboat with a group of friends, and each year we would go boating for ten to fourteen days. Neil had been house boating on Lake Powell since he was teenager. He and his friends had become very skilled at navigating our clunky four-bedroom houseboat through the red rock canyons. The only problem is that there is virtually no cell phone reception in those canyons, and even the emergency satellite phone didn't work much of the time. It made me anxious to be so out of touch with Jack and Brianna, not to mention Taula who was taking care of them.

We always had a good time, though, sharing lots of food and drink, our own private professional fireworks, waterskiing, wake boarding, jet skiing, hiking, and so on. All the out-of-town company stayed at our house before and after the trip, and I always wanted the house to be in perfect order for our guests. Taula didn't always see things the same way.

One year, after a week and half of houseboating, ragged and depleted from partying, we all arrived home after the four-hour drive from Lake Powell.

"Hi," Taula said, as the twins came running into our arms, shrieking with joy that we were home.

"Hi Jack! Hi Brianna! I missed you so much!" I grabbed them and hugged them with all my might.

"They were good. Did you have fun?" asked Taula, yawning as she pushed herself up from where she reclined on the couch. Her husband and her son Falia were lying with her on our carefully chosen sectional. For some reason, that's where they all slept, no matter how many times I told them to use the beds. The couches never looked the same when we returned from trips like this.

And neither did the rest of the house. Clothes were strewn all over the floor, toys scattered everywhere, food splattered on the counters, the stove covered in grease, dirty dishes piled on the sink, hardened food stuck to the tile floor, and I didn't want to know what kind of stains discolored the carpeting. Clearly, Taula had made no effort to take care of the home we took so much pride in. I was mortified, since we had guests staying that night.

And I didn't say a thing because I knew what would happen if I did. The dance with Taula would begin, as it had so many times before. I would let Taula know of my disappointment in what I considered a reasonable tone. Taula would respond as if I had raked her over the coals, running to Neil to tell him I was being mean to her. Neil would roll his eyes and tell me I must be exaggerating, thereby undercutting even the small amount of authority I had left with Taula. A smug smile would slink across Taula's face, and she'd go about her business *her* way. To Neil, these were women's problems, not worthy of his time. The fact that he had to get involved to this degree was just another indication that I was weak and couldn't do my job very well. I couldn't win with Taula or Neil. As the years went by, I learned to have our housekeeper clean the house just before we got home so I wouldn't be embarrassed in front of our guests. We always had to tip the housekeeper more than the usual amount because the house was so dirty.

Over the years I found out just how many parties Taula had had at our house with sometimes fifty or more people without permission. I wondered why I had to have the carpet and furniture cleaned so much in those days. The twins remember the parties. To them they were all good fun. She had giant pig roasts, and many of her friends and family spent the night, sleeping in every room on couches, floors, and beds. Not going on the trips wasn't an option for me, though. There would have been a far greater cost to our marriage if I wasn't on my husband's arm when he wanted me.

Taula got away with whatever she could, extending as little energy as possible for the least amount of work possible. We explained what we wanted the twins to eat or how we wanted their schedules to go on a given day. She looked at me, said "Okay," and did whatever she wanted. This extended to the guidelines for Jack we set up with our team of autism experts. She never followed them. Fortunately, Jack had enough structured time with the therapists that it didn't really matter that much. Taula loved the twins, though, I have to give her that. That's how she lasted eight years. She did it her way, but she always treated the children well, and they loved spending time with her. What kids wouldn't want to do whatever they chose as long as it didn't cause too much effort for Taula?

In other words, Taula wasn't all bad. She helped me survive many parties, guests, and appointments for the twins and service projects over the years. Grateful, Neil and I did our best to care for her and her family in return. She became very ill one time, and I helped nurse her back to health. We also gave her six months off with pay to recover. At one point, I drove her to the hospital, and the doctors rushed her into surgery due to complications from a severe case of valley fever that had attacked her heart. The doctors told me she might not make it out of surgery. I had to decide whether to tell her husband and young son. I decided just to have them go in and wish her well before the surgery and give her a big hug. She recovered just fine, and they never knew how serious it had been.

With Taula, there always seemed to be financial, legal, or health related chaos. Neil and I always tried to help her manage. We helped Taula and her whole family become legal residents in Arizona, for example, and we loaned them all money, if a car broke down or they had other emergencies. Once Taula was having gynecological symptoms I was concerned about. She had never been to a gynecologist, so I convinced her to let me take her to Dr. Foltz. I explained that he would have to examine her and that I would be right there for her. She was mortified, but we got through it. It was a good thing we went because she did require treatment.

About two weeks after our visit, I was putting on one of our many dinner parties. The formal dining room was set just right. I loved decorating the table and always made sure of that. The aroma of homemade tomato sauce and sausage filled the air. Everything was ready for our guests. The doorbell rang.

"Taula, can you get that?" I said. "I think our guests are here."

"Sure, got it," Taula said, then made her way from the kitchen through the formal living room to welcome our guests.

"Oh my God." I heard Taula shriek, and the door slammed shut.

"Taula, what's going on? What's wrong?" I ran to her as quickly as I could.

"It's that man. What's he doing here?" Taula demanded in a panic.

I ran to the door to apologize and welcome our company. It was Dr. Foltz and his wife! It never occurred to me to tell Taula who our guests were that night. Taula kept her distance until it was time for her to go home.

Over the eight years she worked for us, I never felt comfortable with Taula. I always knew she resented me. I could feel it in her glances of jealousy and her stubborn defiance when I tried to push her. She was happier when she could go at her own pace with the least amount of energy. She caught on quickly that I was a people pleaser and took advantage of that, though I have to take some responsibility for that because I taught her how to treat me. But I felt helpless knowing I needed her to keep up the pace of our household. I also wanted to feel as if I was in charge of my own house. Every once in a while, I lost it with her, but that wouldn't change anything. She was most decidedly not a people pleaser, and she never let anyone's energy affect her. She was tough, good at taking care of herself, and I didn't mess with her.

A typical busy day might include company staying with us and a dinner party while managing the schedules of the twins and keeping up our home. Even if we weren't having company, I always had a home cooked meal and a perfectly set table. Taula went at her own pace, no matter what the occasion. My manic intensity never got to her. I unconsciously treated her the way Mom treated me when we got ready for guests when I was a child.

"Taula, we only have two hours until everyone arrives. Why did it take you three hours to run the errands today?" I'd say with frustration and anger. "It should have taken at an hour!"

"I went as fast as I could," Taula would respond, calm, unruffled and indifferent.

If I persisted, Taula would find Neil.

"Neil, she's being mean to me," Taula would say in a young girl's voice. She always talked to Neil like that, as if she were a scolded child going to her daddy.

"Lynn, what the hell? Take a breath. Everything doesn't have to be perfect. Put some paper plates on the table and get over it," Neil would say, now sounding like the parent scolding me. Of course, it didn't matter to him how the table was set or what any of the guests thought about their experience. I knew I had to prepare for our events. They didn't just happen on their own, and, as always, it was important for me to make a good impression. It frustrated Neil that I went to so much trouble for the events, spent too much money on them, and created a panic throughout the household. Looking back, he certainly had a point. I was always proud when our events turned out well, but they came with a price that I was sure to pay.

I learned to keep Taula happy to keep Neil happy so that he and I did not have as many confrontations. This was not healthy, to say the least. Not only was I giving Taula power, but I was also allowing Neil to treat me like a child.

When I finally decided I'd had enough after eight years, I had to tread very softly—or so I thought. The twins were attached to Taula, and I wasn't sure how they'd adjust to the change. I didn't want Taula to take it out on them. To ease the transition, I helped her find a new job. I put the word out, and a good friend said one of her friends was looking for a nanny. We knew this family. They were acquaintances from EO and very accomplished entrepreneurs. They had just adopted an adorable baby, and Kelly, the wife, needed help right away so she could continue running her restaurant business. I have always had a lot of respect for Kelly, who is beautiful, strong, and confident. She and her husband hired Taula based on our recommendation. After some months of employment, Kelly called.

"Lynn, what the hell! Why would you send over that lazy manipulating bitch?" Kelly was furious. "She has been manipulating my husband and causing a huge amount of bullshit around here. She has this thing against affluent women. It's like a fucking game with her. How the hell could you do this to me? You had to know."

Actually, many people treated me as Taula had, but I thought it was my fault, which is how victim-martyrs think. I wrongly assumed she'd be different with another family. Kelly fired Taula. She and her husband divorced shortly afterward. I am sure Taula wasn't the real cause, but she sure didn't help. I felt terrible. I was lost in my own dysfunction, and it caused unnecessary conflict in another family's life, and I was embarrassed by my unconsciousness about the unhealthy dance that Taula and I had played for so long. This was a time when my enabling and people pleasing hurt someone other than me. I should have been stronger, seen what was actually so, and fired Taula myself. I believe that my unhealthy patterns got the best of me. I wanted to ease the transition in my own home and did not consider, as I should have, what she would inflict on another family.

I not only tried to keep pace with Neil to please him, but I also wanted to please everyone else too, even people I didn't know. I invited two hundred people to the house for the twins first birthday. Years later, I held a carnival at our house for over hundred children from their elementary school. I had a camp out with over twenty five ten-year-old children. I gave parties for friends, parties for charities, parties for holidays. And every party had to be just right. I put so much pressure on myself that I was a wreck beforehand, just as my mother had been. You'd think I would have learned a different lesson from those experiences with her.

In the end, the parties I threw always came together, and once they began, I even managed to have fun. One of my favorites was Neil's fiftieth birthday, for which I chose a Woodstock theme and invited more than one hundred and fifty friends. I planned for months and months, attending to every detail. On the invitations, which looked like a concert poster from that era, I asked each guest to dress in theme. When they came through the front door, they saw a life-size cardboard cutout of Neil in Woodstock attire. It was a surprise for Neil, and once everyone jumped out and yelled "Happy Birthday," I whisked Neil off to put on the costume I had laid out for him.

Then, throughout the backyard, I had small tents set up and Woodstock signage for ambience. Each cocktail table had its own bong and dime bag of real marijuana. Trippy psychedelic lights strobed throughout the yard. On a stage was set up a movie screen with a projector on each side, one showing events from Neil's life and one actual Woodstock footage. A DJ played the best of the Woodstock bands, and our casita was set up as The Bad Trip Casita. We had real pot brownies and the perfect Woodstock birthday cake, with frosted pictures of a VW bug, bongs, a hippy Neil, joints, guitars, all in psychedelic colors with pills scattered throughout. Fake cops raided the party with a made-up noise complaint that caused many guests to jump over the backyard wall in fear of being busted. (That one might have gone too far.)

It was a perfect summer night in June, the backyard was packed, and we were all feeling no pain. Everyone who attended was dressed in Woodstock attire: hip huggers, long hair, colorful clothes with lots of flowers and bare midriff tiny tops. We were all enjoying the music and footage of Janis Joplin, Jimi Hendrix, Joe Cocker, Crosby, Stills & Nash, the Grateful Dead. We had many of his friends stand up to share great memories of Neil. I went last. I had spent weeks preparing my speech so it would go off without a hitch.

I was dressed in psychedelic tight fitting bell bottoms, a matching tiny top, and a head band. I had even spread mud all over my body because there had been a lot of mud at Woodstock. My speech went something like this.

"Woodstock was about Love and Peace, and we have all heard one of Neil's most famous quotes over and over: "Can't we just all get along." The crowd laughed.

"Woodstock was about sexual freedom, and for everyone who knew Neil before we were married, well, nothing else needs to be said." They all laughed harder and clapped. Footage came on the screen of Neil's Bad Dog Days, a video produced by our good friend Jennifer. The video reflected just how "Bad" those "Bad Dog Days" were. It was so well done, we all screamed and cheered.

When the video was over, I replaced the microphone in the stand in front of me. Joe Cocker's version of "With a Little Help from My Friends" came through the speakers.

I turned to the microphone and spoke loudly over the music. "Okay, everybody, in the true spirit of Woodstock, I would like to give my birthday boy a special birthday treat." I turned around, bent over, and wriggled out of my silky bell bottoms. Then I pulled my top over my head, turned around, put my arms in the air and called out: "A birthday suit for my birthday boy. Now let's get naked!" I opened my arms and legs to give every-one a full view, with the footage of real naked Woodstock playing on the screen behind me. Five of my girlfriends joined in and removed their clothes.

The rest of our friends didn't know what to think. Some laughed, some hooted, some whistled, and some just stood there with their mouths open. We had planned it well in advance and wore nude body suits under our costumes, with boobs painted on and big hairy bushes glued to just the right spot (after all, that was the style in those days). It's a miracle we weren't raided for real! One of our friends passed out when he mistook the pot brownies for normal ones and ate three! Fortunately, he recovered. A 911 call might have been a problem. We all laughed so hard that night. That was one party where all my planning paid off.

Successes like the Woodstock birthday party were always just temporary, though. No matter how fast I paddled, it never seemed to be enough. My expectations for myself and Neil's for our life together were pulling me under. Neil criticized me the way his mom and dad criticized each other. It was as natural as breathing to him, as well as a way to control me. I took everything to heart, and genuinely tried to do better. I so wanted his approval early on (I'm much better now at not giving oxygen to the criticism), but no matter what I did, it was ever good enough. If I did too much, he told me to stop stressing about being so damn perfect. If I didn't do enough, he told me I was doing a shabby job. It was a no-win situation.

I recall one trip to San Diego. Neil, the twins, and I rented a beautiful condo overlooking the bay at Mission Beach for a few weeks. For Neil, vacations weren't for relaxing. They were for experience, for cramming as many activities as we could into the allotted time—and then a few more for good measure.

On this trip, he wanted to visit at least five different amusement parks. Two of Neil's best friends joined up with us, but after a few hours at Neil's pace, they tried to talk him into slowing down—they wanted to have some down time. Neil was having none of that, so after a while, the friends stood up to Neil and took off to enjoy Mission Beach their way.

Though I felt somewhat validated by the look of sympathy they gave me when they left to do relaxing vacation activities, standing up to Neil was not really an option for me. It only resulted in Neil's scathing disapproval and fights I really had no hope of winning. It was easier to just go along with him and avoid the conflict and bad feelings altogether.

I realize now (I realized, then, too, I just felt I couldn't do anything about it), that I was teaching the children unhealthy communication—that it was okay for one partner to steam roll the needs of the other and for the weaker partner (as they would have seen it) to let the resentment build up until it exploded. The children and I have talked about these dynamics since then, and I'm hoping they'll learn from my mistakes and make healthier choices in their own lives.

There were many examples of the dance Neil and I had become accustomed to over the years. On that same trip we took each year to Mission Beach, a few years later, the twins brought up an issue I thought we had already settled. They wanted another dog even though we already had one. They were fifteen.

"Mom, please, please," Jack and Brianna begged. "Another dog would be so much fun!"

"No, we're not getting a puppy," I said. Our schedule was already crazy with all of Jack's therapies and Brianna's activities, and I knew I'd end up taking care of this dog the same way I took care of the dog we already had, an adorable labradoodle. "We can barely keep up now. And Cooper is only two!"

"But Mom, Cooper needs company. It's not fair we can't get a playmate for him. Please, Mom."

Neil came into the argument, but not on my side. "Kids, I want to get a dog as much as you do. It's Mom who doesn't want one. You're going to have to convince her." He shrugged, as if it was out of his hands.

This time I stuck to my guns, and we didn't get a new dog. Neil may have wanted a new dog as well, but the way it was handled left me feeling as if we were not a unified front and that if I ever dug my heels in, there would be a price, a price I most often was not willing to make because the cost left me feeling as if I was the bad guy. It was most often more important to me to have the approval of both Neil and the children, even if many times it was at my expense. Because I had remained firm on this position, I wanted to explore it more deeply to see if I had asked too much for myself. I needed to reach out to a professional that Neil respected for his guidance. I was determined to explore healthier ways to communicate so that I could feel as if I had a voice without having a conflict as a result.

A therapist we saw together and separately opened a glimmer of insight for Neil by appealing to his business sense. Neil had a partner, Mike, whom he respected and worked well with. "Neil, when you have conversations with your family, as in the example of getting a new dog, and you side with the kids, it's like having a meeting with all of your employees and telling them that you'd love to give them all a huge raise but your partner, Mike, doesn't want to. That if it were up to you, they'd all be making tons more money, but you're very sorry, no raise because of Mike." Here the therapist paused to make sure Neil was taking it in. Then he asked, "Would that be a good way to run a company?"

"Well, no, of course not," Neil said. "Leadership has to have a united front."

"Exactly," the therapist said firmly.

"But that's diff—"

"Not really," the therapist said.

Neil nodded thoughtfully.

Our therapist was a man, and Neil respected him. Sessions like this are slowly dispersing the fog of dysfunction in our family. One thing to say about Neil, he has never shied away from reaching out for help if any of us needs it, from Jack's classes and therapies to our own marriage counseling, to rehab for me, which I'll write about in an upcoming chapter. We've had some wonderful therapists over the years who have helped us approach challenges like these as a team, as a family. For many years, we have had a plaque in our kitchen, the center of our home, that reads: "We May Not Have It All Together, But Together, We Have it All." Neil and I both continue to push forward to gain insights for our own journeys and to be better parents to Jack and Brianna—and Cooper, of course.

Having children later in life gave me a whole new understanding about the responsibility of becoming a parent. Given the chaos of the home I grew up in, creating a warm, comfortable, and safe home for our family was my first priority. From the day our children were placed in my womb, they were more important to me than anything. I knew it wasn't about just me anymore. I have a new appreciation for the hard work it takes to care for children and a home. For years I had heard mothers talk about getting a break when they came to work. I was beginning to understand what they meant.

The moment I laid eyes on my children I decided I could never divorce, because I would never be able to give them up half the time. I knew Neil would be a good father. He would take parenting very seriously, and I was certain he felt the same way that I did. Neil and I would just have to find a way to make it work, no matter what was going on personally and in our relationship.

This put me at a disadvantage in many ways, the disadvantage women have faced for thousands of years. Because we have the babies, many of us have had to take a subservient position in marriage and society. As a forty-three-year-old woman, I knew the difference between independence and the choice I had made to become more dependent on my husband because I had been on my own for a long time. But I was willing to give up control to some degree to protect my children and marriage. So even now, in the twenty-first century, when the husband is a successful and driven type A personality, Neil and I fell into a very traditional marriage, both legally and financially. Entering into a marriage late in life, as I did, puts many women in an even more vulnerable position if they decide to have children and the wife decides to stay at home. Neil had to protect his wealth before our marriage, and with our prenup, he was fully secure. I, however, did not have the same circumstance. Neil insisted that I put the majority of the funds I had left from the sale of my business as my portion of the down payment on our house, which left me with little security of my own, other than, of course, owning half of our home, which, back then, had a large mortgage.

Now don't get me wrong. Neil is a generous man, and he loves me and the kids. We don't have to worry about money. In my situation it was imperative that I give up employment in order to stay home with our children and keep up the busy travel schedule that Neil wanted to continue. As a result, our parent-child relationship was set in motion, and the insecurity began to fester within me. I pointed out multiple times that many of our married friends were both protected legally and that they both shared and benefited equally in all their financial decisions. I told Neil that I believed that made them more equal and healthier as a couple. I didn't want to take advantage of Neil. I just wanted to know that he trusted me and respected me. "Those couples were married before they had any significant means," Neil would always remind me. "Their situation is very different from ours. You'll just have to live with that."

Today, I am more than grateful that our marriage has survived, but there were many times that I felt if he ever decided to leave me, I would not be able to provide for the children in the manner that they had been raised. It left me feeling quite vulnerable, powerless, and in a subservient position. Neil had the final say over our financial life. We've had an abundant life with beautiful things and adventures, but the inequity has taken a toll on our ability to have a deeper connection with each other. Achieving equality was another part of my journey in finding my own voice and my own authentic power.

As the years went by, I gained more courage and began to express my desire to have more security for myself. Neil had many investments, but each of them was made in his name only, even those made during our marriage. When we bought our second home after fifteen years of marriage, Neil was going to put the home in his name only. I pointed out to Neil that my broker's license had saved us many thousands of dollars when purchasing our homes, so I was finally able to convince Neil that I deserved to have my name on the mortgage as well. I told him that I would not broker the deal otherwise. I have been blessed to live a wonderfully comfortable life without paying bills or overseeing what must be done to maintain our lifestyle. Still, I believe the cost of an unequal partnership like ours is a very high price to pay for staying married. Many times, that price can become the relationship itself and the emotional security of the whole family. Marriages that are set up in this unequal manner have had a firm grip on women married to affluent men for generations. Because financial security is a healthy and important part of life, it would be another difficult stepping-stone in our journey to find security, respect and trust in our marriage, a dilemma that many women over the years have faced in order to have children and live in the world of a successful entrepreneur.

When you marry a successful entrepreneur, you're marrying into the business whether or not you become an actual employee. Maintaining a successful business is not easy. There is a certain responsibility that comes with being part of a business family, and the entire family must make sacrifices to keep the business going, especially the way Neil operates. Neil's mantra is "Sales is really only relationships," and he means relationships for the whole family.

For example, a big part of Neil's business was franchising, and he ran a training program for all the new owners. The signature event of the training was the graduation, which Neil always liked to hold at our house to provide the personal touch. He was like a god in the closet industry, and the new dealers loved getting up close and personal by coming to the house and meeting the family. Neil always knew how to balance the relationships in business and friendship with such brilliance.

I didn't have a problem with that, except it was up to me to see those events came off without a hitch. It wasn't optional and it wasn't easy.

"Hi Lynn, it's Alicia," a typical event would begin. "We have a big group in training this week. You can plan on fifteen to twenty." Alicia was Neil's assistant, and we had gotten to know each other well. She had worked out of our home with Neil for a few years before they opened a separate training office.

"I'm on it," I'd respond, sometimes more enthusiastically than others.

No matter what was going on in our crazy household, I would make sure the house was decorated and the food and drinks were in perfect order. Other times, I was expected to attend conventions and dinner meetings. Business guests also stayed with us. It was like running a bed and breakfast. I loved getting to know the people Neil did business with. Most of them became family friends. Keeping up took its toll, but when the doorbell rang, I answered the door impeccably dressed and with a smile on my face because I knew this is how Neil did business, and it was an important way I could help him.

That's why to me, during the duration of a marriage, each spouse should equally benefit from the family businesses and any investments that result, because there's no real boundary between family and business. Otherwise, you risk establishing a marriage of unequal partners, whereby one of the spouses becomes the parent-employer and the other the child-employee. This is not good for the marriage or for the family as a whole. What does it teach the children?

As I write these pages, Ruth Bader Ginsberg has just passed away, and I'm reminded of how she fought so hard for women to be equal before the law. Treating each other as equals during marriage creates trust and respect for both parties. That way, neither partner is the boss. I am very fortunate that in my marriage I have never really wanted for anything. I bring up our legal and financial agreement only to reflect that I realize there has to be a business component when entering into marriage, but it must be consciously agreed on to ensure that each partner is respected and can trust one another. I believe our current culture is beginning to change with more men staying home as well, and whether it's the man or the woman, I believe each partner should feel in control of every aspect of their lives. This kind of relationship breeds a spiritual connection that is much more important than the security of things that are obtained during a marriage.

Of course, there are many perks of being married into a business as successful as Neil's, and traveling is a big one, whether for business or for fun—and often both on the same trip. We've taken some wonderful business trips together. One of my favorites was a trip to Venice and Pordenone, Italy. An Italian manufacturing family who was trying to get Neil's account as well as that of a friend of ours had invited Neil, me, Randy and his wife

Karla as their guests to Italy to make their pitch. The twins were still quite small, maybe around two, so they stayed home with Taula.

I had never been to Italy up to then, and I was beyond excited. Both of Dad's parents were Italian, and we were all very proud to be Italian, especially my dad. He told us stories about Italy all our lives. He had always said when he was in Italy, he felt like he was home, although he had never lived there. Dad was as excited for me about the trip as I was, and I thought of him the whole time, thinking he'd like that café or restaurant, that cathedral, this palace. It was as if he was with me every step of the way.

Tony, the patriarch of the Italian family that invited us, was the same age as my dad at about sixty-five. He was the perfect Italian man, so gracious and respectful. He had two very handsome adult sons who were just as gracious. The family wined and dined us with five-star attention the length of our stay.

Our journey started in Venice for a few days before we met with them in their hometown of Pordenone, an hour's drive away. Tony had selected the perfect suite for us on the Grand Canal thorough-fare. Our flat overlooked the famous Rialto Bridge that reflected the glory of the renaissance. I loved watching the gondolas and row boats plying the canal just below our windows. Venice was my first authentic Italian cuisine (though I'm sure my dad would have argued for his mom's homemade sauce). We enjoyed several grand dinners on the ancient gothic patios that reflected the splendor of the 1,200-year-old city. We walked through the central square at the Piazza San Marco and gloried in the lovely cafes and shops and the breathtaking Saint Mark's Basilica. It was so romantic; the perfect way to experience Italy for the first time.

Pordenone is a magical place as well. Tony and his family had lived there for generations. Our hotel was in the center of town, steps away from the finest shopping lining the cobblestone streets. One evening we had an eight-course Italian dinner I can still taste today. The family gave Karla and I sterling silver tokens laid in silk lined boxes. The tokens depicted the grapes the region was famous for. I still display it in our living room china cabinet along with others of my most cherished mementoes.

Tony, Randy, and Neil did come to a business agreement, and Tony's company manufactured materials for Neil for several years.

Neil has a separate reality from mine. He wants to do well in the world, and he's not much for the spiritual realm. He jokes that he's not a deep thinker, that he's actually quite shallow, uninterested in deep conversations about emotions and the spirit and so on. I don't agree that he doesn't think deeply, but I'm not going to argue. He lives in his reality.

This I do know. Neil works very hard and always has. He strives for approval in the world for what he has accomplished. He loves recognition, and it is very important for Neil to be respected. Neil is a powerful man who was raised to believe he was special and should be treated that way. He wants to create a wonderful life for his family, but he doesn't want to re-create what his parents had, with their conflicts and constant fighting, so he chose me to marry, someone, he thought, who would listen to him with-out conflict.

For a while, I was that woman (and sometimes still am—confronting that weakness is one of my lessons for this lifetime). When I became a parent, it became harder for me to find my own voice and honor my separate reality. That wasn't Neil's fault. He's on his journey, and I'm on mine. We are the perfect example of a couple with completely different lessons to learn.

My early life with Neil was such a paradox. I was living the life of *The Rich and Famous*. Who was I to complain about anything? We traveled the world, we had a nanny, I had two beautiful children, I lived in a beautiful home—but I knew our relationship was not one of equals. I knew I had betrayed myself, all the while knowing I adored this man. Did he adore me?

Yes, I think he did and still does. We are the perfect couple, both of us having gifts the other does not. Our souls were supposed to learn from each other. I can only speak from my reality, but I know that I had become the epitome of a people-pleasing martyr with a victim complex. I lived in my past and re-created all the lessons I still had not overcome. I complained and whined and took no responsibility for what I had created. My past beliefs were holding me hostage. I believed that I didn't have a voice—that I *couldn't* have a voice, that I wasn't worthy to have a voice. These were the patterns of my childhood. I was raised to believe my purpose in life was to please others and keep the peace. I ignored my needs and feelings, the very essence of who I was. I thought that was the right and moral thing to do. Aren't we supposed to give to others? Take care of others?

Yes, of course, but not at the cost of our essential being. It has not been easy for Neil to watch me bend over backwards in unhealthy relationships, especially with members of my family, and then whine and complain about it. I stuffed down my genuine feelings for long periods of time and then went off. It was never pretty and caused a good deal of pain in our marriage.

Joe Bailey, author of "Slowing Down to the Speed of Love", writes that "ignoring emotions or feelings is like ignoring the clicking engine in a car. If you continue to ignore it, it will be a broken car or a broken marriage."[15] Until I became a mother, I ignored what was going on in our marriage—the patterns of inequality and how that made me feel—hoping it would go away. That wasn't going to happen, of course. I needed to give myself permission to find myself again.

Our beautiful twins were the beginning of the answer, the blessing that helped Neil and me see how important it was for us to grow and learn. I may not have been able to have children with my own eggs, but God gave us the gift of Jack and Brianna for a reason. Our love for them broke us open to parts of ourselves that had been hidden away, gave us both our purpose to push ourselves along on the journey to become our true selves. We wouldn't have been strong enough to grow without them. We were meant to go deeper, and parenthood took us there. That is why soulmates connect, to grow. It can be—*will* be—painful, but if you can walk through the pain, you will grow closer to becoming your true self.

Relationships evolve when we realize that trying to fix the other person rather than ourselves does more harm than good. Our experience is simply that, our experience. When we believe that our personal belief system is the only truth, it may make us feel safe, but it's an illusion. When we evolve, the need to be right dissipates, the need to control dissipates and only kindness remains. When we learn to treat each other as we would like to be treated, healing occurs. In the end, we are all one, here to learn and love one another.

In his book, *Getting the Love You Want*, Harville Hendricks observes that only when we work through the power struggle so many relationships are built on and begin healing will we evolve and grow.[16] In my case, if Neil and I can get it right in this lifetime, we will experience the joy we deserve and only love will remain.

Chapter 12
MY BREAST CANCER – THE WHISPER BECOMES A BOULDER

Mark Nepo, the author and poet, observes that there are two virtually universal ways we grow as human beings: "We are broken open, or we willfully shed" what isn't working.[17] I have always loved that quotation and have it hanging in my writing studio, along with Oprah's observation that God tries to get our attention first with a pebble, then a stone, and then with a brick to the head. What both demonstrate is that we are given life not to make us happy, in the sense of always feeling comfortable, but to make us conscious, to evolve to our true selves. God puts the lessons in front of us over and over again until he has our attention, and we begin to heal.

Our deepest feelings point to these lessons. They are one of God's most important ways of getting our attention. When we ignore these feelings, at best we lose touch with our true selves, at worst we literally make ourselves sick. Up to this point, I had spent a life-time ignoring my feelings, not paying attention to God's lessons for me. It was time to be broken open, time for a brick to the head. Breast cancer was one of my bricks to the head.

One summer night in 2007 we had been hanging out in Parker, Arizona for Father's Day, a tradition of Neil's since his teen years. For some reason that year, there were lots of mosquitos, and they had eaten me alive. When we came home, I itched like crazy. As I feverishly scratched my body, I found a lump in my breast that I knew no mosquito bite caused. I wasn't that concerned about it, but I knew enough to make an appointment for a mammogram and went to a medical imaging clinic to have it checked out. They ran all the tests on me, including an ultrasound. Then they asked me to come into their office where they read the scans. The dark room felt damp, even cold as I walked in with reluctance and curiosity all at once. There were probably ten people in the room, none of them showing the least bit of emotion, just all working on their own projects.

One of the technicians, sitting across the room, barely made eye contact, then announced, "You have cancer. You will require a little surgery, a little chemo, and some radiation, and you'll be good." He gave the news as if he was repeating a takeout order for verification, then went on to the next image. All the technicians were within hearing. I was stunned. I felt as if I was about to throw up. Was this real? Was I imagining it? Why did they think it was okay to tell me this earth-shattering news in this disrespectful, casual way in front of everyone else in the room? What was I supposed to do? Shrug and say, "Okay, thanks for letting me know!"?

I got in the car, borderline hysterical, and after trying to calm myself with deep breathing, I phoned my husband, sobbing into the phone, barely able to get the words out. "They said...I have cancer."

Neil got me calm enough to drive home, where he met me within moments of my arrival. It was a comfort that he had stopped everything to be there for me. I knew I would get through it with his support.

In the end, it was true. I had cancer, no matter how unprofessional the delivery of the news. The hardest part is hearing those words for the first time. *Cancer. You have cancer.* The words repeat in your mind like the needle skipping on an old record player as you begin to process the magnitude of what you just heard.

When I was first diagnosed, I didn't know the extent of the cancer or what my future had in store. It's that fear of the unknown that creates the emotional upheaval. The world stops. All you know for sure is that people die from cancer, even after they are treated. My father had died from cancer just two years before.

My diagnosis became a significant turning point in my relationship with Neil. When I was diagnosed, he took it very hard. When we went to the oncologist accompanied by our primary doctor to get the run down on what was next, Neil couldn't stop crying. I knew my husband loved me, no matter what the issues in our marriage. That's what carried me through. Knowing he loved me overrode the fear of what lay ahead.

The good news, I was told, was that we had found the cancer early. The oncologist recommended a double mastectomy. I called Dr. Foltz, my close friend in addition to my ob-gyn. He told me that he had seen too many patients who only had one breast removed back in his office with a recurrence of the cancer. My kids were small, and I trust Dr. Foltz with my life. I agreed to the double mastectomy. I didn't want the kids growing up without a mother.

After surgery, I didn't require chemotherapy, radiation, or even the hormone medication many women are treated with. I was lucky. My doctor said, "If you're going to get cancer, you got it in the best way." This was a small win, but real, and I took it with genuine gratitude.

The treatment took three surgeries. The first surgery, during which my breasts were removed, took eight hours. The second was to take out the expanders and do the breast reconstruction. The last one was to create new nipples. After the first surgery, the build-up of fluids in my chest had to be drained or it would become quite painful. For this reason, and the fact that I had undergone major surgery, recovery for me was toughest the first few months.

But, as usual, I made it tougher than it had to be by not asking for what I really needed.

Every summer, we have a full travel schedule. Within two weeks of the surgery, I was on a plane to British Colombia, Canada. Yeah, I know. But it was already on the schedule, and I didn't even think to question it. I just did what I always did, stuffed down my feelings, soldiered through the pain, and got on the plane.

During the flight, the pressure built up in my breasts from the altitude. It was like the pressure you get in your ears, times fifty. It hurt like hell. What's more, Jack, four at the time, was completely out of control, screaming at the top of his lungs. Autism coupled with ADHD is a difficult combination for flying, what with the noise of the engines and being trapped in a seat. We always passed out cards to everyone that had seats around with a brief description about autism so that they would have more compassion. But on this day, the cards didn't work. We had asked Cassie, my fourteen-year-old niece, to come with us to help out. She wasn't used to Jack's behavior and didn't understand autism or the degree of recovery I required and wasn't very much help because she simply didn't know what to do. It was a very long three hours. By the end of it, I ached like I'd been worked over with a baseball bat. When we arrived, I was in pain and exhausted from the flight.

Our condo was on the majestic Wood Lake, surrounded by the mountains of the Okanagan Valley. We went there each summer to hang out with friends and their families. It always turned into a big party with lots of boating, water skiing, drinking, and adult play. Our children were the smallest in the group and required the most attention, which fell to me, as did all the usual housekeeping duties. It was my job to make sure the kids were fed and cared for, and a little thing like major surgery two weeks before wasn't going to change that because I was the consummate victim-martyr.

When we arrived at the condo, my first task was to shop for groceries. I walked the aisles barely able to raise my arms to reach the items on the shelves. Pain shot through me each time I took a step or moved my arms. I cried through most of it and didn't think I'd get through it, that I'd collapse on the floor to be taken away by ambulance. But I knew I had to take care of the kids and Neil, so I bucked up and gritted through it. Back at the condo, I took a few pain pills, put the groceries away, unpacked our bags, made dinner, and watched over the children.

The pain grew steadily worse. I thought it was all the activity, but I couldn't stop doing what I had to do. Most of the couples on the trip had been married for many years, and all the other wives seemed to have it way more together than I did. They prepared wonderful, tasty, healthy dishes, kept their condos clean and well-stocked, and still managed to hang out and have some fun themselves.

Then there was me, the one who didn't have children until I was forty-three years old. As a hard-working business owner, I had never really learned to cook. I'd be lucky if I had coffee, wine, and hot pockets in my kitchen. I eventually became pretty good, but there was a learning curve, and cooking always made me very anxious. Would I measure up to the other moms? Would the meals I make look and taste good? I *had* to win the other moms' approval.

What other people thought of me was always more important than how I treated myself. The cancer was trying to teach me another lesson, but I wasn't listening. I sucked it up and carried on. I kept our condo in perfect order, cooked all our family meals, did the housekeeping, and minded the twins, while Neil hung out on the water and partied with our friends. Cassie was having a blast hanging out with all the other kids her age that came each summer. She loved them all, and they loved her. Cassie spent most of her time with all of her new friends, which were all children of our friends that she is still friends with to this day. She was too young and didn't understand what was required to care for Jack, and certainly didn't understand what it felt like to have a double mastectomy, so I was on primarily on my own.

Anyone in their right mind would never have tried to go away two weeks after a surgery of that magnitude. I should have been at home healing, not catering to the needs of others. My role as a martyr was firmly ingrained, though, and I didn't even think to ask for what I needed. A very insecure part of me thought that if I didn't keep up with Neil (and keep an eye on him), I would lose him. If he wasn't happy, and we divorced, then I would lose half of my time with the children. That fear of abandonment dominated many of my decisions at the time. I was terrified of anything that might undermine my security. I was lost, repeating and magnifying those patterns established as a child in my marriage and many other relationships in our circle. I didn't believe I was good enough in myself, so I had to do twice, three times, ten times what everybody else did. Then maybe I would earn everyone's respect and love. I didn't know how sick I was, and it wasn't from the cancer alone. God was trying to get my attention, and I still wasn't listening.

I did have what I call a tea kettle experience on this trip. Whenever I hold my feelings in too long, the tea kettle boils over in a shrieking whistle of anger and frustration. This boil over was a big one. I had been chasing Jack around for days. I was exhausted and in a great deal of pain, and livid with Neil, who was on vacation and enjoying our friends. Sure, he was playing with and entertaining the twins, but it was on his schedule, not mine. I had taught him how to treat me, and he got an "A" in the course. I was also angry at my niece, but I wasn't asking her for what I needed either.

The condo was on a grassy area that overlooked the lake, an ideal gathering place. Neil and a large group were enjoying the day on the lawn chairs just off our patio. It was Scott's fiftieth birthday. The twins were inside, and Cassie was outside celebrating with the rest of them. I had had a tough day keeping up with them, and the tea kettle was in a rolling boil. Then it blew. "Cassie, get the hell in here, right now!" I screamed with a rage that sounded too much like my mother. "I have had it!" The blood rushed to my face, my eyes about to pop out of my head like a cartoon character. As the rage poured forth, my friends on the knoll regarded me with a mixture of shock, disbelief, concern, and disdain. Few of them had ever seen me like this.

Cassie scurried into the house, where I continued to berate her. "Who do you think you are? I need help! That's why you're here. I'm in pain, Goddamn it! Stop your damn partying and help me take care of these kids!" It was ugly. I had completely lost control. Cassie looked at me in horror, not knowing whether to run, burst into tears, or take the kids for me.

I looked up and noticed through our open screen that everyone stood in wide-eyed silence. Once I took in their reactions, I let the rest of the steam escape and apologized to my niece profusely. (Since then, I have apologized to her many times.) I was in tremendous pain both physically and emotionally, and I took it out on the closest, easiest target. I was embarrassed and exposed. She was a teenage girl. It was not her responsibility to understand what it was like to go through a double mastectomy or to understand the needs of a four-year-old with autism. I should have instructed her, led her through it step by step instead of seething in resentment that she didn't automatically know what to do.

Even with her help, the pain only increased throughout the day and night. Neil took me to Kelowna General Hospital the next day, where they drained fluid from my chest, which relieved much of the pressure causing the pain. We were scheduled to leave the next day, and we did, Cassie confused and hurt, walking on eggshells around me, Neil irritated that I had been a downer on what was supposed to be a fun time.

That was one trip I never should have taken, but I was so broken, I didn't realize that until well after the fact.

From the time I had begun the fertility process in 2002 through 2009, I had over fifteen surgeries:

- Five surgeries to become pregnant.
- A c-section to deliver the twins.
- Three breast augmentations after the twins were born; the doctor had done a terrible job the first time and needed two more times to correct it.
- A partial hysterectomy due to a fibroid cyst the size of a grapefruit.
- Three surgeries for the double mastectomy.
- A complete hysterectomy two years later to take the ovaries because they had found pre-cancerous cells.
- One hemorrhoidectomy in 2009, the worst and most painful recovery of all the surgeries, believe it or not.

In Brené Brown's book, *Rising Strong: How the Ability to Reset Transforms the Way We Live, Love, Parent, and Lead*, she paraphrases Bessel van der Kolk from his book *The Body Keeps the Score*: "Your body keeps score, and it always wins."[18] She was talking about how trauma literally rewires the brain and body. With fifteen surgeries in seven years, my body had undergone serious trauma, which I chose to deal with in a very unhealthy way that rewired my body and brain even more. Instead of looking within myself, I tried to find the magic pill outside myself that would make it all better. Literally. Beginning in Kelowna, I began using prescription pain pills to deaden the pain and keep my feelings at bay, often followed by an alcohol chaser. I enjoyed the time out this combination gave me, the fuzzy bubble of (false) protection. Instead of addressing what was in front of me, whether that was a disagreement with Neil or a tough day with the twins or my family, I kept the peace and the pace by opening the medicine cabinet for a magic pill, a glass of wine, or both.

God was still trying hard to get my attention. I was still not listening. So he changed track and went after Neil.

Chapter 13
NEIL'S CANCER – THE BOULDER BECOMES A BRICK WALL

In the summer of 2013, we had our usual heavy schedule of business trips and vacations. The twins were ten years old. Neil's back was hurting, but he had had two back surgeries over the years, and we figured something was off again. While we were in Oregon with friends, though, he had to cancel a rafting trip that all the men had been looking forward to. That wasn't Neil, but he was in too much pain for such a physical activity.

Even though the pain increased, he insisted we stay on schedule and go on the next trip as well, the annual week in Wood Lake in British Columbia. That was Neil. Most people would have gone home to the doctor, but nobody told Neil what to do, not even his body. In Canada, though, the pain became unbearable. We realized he had broken several ribs just by bending over. Now we were scared; something was wrong, and we had to get home.

At home in Arizona, his condition grew worse fast. It got to the point where he couldn't even walk. We got him in for testing. As we waited for the results, Neil quickly deteriorated even more. I had to buy a walker and a portable toilet to put next to the bed. We were terrified and confused. What in God's name could take over his body and with such vengeance?

I was in our bedroom when I looked up and saw my formerly strong, confident husband clinging to his walker as he pushed toward me. He had been on the phone with his doctor and barely got to the couch by the entrance of our bedroom before he dropped onto it. Tears streamed down his face; his body shook. I could barely understand him when he said, "I have cancer," with a look of panic, disbelief, and fear that still floods my heart. The vulnerability he showed at that moment deepens my love for him every time I remember it.

Life had come to a stop once again. God had our attention.

Neil was diagnosed with multiple myeloma, a cancer of the blood in the leukemia family. It affects the plasma cells in the bone marrow, often resulting in fragile bones that easily fracture, as Neil found out the hard way.

When Neil got sick, I got sicker, too, not physically, but emotionally. Neil was losing control of his body; I was losing control of myself. We locked more tightly into our dance of codependence and deepened the wounds as we sank deeper into fear. Fear is like an alarm clock that keeps ringing. Ours would continue to ring for the next four years. God had brought us to the most critical time of our growth as a couple.

Neil's cancer was in the final stage of this type of cancer. His bones were losing calcium and weakening, and he was in tremendous pain. As a caregiver, I went immediately into sacrifice mode. I knew I would do absolutely anything to make it better for him in any way I could at my own expense. In this way, I quickly regressed to my familiar unhealthy patterns.

I do not want to speak to Neil's lesson through this experience, but I agree with Michael Douglas, who famously said that "cancer didn't bring me to my knees; it brought me to my feet." In other words, Neil's multiple myeloma woke us up in a way that my breast cancer had not.

The next years would be filled with bone marrow biopsies, stem cell transplants, chemotherapy, radiation, many illnesses due to a weak immune system, care classes and many, many days spent at the hospital. When multiple myeloma is this advanced, a bone marrow transplant is the primary treatment, but it comes with great risk. In the procedure, the patient is essentially killed, then brought back to life. They even give you a new birthday because every cell in your body has been replaced. After the procedure, Neil had to stay in quarantine for one hundred days to avoid infection. It's quite an ordeal. In our case, the ordeal was made easier by the waves of support we received from friends and family. I started a CaringBridge web site to let people know how Neil was progressing. We had over 6,000 responses of support. Plenty of visitors brought meals to the house, helped with the twins, sat with us. They talked when we needed it, listened when we needed that, and provided anything else we needed. We were and are very blessed and will be forever grateful.

Neil tried his damnedest to maintain a good attitude. We both tried to keep it as lighthearted as we could, especially for the twins. For the first transplant, Neil colored his hair purple and got a mohawk. We all followed suit by putting purple in our hair as well, even the dog. Jennifer Carroll (of Woodstock party fame) produced and shot a wonderful video we posted on our CaringBridge site. People from all over the world started coloring their hair purple in honor of Neil. It made a very difficult situation easier for all of us.

While all this was going on, of course, our life didn't completely stop. We still had businesses to run, Jack's autism to address, issues with my brother that I'll write more about later, and so on. Sometimes these other tasks were a welcome relief from cancer and hospitals; other times they were distracting burdens that weighed on us heavily.

With Neil's fighting spirit and the miracles of modern science, we thought we had a good chance of beating multiple myeloma. Neil had had two bone marrow transplants between 2013 and mid 2016 before going into remission for the second time. We were told he could only have that procedure twice, though, and if he relapsed again, there wasn't much more they could do.

To our dismay, Neil relapsed a year later, in late 2016. We were devastated. Was that it? Did we have to bow to the inevitable?

We were losing ground, and we were scared. Neil sold his company and retired to spend what time he had left with us. Did he hunker down at home waiting to die? Of course not! That's not Neil. He accepted that his time on earth might be running out, but he didn't give in to it. What he loved most in the world was to travel. This was perhaps the last chance he had to show the kids all the places in the world he had explored and loved over the years: Europe, Asia, Australia, Africa. So that's what we planned to do.

We would withdraw the twins from school for eighth grade to take a trip around the world.

Neil is truly a phenomenon, with a rare focus and determination. He planned the whole trip himself, down to the smallest detail. With his gift of persuasion, he got us all to accept the reason for the trip and to be excited about the trip itself. He must have been terrified, but he was going to make sure we had a beautiful family experience no matter what happened next. I was very proud of Neil for this and loved him even more if that was possible. He is such a wonderful father.

He wasn't deterred from going, even once his doctors told him that, given his compromised immune system, he shouldn't travel in third world countries. Okay, he decided. We would travel through Europe for the summer instead, and the twins could still experience eighth grade at home. We could make Barcelona our home base, since we had good, good friends there who would let us stay in their summer house north of the city. Neil's doctor reached out to a doctor in Barcelona who could keep an eye on Neil while we were there. The Balter Summer Tour was on!

The trip was a fairytale experience. Our friends' home, a literal palace that overlooked the Mediterranean Sea, was just north of the city in a small town in the coastal region of Catalonia in Costa Brava. The quaint beach towns with their narrow cobblestone streets brought the glory of old-world Spain to us each day. When we weren't on the road and wanted a change of pace, we stayed in their apartment in the city. Now those are friends!

We even created a website so our friends and family back home could follow our progress. I wrote a blog in each city we visited. (That's how I discovered I might like this writing thing.) In two and a half months, we traveled to seventeen cities and five countries; had twenty-one flights, one bus trip, and three train trips; stayed in eighteen different rental apartments; rented thirteen cars; took six bike tours and hired three historians. We visited Barcelona, Granada, San Sebastian, Marbella, London, Florence, Rome, Pompei, Venice, Paris, the South of France, Normandy, Berlin, Munich, and Morocco across the Gibraltar Strait.

In almost every city we visited, we had friends who either lived there or would meet up with us. Neil and I have been blessed to travel the world, and between YEO (EO), Neil's travel setting up California Closet franchises, and the travel we have both done, we are fortunate to have wonderful friends in many beautiful places. Not only did our children have the benefit of learning firsthand about each city we visited, but they also spent a lot of time with friends and family. We were able to experience the real flavor of local living in towns and cities across Europe.

I could write chapters on the glory of each city, but that would be a book in and of itself. One of my favorite cities was Granada, Spain, called the Moorish Jewel because it was an important center of Islamic rule in the early Middle Ages. The city sprawls at the base of the Sierra Nevada Mountains with their deep canyons and jagged peaks. The high point of the city, both literally and figuratively, is the Alhambra, a walled town with a castle and fortress built on a plateau in the southeastern part of the city. It was the royal residence of the Muslim rulers and has a beautiful garden complex called Generalife with gorgeous cypress, pomegranate, walnut, cherry, orange, and almond trees, oleander and rose bushes, and climbing vines, such as jasmine wisteria, and ivy. I shared that trip with two of my sisters, Darline and Lisa. My dad actually adopted Lisa with his fourth wife, Darlene. Lisa lives in Marbella, about two hours southwest of Granada. We stayed in the most delightful Spanish home deep within the streets of the famous city and, while we were there, she introduced us to her friends and the local culture.

Our trip to Europe was the adventure of a lifetime, and we all had a glorious time soaking in the natural and cultural sites, eating great food, learning more about Europe than you ever could in a book, and spending this precious, intimate family time together.

Hanging over it all, however, was Neil's terminal illness, which sent Neil and me retreating to familiar, unhealthy patterns. The last thing I wanted to do was to make life more difficult for Neil. I tried even harder to make sure he was happy. My world revolved around Neil and what he needed. It had always been like that, but when he was ill, that dynamic multiplied times ten—or one hundred.

When someone like Neil, who has always been in control of his life, has a serious illness, it rocks his world, and thus, it rocks everyone in his world. Not being in control of his future was especially difficult for Neil. He had worked hard his whole life and achieved monumental success by planning everything to the smallest detail. But he had not planned for this—who does, no matter how many Sunday sermons you listen to? Controlling events, negotiating, and winning arguments are fundamental to Neil. He was used to winning at this game of life, and now it looked like he was losing. He wasn't in control of his health or even his time on this planet. So he unconsciously doubled and tripled down on what he could control—me.

Perhaps it's the ADHD, but Neil doesn't like to sit still. He always has to be doing something, whether for work or recreation. He's an extrovert, not one for contemplation or looking inward. Alone time is his idea of hell. And like many extroverts, he doesn't understand why everyone doesn't see things the same way. Don't be so boring and lazy! Get out there and do something! You don't know what you're missing!

Often what I was missing was a good night's sleep or two seconds to myself. I'm an extrovert too, but I need downtime and inward time every once in a while.

The trip only intensified Neil's go-go-go mentality, even when that wasn't the best thing for him. We were running constantly, and his health couldn't always keep up. I was like a combat nurse or athletic trainer, taking care of Neil when he fell ill from the pace or the side effects of the medications, patching him up so he could get back out on the field. And only rarely did he think I did things to his satisfaction. He criticized me mercilessly, the dance he had learned in his family of origin. And I felt now even less able to speak up and ask for what I needed. Neil was going to die. What right did I have to take care of my needs? I was the child again with the weight of the world on her shoulders.

But I wasn't a child anymore, and I knew I was betraying myself. But I couldn't really help it. It wasn't a good time to change, I told myself. It's not what Neil needs right now. When Neil gets better, I'll take care of myself. But not right now. Right now, I need to take care of Neil. That's all that matters. To get by, I drank and medicated myself, a habit I had begun during my own pain-filled illnesses. I even "borrowed" Neil's pain medications sometimes.

I generally kept the substance abuse under control, but sometimes it got out of hand. On that trip, Neil and Jack had travelled to London to visit a tank museum, while Brianna and I, who couldn't have cared less about tanks, stayed in Barcelona. I went to dinner with some friends and Brianna remained home with the family we were staying with. We dined at an elegant restaurant overlooking Ciutadella Park, a breathtaking green surrounded by many delightful Spanish homes.

We went through a few bottles and after dinner drinks before heading for a hip bar on Barceloneta Beach, with its beautiful boardwalk lining the city of Barcelona. As I entered the bar with crowds of people, I found it difficult to keep my bearings amid the wild drunken dancing and singing. I soon lost track of my friends, grew more confused and woozy, and instead of trying to find my friends through the endless crowd, decided to head home.

I made my way outside to find huge lines of partiers waiting for taxis. I just wanted to get home. In my drunken state, I walked up to three men and asked them to share their cab. The taxi driver was disgusted with the state of all four of us and threw us out of the cab. Now I found myself walking the streets alone in the middle of Barcelona at three in the morning. I finally found another taxi and made my way back to our friend's apartment. My spirit guides were watching out for me that night.

The next morning, I woke up and went out to the living room where Brianna was hanging out.

"Hi Honey, sorry I slept late. What time it is?" I groaned, holding my throbbing head in two hands. I had seen in the bathroom mirror that my face was smudged with mascara.

"Mom, it's two in the afternoon," Brianna said with teenaged contempt for all things parental.

"What?" I said mortified, as if I were the child and Brianna the mother. I had never done anything like that before. No matter how hard I partied, I had always answered the bell in the morning, at least until then. I will be forever ashamed of that night and the day following.

It was just another sign I wasn't taking care of myself. I had gained weight and grown puffy from the alcohol. I looked terrible. The self-medication to numbness had stopped working (if it had ever worked at all). Every time I brushed my teeth, I wondered who that woman in the mirror was. When I see the pictures taken toward the end of that trip, I wince at just how badly I was treating myself and my family. I was so busy taking care of Neil, Jack, Michael, Brianna, my mother, and everyone else, that I had nothing left for myself. I was self-medicating and exhausted. In Oprah's terms, a huge boulder was coming at me, one that might crush me for good.

When we returned, Neil's health deteriorated quickly. He was often sick and uncomfortable. I was just trying to survive every day—every hour, really—and make him as comfortable as I could. But I know that though I was always there in body, I wasn't always there in spirit, self-medicating as I was. We did our best to make sure the children were not affected.

Around this time, Neil's doctor told us about a new treatment that might help: a clinical trial for patients with late-stage multiple myeloma who have relapsed after having the limit of two bone marrow transplants. We were blessed to be in the hands of Mayo Clinic, who gave us the benefit of all the latest advancements in the treatment of multiple myeloma. The intramural therapy would help a patient's cells fight the cancer with a weekly infusion of daratumumab. The clinical trial gave us a bit of hope, but it was such a new treatment we didn't put too much stock in it. Even the doctors told us we should "start making arrangements." Neil might have just about a year or so left to live.

With the first round of clinical trials, though, Neil showed good progress and started feeling better, more like his old self. This was good news for him, good news for us, and good news for me. The boulder had been rolling toward me for a while, and now that we had a bit of a breather from the cancer, maybe it was time to do something about that. In other words, the early success of the clinical trials gave me the space—and the strength—to take the radical step to heal myself that I had been thinking about for some time: rehab. It was time for me to go inside myself to heal, to "willfully shed" the pills and alcohol that only masked my pain. I had to find a way back to my true self.

Chapter 14
HOW DO YOU GET A BREAK AROUND HERE?

It was 6:30 a.m. on a fall day in 2016. I rolled over, looked out the window, and basked in the sunrise of the most incredible pinks and yellows blended into a radiance that expanded over the Gulf of Mexico—still, gentle, and vast as it lapped against the Florida panhandle. The seagulls swayed over the water on the lookout for breakfast. The view looked beautiful, comforting, and breathtaking. As I roused myself from a night's sleep, one of the best I had had in a long time, I remembered where I was: in rehab, at Gulf Breeze Recovery at the western tip of the Florida panhandle. I chose to be here. I was finally safe to heal.

After reading an article in *Spirituality and Health*, one of my favorite magazines, about Gulf Breeze Recovery, I realized the two-month program was tailor made for me. Their goal was teaching participants to heal the wounds at the foundation of their addictions rather than just put a band aid on the outward symptoms. The program was meant to give power back to anyone who had the courage to dig deep enough to learn and grow. In fact, its principles seemed to be based on the teachings of many of the authors I had been studying for years. *This is what I need*, I told myself as I read the article. I was exhausted and stressed, stretching myself thin taking care of everyone else, drinking to numb myself to it all. I felt lost. I needed the time to find my way back to myself.

I had been trying to justify entering Gulf Breeze for months, but I had come up with nothing but excuses. What wife and mother has the right to step away from her family to "find herself?" Could I be more selfish and self-indulgent? Neil's new treatment was working, but was it too much to leave Neil alone with the twins so soon? What would my children think of me? Did I have the courage to face not only my own family but the judgment of everyone else in my life? I had just had the trip of a lifetime, at least from the outside. Did I have the right to go away again? My answer: I had turned to these excuses for far too long. Neil was doing much better. This was the perfect window of opportunity. If I didn't get healthy myself, I would be no good as a wife and mother to the very people who needed me.

Oddly, rehab is a socially acceptable way of taking care of yourself, almost a permission slip. Rehab gave me the permission to do what I desperately needed to do—dig myself out of the hole I had climbed into. During our family trip through Europe, the unhealthy parent-child patterns that Neil and I had established so long ago were amplified, as were Neil's criticizing and gaslighting. When you experience those demeaning behaviors for years, you start to question your sanity. We were both exhausted and unsure of the future. Yes, I had been traveling to many wonderful places, but as each week passed, I fell deeper into despair, completely beaten down, drinking too much just to numb the pain. By the end of our trip, I looked and felt terrible. I was puffy from drinking and eating badly. I wasn't exercising and had gained twenty pounds, some of which I believe had become a layer of protection. I had given up on myself. I wanted to escape from the world. Every day was just another slog to make it to the end of the day.

Two weeks after we returned from the family summer tour, Neil and I flew to Europe again, this time to Croatia with our EO friends. Neil continued to improve with the infusions from the clinical trial at Mayo and was ready to celebrate with our friends. They were all so excited to see how well Neil was doing, and we all celebrated accordingly.

At dinner one night in the historic walled town of Dubrovnik, we went through ten bottles of wine at our table. I got drunk, Neil and I had decided to walk home and leave the dinner early. On the walk home, my tea kettle went off.

"I can't do this anymore," I said to Neil. "I'm exhausted, and I feel like crap. I'm worried about you and the twins, the future and how we have all been affected by the last few years. Scared, in fact. Scared out of my mind.

What are we going to do if something happens to you? I'm running on fumes, here. I've got nothing left."

Alcohol had become my courage in a bottle, and everything I had been holding in since Neil's diagnosis came spewing out. "What the hell, Lynn. Are you drunk again? What is wrong with you? You look terrible. I'm sick of your drinking. Get your fucking shit together!" Neil went on the attack as was his way.

The people on that magnificent stone walkway along the shore of the Adriatic Sea heard every angry word we hurled at each other. Thank God it was only a mile to our room, and we had spared our friends this ugly brawl.

I woke up the next morning and told Neil he was right. I needed to get my shit together. When we got back to Arizona, I was going to pack up and head to rehab. I told him what I had found out about Gulf Breeze Recovery and that I would sell some jewelry his mom had given me to pay for it if I had to, but I was going. I wasn't usually that direct with Neil, but I knew what I had to do. He got angry, of course, as people do when you change the dynamics on them. He yelled about how expensive it was—his go-to argument for things that I wanted to spend money on. When I pointed out we had spent way more on our summer trips, he switched gears, arguing that I was selfish, how could I take so much time away from them when he was still trying to recover? Our room over looked the vivid blue sea and the wonder of the Croatian mountains. It was a romantic vista, but there we were, going at it.

I was conflicted because I had some of the same doubts Neil had. Who in the world did I think I was to take two months away from a sick husband and two children, one of whom was autistic? On the other hand, I knew that for my mental health I had to do just that. We wound down our "discussion," and went to breakfast with our friends. While eating breakfast, it struck me how I could make this happen. Without preamble, I announced my plans to the table. This was manipulative, I know, but I was determined to go, and I knew Neil would get behind the need for me to go with our friends' support.

Most of our friends were taken off guard, but once it sank in, they all clapped for me. This group of friends knows us well, and they were aware of the unhealthy patterns that Neil and I had fallen into. Our friends were proud of me for asking for what I needed, and Neil agreed that it was probably a good idea. Always one for the grand gesture, he offered to pay the cost as well. Once Neil got on board, I was more than happy I'd be going to Gulf Breeze. I had been caring for Neil through his illness for four years. The child-parent dynamic between us had only grown worse. I felt as if I couldn't tell my truth without a huge fight. I had simply shut down, walking through the days unaware and unconscious. I had climbed so many mountains to be free over the years, but the same patterns of dependence and people pleasing occurred over and over again. The past can hold you as a prisoner, and it had a firm grip on me. I had betrayed myself, which made me no different from those who had hurt me. I wanted desperately to wake up, but to do so, I had to go back to school. I wanted to be Mary Tyler Moore again.

My decision to go into rehab came as a surprise to many friends and family members. When we returned from Croatia, I first had to tell the twins, who were now almost fourteen. It was one of the hardest things I've ever done. It wasn't as difficult for Jack as it was for Brianna. Jack's autism made it factual for him. Mom is going on a trip to feel better. Brianna was taken completely by surprise, though, because she wasn't aware anything was wrong. Even that day in Barcelona, she had just thought I had been really tired.

"Brianna, Mom has to talk to you about, something important," I said, looking deep into her eyes.

"What, Mom? Are you okay? Is everything okay?" She looked at me with concern and surprise. I didn't usually bring my problems to her.

"Honey, I have not been taking good care of myself. I've been making bad choices and using alcohol to avoid my feelings. I've made a big decision that will take me away for a bit so I can take care of that."

I held my breath for her response.

"Oh," Brianna said. "Brook's Dad just got a DUI, and their family's getting through it. We will too. I love you, Mom." She fell into my arms with tears of uncertainty and confusion.

Brianna had lived in a child's world until that day. Yes, she knew of cancer and autism, but those were things that happened to you not something you created yourself. I was honest with Brianna and told her that sometimes you have to reach out for help and that I would be okay. She grew up a lot that day. I had hurt her into that growth by shaking her world, and I will always have to live with that.

I left the next day, September 19, 2016.

I wrote a letter explaining my choice to well over a hundred of our friends before leaving. I didn't want my family to think they had to lie about it. I also had to explain to many others outside our inner circle why I wouldn't be home for the next two months, as I had many responsibilities. I wanted to eliminate shame and judgement by showing my truth. To do that, I had to be vulnerable. I hoped to change my patterns of silence and shame from the start. Brené Brown writes, "The addict needs shame like a man dying of thirst needs salt water."[19]

That's where my friends came in. The love and support I received from so many on that list was the opposite of shame. I was in trouble, and they were cheering me on, giving me the courage to move forward. My secret was out. I was drinking too much. I was an addict and had many addictions that went far deeper than drinking. I was addicted to hearing the voices of others before my own. I was addicted to being a victim, a martyr, and a people pleaser. I had to take the risk to be vulnerable and attend the program at Gulf Breeze or I would move no closer to my true self in this lifetime.

I was fortunate to receive the support of my circle, but not everyone is. As a society, we have to work harder to create a culture that allows people to get help when they need it without the label of shame. Many people don't seek help because they don't want to be called addicts or alcoholics the rest of their lives. It shouldn't be a life sentence. It takes courage to go inside yourself to heal. It is my prayer that we can create a culture that allows people to feel safe getting help, to stop the secrets, to stop the judgment of those treated for alcohol and drug addiction or other mental health issues. In recent years, quite a few wellness centers have opened up. We are finally realizing that we should all have permission to step away when we notice that we are too close to the edge. And don't get me started on how expensive these programs can be. My program cost over $20,000. I am blessed that we were able to pay for it. Not everyone is. We have to find a way in our culture to change this dynamic and provide programs just as wonderful as Gulf Breeze to everyone who has the courage to ask for help.

To truly help ourselves, sometimes we have to leave the environment we live in so we can see ourselves more clearly. When I arrived at Gulf Breeze, I didn't require detox. In fact, according to a report they ran, I would have been fine doing outpatient treatment (that's why our insurance company wouldn't pay for any part of my stay, no matter how hard Neil tried). But I knew that for me to heal, I had to get away. I had to have time just for me. An outpatient program from home never would have worked because the patterns I lived in at home were unhealthy. To change them, I had to get away. I knew that was the only way I was going to heal.

Gulf Breeze works with the psychology of addiction, teaching us how to look at the foundation of the addiction, not just the symptoms. At Gulf Breeze, we were nourished, not punished. They started by nourishing our bodies with healthy meals and detoxifying our bodies with saunas and other natural methods while filling us with wisdom and inspiration from the inside out. They didn't try to apply ready-made solutions to fix us as if we were broken machines. They helped us heal from within. As Jesus says, "The Kingdom of Heaven is within You." When you go deep inside, you move from an intellectual understanding to an understanding of the soul, from information to wisdom.

Gulf Breeze teachings are based on The Three Principles of the Divine Mind (or universal intelligence of our souls), Consciousness (or gift of awareness), and Thought (streams of thought and worry based on the past that can get triggered), originally developed by Sydney Banks in 1973 and brought to the world by many other teachers since then.[20]

The Three Principles are simple to list but not so simple to practice. Michael Neill, Elsie Spittle, Amar Karkouti, Jack Pransky, Joe Bailey, Linda Quiring, and Allan E. Flood have all written with their own interpretation of the Three Principles. This is my interpretation through the teaching that I was fortunate enough to receive at Gulf Breeze:

1. **Mind:** Mind refers to the Divine Mind, Spirit, the universal intelligence of our souls. We are all part of the Divine Mind, the universal knowing that we are all one. All of our souls participate in the Divine Mind. If we can tap into the Divine Mind in our human form, we move closer to our true spiritual selves.
2. **Consciousness:** Consciousness is the gift of awareness, knowing that we are alive in our human form. There are many levels of consciousness and as our consciousness grows, it allows us to access greater wisdom. There are also many ways to grow more conscious through meditation, study, and the ability to tap into the Divine Mind.
3. **Thought:** We all have thoughts that come and go within our human minds. They come in a constant, distracting stream. They are not of our true selves. They are of our personality and ego, not our soul. The soul knows better. Many thoughts are determined by our past—the way we grew up, the patterns we learned from our families, our socioeconomic status, our education—and many others are governed by worry about the future. These thoughts are not real. They are not of our soul, but are triggered by outside forces. When we truly let go of the worry about past and future, we set ourselves free. As we become more conscious, we understand where our thoughts come from and why we respond to them the way we do. When we realize they are just thoughts, we are more able to release them and become our true selves.

How do the Three Principles apply to addiction recovery? Well, you may have the thought to pick up a drink, for example, but when you become aware that it is just a thought, that you don't need that drink, you merely think you need that drink, you can feel the pain of that need and let it pass. The medicine is in the pain. In this way, we begin to recognize that the pain does not kill us. It passes like a storm over the sea. We can no more control our pain than we can stop a storm from moving the waves in the ocean. When we try to control our surroundings, the pain grows worse. When we try to numb the pain, we freeze it in place, and it can't pass through.

But this isn't easy to do, embracing pain and letting it pass through. We are afraid of pain. There's no need to fear pain, though, because the pain comes whether we fear it or not. If we let ourselves become aware of the pain and feel it, then breathe through it, it will pass. We can't ignore pain. Pain doesn't hurt you in a permanent way, ignoring it does. If we tap into the divine oneness, then we begin to heal. Feeling that pain is the price of freedom. In his book *The Untethered Soul*, Michael Singer writes, "If we ignore [pain], it will get infected, like having a splinter in your foot, if you don't take it out."[21] He reminds us that we must feel the pain and breathe through it. If you stay in the pain by trying to numb it, you stay in the addiction. When there is pain, there is a reason, and that reason is to promote growth.

During my stay at Gulf Breeze, I saw people with very serious addictions come through the program in rough shape. They were empty shells of themselves. After they went through detox, I saw these beautiful persons emerge. I'd watch them get stronger from the insights they learned in class, from counseling, from treatment. It was such a miracle to witness these acts of God every day. Of course, some of the people I met were young and not ready for what they were receiving. Some were too broken, and others thought they already knew everything. You can't gain wisdom when your mind is closed.

The Three Principles help us go within ourselves for well-being instead of trying to find it outside of ourselves in all the usual quick fixes. These quick fixes can become addictions before we know it, or at least compulsions. I'm using a broad definition of addiction here rather than the medical one. An addiction is anything we do that is harmful to ourselves or others that we can't stop doing. There are the obvious addictions, such as tobacco, alcohol, gambling, and drugs of all kinds, but other behaviors can also morph into addiction, such as overeating, overworking, people pleasing, controlling and criticizing others, always needing to win.

There was a big sign in our classroom that read, "Life is 10% of what happens to you and 90% of how you react to it." These destructive patterns of addiction create chaos in our lives and ruin relationships. To change these patterns, we need to learn to calm the turbulent thoughts in our minds. What's the first thing a computer tech tells you when your laptop goes on the fritz? Unplug it and reboot. Metaphorically, that applies to us as well. Think of yourself as a snow globe. When a snow globe is all shook up, the "snow" swirls around, hiding everything from view. If you let the globe sit still, the snow begins to settle, and everything clears up. You can see again. If we can let our ourselves be still, then our thoughts will settle, and we will have a clearer idea of what we need to do, how we need to react. We will make better choices.

At Gulf Breeze I learned how to be conscious, to stay awake, to begin to change the patterns of addiction. Miracles were happening within me. I couldn't go back to sleep. I had to embrace change, and in doing so, I began to reveal my true self, my soul state, the part of me that is aware that we are all one and that our purpose in life is to heal the broken parts within ourselves and become whole. William Paul Young writes, "Wholeness is when the way of our being matches the Truth of our Being."[22] I was learning how to do that better and better each day, both by the inspiration, knowledge, and wisdom I picked up in the classroom and by deepening my meditation practice.

I had been meditating for many years and found that I had some of my best meditation experiences in larger groups. In group meditation, the energy grew stronger within me, and I was able to go much deeper. One of the highlights of my days at Gulf Breeze was our daily group meditation. After each session, I felt myself growing stronger and more centered.

One session in particular was a huge breakthrough for me.

A shaman visited Gulf Breeze twice a month. Shamans are healers—medicine men or women. I had never met a shaman before, and I was excited. The staff at Gulf Breeze had great respect for this man.

The shaman held his session in our regular classroom, where we attended class, ate meals, did yoga, and socialized at night. That day the room held about twenty of us, both residents and counselors. The tables were arranged in a circle with the chairs set up so we could all see one another.

We were all seated when the shaman walked into the room accompanied by a beautiful, graceful younger woman in a vintage dress that set off her long auburn hair. She wore no makeup, but glowed with an inner radiance as she gently guided him by the arm. I don't remember his name, but the serenity of his face and gentle power of his presence has stayed with me. He was quite thin and a bit elderly, although he seemed in very good health. His grey hair was long for a man of his age, although it suited him. He was soft-spoken and gentle. I could feel the energy of his compassion and tranquility wash over me as his companion led him through the room to their chairs in the circle where they sat next to each other. His smile took in all of us at once, humble and bold at the same time. I was mesmerized and couldn't wait to devour his wisdom.

He told us a little about his background, that he had been practicing shamanism for many years as well as the practice of meditation. He had traveled the world to share his gifts and we were all about to have an adventure. His soft eyes scanned the room, taking in the energy of each of us.

"Is everyone ready to play?" he said in a voice filled with excitement.

We all nodded eagerly.

"I would like you all to hold hands and close your eyes in meditation," he said with a joyful ease that immediately calmed me. "If you allow yourself to trust and completely give yourself over to our practice today, we can really have some fun."

I don't remember what he said from that point until I came out of the spiritual trance I had fallen into. I had gone into a space of love and peace that was so magnificent I can't find the words to express it. I can tell you that I didn't want to come out of that trance. When I eventually did come back to the room, my eyes still closed, I realized I had been crying. My face was soaked with tears of awareness—everything was all right and always would be.

"Now you may open your eyes," he said as a nurse would say to someone coming out of anesthesia.

When I opened my eyes, everyone was looking at me.

"She really wanted to play," the shaman said as he looked at me the way a teacher would look at a student who just earned an A.

Maybe I should have been embarrassed, but I wasn't. I was grateful. I've heard it said that shamans are healers who can penetrate your spiritual skin. That day I know he did just that for me. It was as if he had gone into my soul and restored a portion of it. He got the healing started.

My time at Gulf Breeze, that miraculous place of healing, was a gift from God for that reason. It got the healing started. The staff and the other beautiful souls I met there will always be special, forever etched in my soul. The experience with the shaman took me deeper within myself than I had ever gone before and revealed the love and wonder of our Lord and the divine energy of the world. That experience enabled me to incorporate everything I had been studying for so long into my everyday life. I felt like Dorothy in the Wizard of Oz. I had been home all along, and home was inside me, not in the outside approval of others. Brené Brown observes that looking for happiness outside yourself is like looking for seashells in a bathtub. The only seashells in the bathtub are the ones you put there yourself.

I was reborn at Gulf Breeze, but I knew I had to go home and do the real work. As Einstein taught us, "The definition of insanity is to do the same thing over and over and expect different results." I couldn't go home and remain the same, but I was scared to face the transition.

I had a panic attack a few days before I was supposed to leave. At Gulf Breeze, I had become my best self. I had agency. I had made my own decisions. I had rested. I had exercised. I had lived life at my own pace. I had learned an amazing amount about myself. But had I learned enough? Could

I take this newfound acceptance and hope home with me? I would be walking into the same storm that brought me to Gulf Breeze in the first place. Would I have the courage and the strength to continue to move forward, continuing to find the well-being I had achieved within the walls of Gulf Breeze in my life at home? Couldn't I stay just one more month? Then I'd be ready to leave.

The woman managing the center came to my room and gave me a pep talk. She assured me that I had to face the real world, and it would not be any easier a month later. She pointed out that the beauty of Gulf Breeze was that they planted the seeds of healing which, if properly tended, would flourish for the rest of my life. With that encouragement, I took a deep breath and let it be.

I returned home just in time for the twins' fourteenth birthday. They were excited I was home in time to celebrate with them. We took a big pack of their friends to a local birthday hot spot with race cars, virtual reality laser tag, a full arcade, and lots of junk food. We all had a blast.

Once home, I continued working with a therapist from Gulf Breeze on Skype. I worked with her for almost two years, but it wasn't long before the old patterns triggered the old behaviors. I had changed, but nobody else had changed with me: Neil was still recovering and unconsciously trying to control everything; my mom still wanted me to make her life better in all ways, large and small; Michael was still an eleven-year-old in a man's body; Jack still needed a team of autism experts to get him through the week; and Brianna—well, Brianna was still her wonderful, beautiful, accomplished self, but she was taking some of her cues from her father and at times reacting to me the way I had taught her father, and now her, to treat me—with disrespect.

When the pain of these old patterns returned, I became overwhelmed. When I was overwhelmed, at times I would slip and turn to alcohol to escape. One day about a year or so after I had returned from Gulf Breeze sticks out in my mind. We were skiing and had taken our lunch break.

Jack was ready to call it quits. "Dad, I'm so tired. Can I please stop skiing?" It was a cold day, and we had been on the slopes since nine that morning. It was now two and Jack was tired. I was proud of him for asking for what he needed.

"No, Jack, absolutely not," Neil said in that tone that brooked no negotiation. "You're skiing until the end of the ski day, and that's that!"

"C'mon, Dad. I'm tired and cold. This isn't fun anymore," Jack pleaded.

"I'm tired, too," I interjected. I know Jack well and can tell when he is genuinely tapped out or just making excuses. That afternoon he was genuinely beat. "It's cold. He could hurt himself. He told me he had not slept well last night. Why don't you all go and get a few more runs in. I'll hang out with Jack at the lodge until you're done."

"You always make excuses for him. Stop enabling him!" Neil said harshly. "Jack, put your gear on now! Let's go!" Neil picked up his own gear and looked at me with contempt. Many times, Jack would use excuses to get out of things—normally to play on his electronics. But I was sure this time was different. I wanted to handle Jack in my own way at that moment. I didn't think it would be safe for him to risk getting hurt because he was tired.

Jack's ski instructor was at the table. She witnessed our dance, and I certainly wasn't leading. Moments later, we were all carrying our skis to the next lift, Jack included. I felt embarrassed, defeated, and humiliated. After all we had been through, I still wasn't allowed a say, even when I thought it was best for the children. I knew Jack had not slept well the night before. I knew he was telling the truth. Yet I caved, stuffed it down in the old way, and fumed for the rest of the afternoon. With each breath, my anger continued to grow. Would I ever be able to have a say? Would I ever be able to make a decision? Would my judgment ever be trusted? I was sick and tired of not having my own voice!

When we returned to the mountain house, I gave in and drank my anger. The only alcohol in the house was a bottle of brandy. Although I hate brandy, in my fury, I drank several glasses while I cooked dinner. Since I wasn't used to alcohol, it hit me hard, and everything came to a head after dinner.

Neil and the kids wanted to play Risk, the board game of war and world domination. I don't enjoy Risk. It glorifies war and makes me sad and a little hopeless about the human race. An overreaction, perhaps, but that's how I feel. If there's one thing I learned at Gulf Breeze, it was to honor my feelings. What was worse, Neil knows how I feel about this game, yet he insisted we play anyway. I voiced my objection, which I might have kept to myself if not for the brandy and the day's pent-up anger. But this is not allowed. I broke the cardinal rule, contradicting Neil and having an opinion of my own. He turned on me with contempt, belittling my beliefs in front of the children.

It was a big trigger, and I blew up, also in front of the children. I let him have it with both barrels about how sick I was of his disdain and superiority, treating me like a child or someone who worked for him. Who did he think he was? yada, yada, yada. None of what I said was wrong, exactly, but the way I said it was. After I lost steam, I was ashamed of myself for drinking and exploding. The tea kettle had gone off again. I simply didn't have the capacity to voice my opinion about sensitive topics without the help of alcohol—and by the time alcohol was a factor, it was too late to do so in a reasonable manner. This was certainly not behavior I wanted to model in front of the children.

The next morning, I walked into the bedroom of my fifteen-year-old daughter to explain what happened—that I had drunk alcohol again and was angry with Dad about the skiing and that was why I had had blown up out of all proportion to the issue. She accepted my apology as graciously as any fifteen-year-old, but I could tell she was disappointed in me.

To get well and stay well often requires those closest to you to take a serious look at their own behavior.

To his credit, Neil agreed we had to start working on the dynamics of our relationship if we were to stay together. It was after the skiing and Risk experience that Neil began to work with Joe Bailey, with whom I also worked. He is one of the founders of Gulf Breeze and has written several books on the Three Principles. We worked together with him for over a year to learn how to support each other. We found his teachings on separate realities and deep listening particularly helpful.

The concept of separate realities explains why so many people find it difficult to communicate even with people they love. Each of us has a perception of life that comes from our background, our experiences, and even our genetics. We see life from inside the tunnel of our egos. Many of us can't even imagine a reality other than our own, and that's how we judge the world and the other people in it. For example, if you see life as a competition that you have to win, you might regard someone who likes to collaborate rather than compete as weak, and even a loser. If you're the one who likes to collaborate, then the win-at-all costs person may seem arrogant and belligerent. It's as if we're from different cultures speaking different languages—because we are. We need to learn how to translate from one culture to the other.

How do we do that? The first step is recognizing that most people do view the world from their own reality, including ourselves. Then we must do the best we can to understand our reality—the 95 percent of our life that is unconscious to us, according to Dr. Lipton. In other words, we need to grow more self-aware. We can do this by learning to be mindful and present, sometimes with the help of therapists, coaches, and so forth, sometimes on our own through meditation and other spiritual exercises. What are our hidden assumptions? Through what lenses do we view the world? When our mind is closed, there is no room for learning.

The next step is to understand the other person's reality, which we can accomplish to some degree by getting out of our own heads and using the techniques of deep listening (no one understands another person perfectly). True strength comes from the ability to see beyond our own perceptions. When we make an effort to understand why people act and react as they do, we learn to take it less personally and respond with empathy rather than ego. When we open ourselves to seeing things in a different light, we grow as individuals and in our relationships.

In our work on deep listening with Joe Bailey, Neil and I learned that when you've been in a relationship for some time, you think you have the other person figured out. As a result, you don't let in new information, and you learn to block the other out, responding to a predetermined notion of what you think is going on rather than what may actually be going on. Not this again, you say to yourself, and the same old arguments continue over and over. That's why new relationships can be so much fun—you have no preconceived notions, you're open to learning about the other person, and it's exciting. As relationships continue, however, we often come to feel exposed and vulnerable. We get defensive and our shadow shelves (that 95 percent we are unconscious of) creep in and start sabotaging the intimacy we're trying to develop.

We all have a shadow side, and in much of our time with therapists, Neil and I are working to uncover ours. We are learning to honor each other's differences without criticism and use deep listening to communicate more clearly—that is, to truly listen without thinking about our response and simply waiting for the other person to stop talking so we can get our point across; to not to interrupt; to choose the right time to discuss whatever needs discussion; to try to understand each other's separate reality; to realize that we can listen without agreeing or giving in to the other's will.

Neil and I are still working hard to end the parent-child dynamic in our relationship. It is difficult to have an intimate relationship when you are figuratively sleeping with your father or mother.

We had a huge AHA (day of awareness) when we studied Harville Hendrix's book, *Getting the Love You Want*.[23] His premise is that we are all children seeking to heal old wounds, and that without even knowing it, we often seek out partners with the same traits as our parents—the same parents who had a part in wounding us in the first place. No wonder our romantic relationships can be so volatile! Once we connected the dots that explained why each of us has certain triggers from childhood and what those triggers are, we were better able to listen to each other in trust and safety—to comfort each other rather than pouring salt in the wounds. Of course, we both slip into old patterns from time to time, but it is a marathon, not a sprint. We are learning, and I can finally say we are learning together rather than working at cross purposes.

What does this have to do with drinking and self-medicating? It's all tied together, believe me.

After the usual teenage experimentation with drugs and alcohol as a high school "freak," I became a take-it-or-leave it drinker. I wasn't a teetotaler. I liked to go out with friends to bars, parties, and nightclubs, and I drank on those outings, but I rarely got drunk. I was there for the fun and excitement, and being with my friends, joking, laughing, dancing. We were young and having a good time.

I didn't start drinking for self-medication until I was about thirty-eight. This was in the middle of the business turmoil with my father. We had $300,000 of debt, and I felt every dollar of it as a weight on my shoulders, a weight my father didn't seem interested in sharing even though the stress affected him as well. This was the first time I used drinking for relief. But once we sold the company, I didn't stop. Now that I had some money, I partied even more, not less. It became a habit. It's what I did.

When I met Neil, the partying intensified. Neil and his friends played hard, and I wanted to keep up. Every social event began or ended with drinks and fun additions at times. We liked having a good time, and for a while, that's all it was, a good time. As the responsibilities and expectations of being married to Neil became overwhelming, however, I fell into the old patterns of people-pleasing and martyrdom, which called up all the old wounds of childhood. I turned to alcohol to numb the pain on one hand and give me the courage to stand up for myself on the other. Of course, when I stood up for myself when I was drinking, I wasn't always in control of what I said. The tea kettle would go off, and my anger would spew forth uncontrollably. I achieved nothing constructive at these times, but I couldn't help myself.

My drinking became an issue in our marriage, and Neil started to exert control over it (as he liked to do with everything else), telling me I drank too much, telling me where and when I could drink, always watching and judging my intake at parties. I began sneaking wine whenever I wanted to just say screw you, you can't tell me what to do—another sign I was falling into the patterns of childhood. That was one of the big reasons I went to Gulf Breeze, to untie the knots of these childhood patterns and how they affected my life even in my mid-fifties.

To stay on track when I returned from Gulf Breeze, in addition to the weekly Skype sessions, I tried AA meetings. The Skype meetings were helpful, but I'm a people person, and I needed the in-person contact to remind me where I had been and where I wanted to go.

I found the perfect meeting, called No Sniveling. The most important rule was not to whine, and the people in this group made sure that no one did so. I don't think I've ever experienced a group of people more in service to one another. There are people in that No Sniveling meeting that have been sober for twenty, thirty, forty years, and they keep coming back to help each other. They were beautiful, caring, and kind as they walked through their pain to purpose and into service. It's then that the real healing begins, and the people in this meeting exemplified that mission. I witnessed firsthand the healing these beautiful folks shared with one another. AA is the perfect example of how to be of service to one another.

Ultimately, I decided AA was not for me. Beginning each meeting with the words "I am an alcoholic" didn't resonate with me. Saying something negative like that about myself over and over bred only shame. I also didn't think it was helpful to me to emphasize that I was powerless. I've had a lifetime of feeling powerless. I want to put that behind me. I want to feel powerful. I guess some people need to remind themselves they're alcoholics, so they don't slip back into denial. It just didn't feel right to me. The meetings themselves sometimes felt like a transfer of addiction, a prison for the rest of your life, and the twelve steps can turn into a checklist to make your way through rather than a heartfelt spiritual practice. Not that I didn't love the beautiful and compassionate people I met and feel their support in the meetings I attended. This is my truth. I want to move forward and continue to grow from within instead of needing support from the outside, in this case an AA meeting.

Or maybe I'm in denial. I acknowledge that possibility. I have not finished this journey, and I still enjoy a glass of wine. My triggers still exist, and in extreme situations, for example, when Neil relapses, I self-medicate. Sometimes, my whiney, victim self wins the battle, and it isn't pretty.

I have been working hard on forgiveness—forgiving myself and forgiving others, letting the past be past, not to stuff it under the carpet, but out of genuine love and compassion. The more I act in love, the more conscious and in control of my own life I become, the less I allow things outside myself to determine how I feel, the less I want to drink when I am triggered.

The habit begins to change when we see a different truth. My truth is that I still enjoy an occasional glass or two of wine and smoke marijuana, and that is part of my journey. I never really smoked marijuana much until I met Neil, but I enjoy it with him, relaxing and laughing before we go to sleep. We are more ourselves. I have made the choice to move forward and accept myself as I am. It is my prayer that I recognize when I am merely enjoying the pleasures of wine and marijuana and when I am trying to numb myself again. I am clearly still on the path of self-discovery regarding alcohol and any unhealthy dependence that may still need to be resolved. In the meantime, I continue to remain open to what lessons I may still need to learn and to refrain from reaching outside myself when I feel the need for comfort.

In her book *The Wisdom of Sundays*, Oprah Winfrey addresses her challenge with food.[24] She tells the story of making eggs years later for the man who molested her as a child, and in that moment realizing how she replayed that type of compliant relationship over and over in her personal and professional lives. By making those eggs in silence and repeating the pattern of repressing her pain, she was betraying herself. When she became upset about something, rather than speaking out, she reverted to the silence of that helpless nine-year-old girl. She finally decided that if she was ever going to have a healthy relationship with her weight, she had to confront whatever needed confronting instead of suppressing it by literally eating it.

That passage hit me like a bulldozer. When you stop betraying yourself, the real healing begins. Some people only love you if you fit into their box. I am no longer afraid to disappoint others, well, at least most of the time. I am learning to tell my truth in the most loving and compassionate way I can.

If not for Gulf Breeze, I don't think Neil and I would be where we are today. That wonderful experience took me out of the woods so I could see the spectacular trees of the forest and the beauty within myself. It is said that the sparkle of a diamond depends on its flaws. I'm choosing to highlight the sparkle, not the flaws.

Chapter 15
TRAUMATIC BRAIN INJURY – LESSONS FROM MICHAEL

While I was dealing with my son's autism, my cancer, Neil's cancer, and healing my own unhealthy patterns, another traumatic event from the past re-entered our lives. My brother Michael, who has had traumatic brain injury since he was eleven, took a turn for the worse. I had been helping with his care since 2006, but things reached a crisis level in September 2019. Over those thirteen years, I had climbed an enormous mountain helping my brother, finally having provided Michael with a beautiful, fun, productive life when he was accused of sexually assaulting a young woman. I later learned that he had made advances toward other women with special needs while at work as well. I had worked very hard to give him what I thought was the perfect life. This awful news brought me to my knees, heartbroken.

After Michael's childhood accident on his bike in 1991, my mother and his father, Frank, cared for him when he left the hospital and throughout high school. Since my mother was in the insurance industry, the people she worked with helped her set up an annuity for Michael that serves him to this day. In 1999, when he was about nineteen, they bought him a small patio home with some of that money. Michael's house was a few miles from theirs; easy for them to keep an eye on him.

After Michael settled into his new house, though, within a few months Mom and Frank moved an hour away from him. At the time, I was busy in my own life, having just gotten back together with Neil. Then Neil and I got married, and we had the twins in 2002. I was adjusting to life as a mother and didn't have much time to spare for Michael, Mom, and Frank, but everything seemed to be under control. They seemed to know what they were doing.

As time went on, though, Michael received less and less attention from Mom and Frank. They visited him at his house on occasion and took him to dinner, picking him up for the big holidays, but he was on his own for the most part, and while he had an adult body, mentally, he was still eleven.

During this time, my son Jack was diagnosed with autism, and Neil and I set off on that journey. When I saw what so many families in that world did to take care of their adult special needs children, I realized how neglected and vulnerable Michael was. These families showed me by example how a special needs person can have a productive and safe life. Though Michael didn't have autism per se, many of the effects of TBI are similar. By the time I checked in with him, I literally needed to shovel out his patio home it was so filthy. He was living in chaos and squalor, with little structure. Few of his medical needs were being met.

I had moved out of Mom's home when I was seventeen, gone to college, and moved to Arizona to make my own way, but the responsibilities of my family continued to pursue me. I tried to fight it—Michael wasn't my child, after all, and both his parents were alive. Wasn't it their responsibility? When I really thought about it, though, I knew I couldn't live with myself if I let my brother live like that. Since no one else was stepping up, it would be up to me. In my soul, I knew we had a responsibility toward those more vulnerable than ourselves. I couldn't, in good conscience, turn my head and pretend it was okay for Michael to live in such conditions by saying, "Not my job."

When something like this shows up in my life, there's a bigger plan, and I had to trust that. His parents—my mother and Frank, his father—did not have the capacity to take on his many needs. As Maya Angelo says, "When you know better you do better," and they certainly didn't know any better. He was my brother, he was alone, and he would always be eleven. As often happened in my family, it fell to me to take charge. This was around 2006.

The next fifteen years were busy with everything I've been writing about in this book. I was trying to manage the needs of Michael and my own family, to meet the requirements of my husband, and to live up to the unreasonable perfectionist expectations I had for myself.

A special-needs person like Michael has a long list of requirements. I tasked myself with helping him manage his morbid obesity (without supervision, he ate whatever and whenever he wanted), medications, doctor and dentist appointments, household needs, social life, and hygiene. To find him work, I put him through two different vocational programs, but they deemed him unemployable due to his temper. I also tried to manage his mental health, finances, and transportation, and to protect him from those who tried to take advantage of the money from the annuity my mother set up for him as a child to support him throughout his adult life.

I also tried to engage other family members in Michael's care. My youngest sister Darline tried her best to help, but it was too much for the rest of our siblings, just as it had been too much for Mom and Frank. When I pushed for more help, I caused a great deal of resentment and animosity in our family—some of it from me! I had to realize that just because I felt the need to intervene did not mean anyone else had to feel the same way (no matter how much I wished they did). I made the decision to care for our brother, and it was not my place to expect the same of them. Most times I was strong enough to let it go and let them be. That's when I achieved a degree of peace within myself. When I tried to control, shame, and judge them into helping out, though, I grew angry and resentful.

As I learned with my son and autism, I had to immerse myself in the world of traumatic brain injury to provide Michael the best, most stable life possible. The easiest way for me to manage these areas of Michael's life was to obtain legal guardianship. When Michael was legally responsible for himself, the only tool I had to help him was persuasion. It was often a difficult battle to get him to sign papers and take even the simplest steps to do what he needed to do. With legal guardianship, I could do all that for him.

Obtaining guardianship of a special needs person who was never legally registered as special needs is very costly and stressful. It's difficult to prove to the court that your family member needs legal guardianship after the fact. This task consumed me and our family for six years from 2010 to 2016, requiring thousands of dollars in legal fees and many emotionally exhausting court appearances. My brother, of course, didn't see the need for any of this. It was a very dark time for him and created a great deal of chaos and pain for everyone involved. I finally became his legal guardian in 2016.

But it wasn't only Michael I had to worry about. Just before I came back into the picture, Michael had met a woman online who was as lonely as he was. They got together and decided to marry. We all thought maybe this was the answer. She was neurotypical and maybe she could take care of Michael. Then we'd be off the hook.

The marriage lasted just six months, during which time she got pregnant. With TBI, Michael had little impulse control, and thus, no control over his emotions, particularly anger. He regularly raged about what we would think of as the smallest things. If you suggested better food choices, if you commented on clothing choices, if you mentioned his hygiene, if you ever said anything in an angry tone, he would spiral into anger himself, so you had to be very careful about your tone of voice and how you approached any conversation with him—then and now. We had all faced the brunt of his anger, but we were used to it and didn't have to live with him. His new wife had no idea what she was getting into until it was too late. When she left, she claimed Michael had raped her and filed a restraining order against him. After she left, she gave birth to their son, Eli, in 2008.

Eli now lives with his mother and her family. My mother and Frank have nurtured the relationship with their grandson and have been very good to Eli, providing love and support, gifts for special occasions, and financial support when he needs it for things like clothes, school supplies, and electronics his family otherwise couldn't afford. They also make sure Michael maintains his visitation schedule with Eli, so Michael and Eli continue to have a relationship. My parents and I are also both close to Eli's mom, who is a wonderful person and a great mother.

It is my prayer that Eli and Michael have a healthy relationship once Eli is old enough to understand TBI and Michael's limitations, which will likely be tough on Eli. I will have all the measures in place to ensure that Eli can be as involved in Michael's life as he wishes as an adult. Caring for a parent who was never able to take care of you is certainly a difficult and emotional decision, and Michael isn't making it easier. Michael treats Eli poorly at times and because of his anger issues, his visits with Eli must always be supervised by me, Mom, Frank, or our siblings. Some of the things Michael has said and done have had a profound, perhaps even traumatic effect on Eli. Eli's mom found him a therapist that is helping him process the complicated and emotional toll that having a special needs parent can have. As Eli grows older, he will recognize how serious Michael's condition is. Caring for someone like Michael is a large burden to put on any one person (a burden I know firsthand). By the time Eli is old enough to make his own decisions, he will have the support to make an informed decision based on what's best and healthiest for him. To protect Eli and honor his choices, I have to plan ahead to be sure that Michael is cared for when I am gone. As a result, I have hired a private fiduciary that I love, and I'm building a relationship with her and her company so that Michael will be in good hands throughout his lifetime.

Before I became more involved in Michael's life, three special people helped Michael from time to time, not in a professional way, but by offering him their time and friendship: Carolyn; Jason, his best friend from high school; and Katie, who brought him into the Mormon church. The church has been good to Michael, offering both stability and support when he needed it. All three of these friends were supportive and kind. They hung out with him as friends do, took him to restaurants, church, and Zumba classes, invited him to attend some of their family gatherings—all the normal, everyday activities we take for granted, but that Michael couldn't do on his own. Their service made a big difference in Michael's life. I hope they know how special they are.

On the other hand, there were also a slew of scammers over the years who tried to take advantage of Michael since he had his own house and an income from the annuity. One of the worst was a woman named Zenn, whom he met through an online dating service at a time when Neil was undergoing cancer treatments, and I wasn't as involved in Michael's life as I had been. Michael and Zenn are the same physical age, in their late thirties now, and because she has special needs herself, their emotional age is also about the same. They have many of the same interests and struggles in life. The difference is that Zenn had zero support from her family and came to see Michael as a meal ticket. She moved herself, her boyfriend, and her two dogs into Michael's small patio home with the intent of making it a permanent arrangement. During that time, we were in the middle of trying to obtain guardianship, Zenn even testified in court that Michael did not require any support from us and certainly not guardianship. Zenn knew her meal ticket would come to an end and the judge saw right through her ploy. In the end she complicated the process through the courts, which added up to additional legal fees and more emotional hardship for our family, especially Michael.

The house was filthy when Michael lived there alone, and it only grew worse with all of them living there. Zenn and her boyfriend convinced Michael to buy all the groceries and pay for all the living expenses. I was concerned that she might even try to get pregnant, so I convinced Michael to get a vasectomy. I had to protect him, and I could do that only once I received guardianship.

After obtaining guardianship, I was able to move Zenn out of the house. I treaded very softly, as I knew it would break Michael's heart if I didn't. I moved her belongings myself and paid to have them all delivered to her new apartment, which I carefully maneuvered without a legal dispute. Here's the kicker. Despite all that, Michael and Zenn are better friends now than ever, even though Zenn lives in New Mexico. They are both lonely and seem to care for one another. What started out as a scam has turned into an authentic friendship over time, which Zenn has proven over the years. They text each other daily, and Zenn visits once a year. Indeed, before Zenn left for New Mexico, she virtually became part of the family. I invited her to holiday functions and Michael's birthdays, and occasionally took them both to dinner. Zenn could no more take care of herself than Michael could. When I picked her up from her apartments (she moved often), they were always run down and filthy. Sometimes I took her out for a nice meal or gave her items from our home to help out. They are two peas in a pod, and I'm glad they have each other for support and friendship.

Around this time, Michael had some health scares due to his weight and the filthy conditions he had been living in. He was hospitalized twice. When I took over, my goal was to uphold Michael's independence and keep him living in his house, so I hired a caretaker to try to get the situation under control. But we soon realized that keeping Michael in the house was untenable, given his lack of impulse control and inability to attend to even the simplest of household tasks. We had to find another way for him to live. Once Zenn was out of the house and we received guardianship, my sister Darline and I worked to sell Michael's house and move him into a group home. Darline was a great help at this time, as was Neil, who paid the legal fees. I couldn't have done it without them.

The responsibilities of guardianship and the hoops the courts make you jump through become a full-time job in and of themselves. A typical family without the financial resources and the education to understand the red tape would have a hard time caring for a family member with special needs. My parents are a good example of that. It is frustrating, wearing, debilitating, and emotionally draining work. No wonder we have so many people with TBI or mental illness living on the streets. The dearth of options for their families, especially a safe place to live, is criminal. These serious cracks in the system must be addressed. It must become easier to apply for and afford long-term care, and there must be more options for living spaces. Even if you can afford to pay privately, there is little to choose from.

Finding Michael a group home was painful for two reasons. One, I felt heart-wrenching guilt for forcing Michael (as he saw it) out of the house where he had lived independently for more than fifteen years. And two, it was plain hard work. The state gave me a list of group homes in metropolitan Phoenix, but each one was worse than the last. Some of the owners may have good intentions, but most seem to be in it for the money with little concern for their residents. Every dollar they spend on the residents is one dollar less in their bank accounts, so once they meet the minimal state standards, many are done. As a result, the employees are underpaid and under qualified. The homes, which are usually in dangerous neighborhoods, are shoddily maintained, with peeling paint, leaking roofs, spotty plumbing, bugs, and so on. They are also badly equipped—stained bedding, unhealthy processed food, sandpaper toilet paper, with no curtains or blinds for the windows. Honestly, often the conditions of these homes made living on the streets seem an attractive proposition.

The best option I could find for Michael was in a decent neighborhood, but the house itself was in terrible condition, just barely meeting the state criteria if it met them at all. Before moving Michael in, I had the entire house refurnished with sofas and chairs and a new stove put in the kitchen. I had new doors hung for the rooms without them, a new toilet installed, the filthy bathrooms scoured, new carpeting laid down in the common rooms and piles of garbage removed from what would become Michael's bedroom. The house was poorly managed, the workers both indolent and insolent, making little effort to actually serve the residents. It was degrading to be treated with such disrespect by the staff. I betrayed myself by letting them exploit me. I kissed a lot of ass in that house and spread gratuities around like candy so Michael would have a chance of being treated with dignity. But who knew what happened when I left?

The care was so bad I had to hire a caretaker to stay with Michael twenty to thirty hours a week to keep him somewhat engaged and productive. I am grateful we were able to afford such expenses. Most families cannot, and their family members end up hiding in their rooms or watching

TV all day with no activities to look forward to. Depression is rampant among them.

After Michael moved into the group home, I took him on a trip to New York to help make the transition a positive one. It was just the two of us. He had always dreamed of going to New York, and we did it right, seeing all the sights and shows—the Statue of Liberty, the Empire State Building, Radio City Music Hall, two Broadway plays, *Beautiful: The Carole King Musical* and *Wicked*. It was all about him, and he was happy. At dinner one night, he looked at me and said, "Are you my real mother? Why would you do all this for me? You have to be my mother."

I was touched that Michael said this, but I also grew angry. I wasn't his mother. He had a mother, the same one I had, and she should have been the one sitting here in New York City with her son. I was still wrestling with understanding it and even more with accepting that Mom just wasn't capable of taking care of Michael. Why should she be? She had struggled tremendously to take care of five kids who didn't have special needs. I have learned to forgive her for this and many other things, some of my biggest lessons in this lifetime.

I was always on the lookout for a better place for Michael, and I got lucky. Because of our work in the autism community, Neil and I learned about a wonderful development that was being built for those with special needs. The facility was under construction in Phoenix, a development that would provide housing and support to adults with special needs. The facility would be beautiful and well maintained. Michael would have his own apartment that I would decorate perfectly for him, as well as a support team to help him manage his life. He would love it there and so would I. For the first time in many years, I would have the ability to step back and care more for my own family. He would be safe and attended to there. It was also designed to provide a productive and engaged life within the development and the community.

In other words, it was the polar opposite of the group home Michael was then living in. I knew immediately This new place would be perfect for him. It was the answer to my prayers. My work for Michael was about to pay off for everyone. Michael was going to have a healthy productive life. I was going to get my life back. My kids were going to get their mother back, my husband his wife. I could take a deep breath and relax because I knew Michael would be safe and well-taken care of.

Michael lived in the unscrupulous group home for a year. Then in July 2018, I moved him into this brand new beautiful life. He was one of the first residents. The apartment was perfect, but much of his clothing, bedding, and furniture was riddled with bedbugs from the group home. We had to replace much of his stuff and deep clean the rest. In the end it was just another reason to be grateful for an environment that protected our family members with special needs. My prayer is that we make stricter guide-lines for the care of those more vulnerable than ourselves.

I'm sure Michael appreciated the new place more because of his time at the group home. He even had a full-time job with the help of the vocational department at the home. During this time, Michael would work at three different companies that welcomed and accommodated those with disabilities. Each company had positions tailored to special needs individuals, and each position gave him confidence, new friends, and a productive life. Unfortunately, he was let go from each of these jobs for behavior issues. Still, things in general were going well for Michael. He made many new friends, met a great woman who also lived there, and they began dating. Michael was eating better, exercising, and living a more purposeful life. He was proud of who he was becoming. Most important, he was happy.

And if Michael was happy, I could be happy too. I could let go and let Michael continue to grow. I had really made a difference in the life of someone more vulnerable than I, and I was proud of that! We had done it, and I say we because I had the support of my family periodically along the way. This was God's work. I had walked through the pain of making it happen and found such purpose, the purpose of being of service and revealing to Michael what he could accomplish. It was my accomplishment too, and I was proud of that.

The miracle lasted about fifteen months, until the day after my sixtieth birthday party, September 2, 2019. That birthday party was bittersweet to begin with because we had just lost a dear friend to cancer the day before. Sherry was fifty-five—one of our core friends with whom we had traveled the world, raised our children, and spent much time together talking, partying, laughing. My relationship with her was an important one in my life. Everyone in our circle was numb with grief, but we decided to have the party anyway. It had been in the works for a while, and for those close to Sherry, it gave us the opportunity to grieve together. The funeral would be the following week.

We held the party at our home in Munds Park, just south of Flagstaff in the middle of nowhere, my favorite place in the world. Over one hundred friends and family came. We decorated our house as a convalescent home and had everyone dress twenty years older, except me. My first costume was a schoolgirl outfit with pigtails. After an amazing video my friends made for me and speeches they gave in my honor, I put on a second outfit for the stage: a tight sequin dress, boa, high heels, and a naked body suit underneath. For my entrance, I walked down the thirty or so stairs from our patio to our yard below with "Pretty Woman" playing. Once on stage, I began my speech to thank everyone. During my speech, I came down with a fake hot flash, which prompted my striptease to a ripped swimsuit bodysuit underneath as Joe Cocker's "You Can Leave Your Hat On" wailed through the crowd. Everyone laughed, cheered, and hooted wildly.

Most of my friends rented places to stay in Munds Park, so the festivities lasted all weekend. We all had a blast. I felt like I was on a cloud surrounded by love and blessed to have such wonderful friends. I had never had a party like that. It was magic, a night I will remember and cherish forever. Sherry had intended to come to the party, and I felt her presence as strongly as if she had been there. I knew she would be happy that I enjoyed the party so much. I loved Sherry. She was one of my greatest teachers. We had a complicated relationship, though—one that mirrored the triangulation I had with my father and stepmothers.

Sherry was very close to Neil, and I always felt we were in competition for Neil's attention. She was critical of me in what I'm sure she thought was a friendly, helpful way—about my cooking, my cleaning, how I raised the kids, how I dressed, how I took care of my dog, how I recycled. It went on and on. I valued her opinion as an old friend of Neil's, and I tried to please her to keep Neil happy, but I was always wrong, and Sherry was always right. Sherry and Neil often gaslighted me about this, saying that I misinterpreted what I saw and heard, that I overreacted. In part, I think I responded so strongly to Sherry because I was revisiting the unhealed wounds of my relationships with my stepmothers, who were jealous of my role in Dad's life and worked hard to put me down and keep me at a distance.

At the same time, Sherry was also a people pleaser and a martyr, as was I. This created a bond between us. We understood each other. We both lived with a tremendous amount of anger. She had had a difficult and long battle with cancer, and now she was at peace, no longer in pain. I was grateful for that. But I was also very much affected by her death. She had taught me a lot about myself. We were closer than we ever had been before she passed.

The next day, still raw from Sherry's death but elated from the party, I received the news. Michael had been accused of sexually assaulting a woman in her twenties with special needs. He hadn't been arrested, but I had to return to Phoenix to address the situation immediately. I didn't know exactly what had happened, but I knew it was serious.

This horrible news came as a shock, but there had been warnings. Michael has always had difficulty with impulse control, both with his temper and sometimes with inappropriate sexual advances. Over the years I cared for Michael, he occasionally overstepped with women. I addressed it each time, believing that it was typical of adult men but more complicated for Michael because he had TBI. I had hired a therapist to work with him. I was always sure to inform everyone involved in Michael's care of these issues. We thought we had a handle on it. We thought we were getting through to him.

I will always have to live with the fact that I did not see the importance of monitoring Michael more carefully. After getting this awful news, I felt such a deep responsibility for what Michael had done. I personally knew what it felt like to be violated. How could I allow this, even indirectly, to happen to another woman? It was my fault. I had failed. I had moved him into a facility that he wasn't ready for, where there were so many vulnerable women. I was brought to my knees with grief and guilt.

I rushed home to the chaos and immediately moved him out of his apartment. I knew we had to get a handle on this behavior. Until we could figure something else out, I had him stay at Mom's house. I certainly could not have him at our home with my teenage daughter. I put most of his belongings in storage. We were let out of the lease, and I notified Michael's employer. The family of the young woman filed a police report and requested a DNA kit. We had no choice but to hire a criminal attorney.

My head was spinning. I was overwhelmed and exhausted, and I had to think about Sherry's funeral, which I attended later that week. I made it through her funeral, a beautiful tribute, but I felt utterly debilitated, a feeling that continued for some time. Michael took up every minute of my time for the next few months. Not only did I have to find a place for him to stay (Mom and Frank agreed to keep him only so long), but I also had the legal case to consider.

I had installed an application on my phone that allowed me to read Michael's texts and track his location. I always watched him closely this way, but during my party, I had given myself a break. I read the texts later to piece together what had happened. By text, he had convinced the young woman to come to his apartment, even though he had a girlfriend at the time. This young woman was autistic, and though she was twenty-five in physical years, she was quite young emotionally and likely had no idea what she was in for. But she went to his room freely and willingly. In the end, the text messages on my phone and her response kept Michael from being criminally prosecuted. We did, however, have to pay significant legal fees to ensure he was represented properly.

Michael and the young woman did not have intercourse, but far too much had occurred that she didn't understand, so it was a gray area. Individuals with special needs have many of the same sexual desires neurotypical people do. Many men and women engage in sexually activity when they think they have received a signal, even when they are committed to someone else. But signals can get crossed, as they did in this case. My heart went out to all involved.

After this painful incident, I moved Michael into a senior care center, thinking that would be safer, but he tried to engage with an elderly woman there. I had told the center about his tendencies, so they were watchful. They witnessed a kiss and inappropriate touching but stopped it before it got too far. The woman didn't pursue the issue, but the center asked him to leave. I ended up moving Michael four times in three months, each time returning him to live with his parents. Because I couldn't get him qualified for long-term care funding with the state right away, I moved him into and out of another place as well, beginning the exhausting process of obtaining long-term care, which I had to appeal at least three times while looking for a private fiduciary for support. I knew now that I was in way over my head.

Was I the only one who could do anything? Apparently. The rest of my family was only too happy to let me handle it. *After all*, I'm sure they thought, *Lynn always has! She always gets herself into these messes.* As usual, they all had their own families and jobs to think of, but it would be me and my family that would live through the chaos as I took on responsibilities that other people in the family flat out refused.

When Michael was finally living in a caring, professional environment, I had let myself step back and enjoy the freedom. I had my life back. But now I was in the thick of it again, only much worse. The endless checklists of tasks and continual efforts to determine the next steps took over my life. I grew angry and confused. I was wracked by guilt, and I fell into exhaustion and depression. This time the grief overpowered me.

During this part of my journey with Michael, I had two "bathroom floor" experiences, as author Elizabeth Gilbert calls them—when you fall to the floor of the bathroom, sobbing and depleted. Soon after that happened, I knew, once again, that I was caring for others and seeking approval without caring for myself. I was running on empty, angry that no one else in the family stepped up to help me. That's also when I heard the martyr in me talking again. Did I ask them to step up? Just because I took it on, did it mean that they had to step up as well? I was angry that they didn't seem to care how much Michael's very dysfunctional life was profoundly impacting mine. I was drinking again to numb myself; I was gaining weight; I had no time to care for myself. I felt as if much of the progress I had made at Gulf Breeze had been erased.

Neil had had enough and didn't want to talk about it; he was angry too. He was tired of the role I had taken on within my family, and he was still being treated for multiple myeloma. He didn't have the bandwidth to support me. We even discussed moving out of state so I could free myself of these pernicious family responsibilities.

But they never went away, these family responsibilities. As if all this with Michael's legal case, and Neil's health, and managing my own special needs child wasn't enough, I had to step in to play the rescuer (and martyr) for two other big family events—one funeral and a wedding, to paraphrase the title of the Hugh Grant movie.

Several years before, my thirty-nine-year-old nephew, Brian, had been diagnosed with skin cancer. He hadn't taken it seriously enough, and it progressed until it was no longer responding to treatment. By 2018, he and his family were barely getting by, so I stepped in to do what I could, as did my other sisters and my mom. When the cancer took a turn for the worse, I flew to Michigan to spend time with Brian, his wife and his two boys. On this trip I went alone. (Everyone else came at different times to help as well, but I am me, so of course I had to do more.)

I stayed at a nice hotel, Tawas Bay Beach Resort on Lake Huron and had the boys stay with me to give the family a break. We did all kinds of lake activities—hanging out on the beach, swimming, and playing. I outfitted them with clothes and gadgets and other things they couldn't get for themselves. I also took the whole family out for nice meals. I also did what I could to clean up their house. My sisters had started the job when they had visited, but it was filthy with hoarding at a level I had never experienced.

The next time I flew to Michigan was to be there while Brian was dying. I was in the room with him when he passed on January 20, 2019, at only 39 years old. I did my best to comfort his wife and sons and especially my sister Lori, his mother. I wanted to do anything I could to make it better. My little sister had just lost her only child, and she was beyond devastated.

While there, my sister Michele and I planned and provided a funeral that ensured Brian was honored in a magical way. The funeral was beautiful. Each room within the funeral home was bursting with all those that had come to show their respect. My sister Michele, Brian's wife, and his boys were comforted by the compassion and love that they all received during this very difficult time. In my traditional fashion, I was sure to manage every detail down to assuring that Michele and the boys were dressed properly and that we could all stay together in an apartment-style motel located close to the funeral home. Brian's family as well as my sister lived up North in Michigan, but we were sure to have the funeral in the city that Brian had grown up in.

Before Brian died, and the last time I would have a conversation with him, I had promised him I'd bring the kids to Arizona for all the fun things they'd never experience otherwise. A few months after the funeral, I flew Beth and the boys to Arizona to stay with us and kept the boys very busy with all kinds of fun activities, like swimming in our pool, indoor parachuting, car racing, virtual reality games, Top Golf, and many others.

That was the funeral, a heart-wrenching but wonderful tribute to my nephew. The wedding was Lisa's, my younger stepsister from Dad's fourth marriage, though she is a true sister in every sense of the word. She lives in Spain, where she was getting married, and her job takes her to third-world countries as a relief worker. I have always been in awe with the work that Lisa and her now husband Luca have done in service throughout their lives and have a great deal of respect for them. This was October 5, 2019, a month after I had to move Michael from the home that I dreamed for him. We had also just buried Sherry, (Brian had passed away that January), and I was having trouble keeping up with the responsibilities of my own family. I shouldn't have pushed myself to go, but I was one of the main speakers at the wedding, and I didn't want to let my sister down.

The trip out was a disaster with three cancelled flights and someone trying to mug me on a layover in Chicago. I was leaving an empty terminal, but this man kept following me. When he made a move toward me, I screamed and ran, and made it outside. The security guard heard me and got him. Then I raced to the other terminal for a new flight.

The fifteen-hour trip turned into two days, and when I finally arrived in Spain, they lost my luggage! We all have bad trips, but this was the trip through hell!

My head was spinning from so much happening all at once. I had just moved Michael two different times in one month and was working with a criminal attorney. We were all still processing my nephew's death and I was processing Sherry's. I was exhausted from all that I had to accomplish and from the terrible flights to Spain. I could barely breathe.

The one thing that went well was my part in the wedding. I wrote my speech on the long, long flight, sharing many wonderful memories of Lisa and Luca. Once I arrived, I prayed to God and summoned every last ounce of energy and was able to turn it on when I had to. The outdoor wedding was magic, overlooking the Mediterranean Sea with sunflowers throughout: perfect weather, a perfect venue, the most beautiful perfect bride. I ran the entire wedding with her husband's best friend, who shared the ceremonial stage with me and honored them with his memories as well.

After the wedding, though, it didn't go so well. All my sisters (except for Lisa, thank God) and my niece were there. I resented everyone who wasn't feeling the same exhaustion I was. Suffering terribly, I wanted the luxury of putting myself and my emotions first. When was someone going to take care of me? When was someone going to lift me up? I was raging inside, both at myself for foolishly taking this all on and at everyone else who let me.

The night after the wedding we all went out to dinner, with a wonderful group of Lisa's and Luca's friends who had traveled from around the world to attend. The dinner was wonderful but what happened afterwards wasn't. I had a few glasses of wine with dinner which only enhanced my reaction that led to a terrible night. Once we arrived back at the rental home my sister's, my niece and myself were staying at, I brought up a conversation that should have never been discussed in my state of exhaustion. I asked one of my sisters how we were going to take care of our mother, whose health was deteriorating. She made it clear that she couldn't be counted on to do much. Well, that was all I needed. The tea kettle went off. It was ugly, vile. I called everyone every name in the book. I wanted to release myself so desperately from the suffering. I wanted someone to open their arms without judgment and care for me.

I'm still ashamed that I broke down that night, and I'm glad Lisa wasn't there, though I'm sure she heard about it later. It became a huge screaming match, and I was certainly seen as the villain, though I have always been the good sister, not the one causing the problems. The next day we all went to Ronda, a mountaintop city in Spain's Malaga province, a magical 15th century town that would make a normal day extraordinary, but not today. My sister, my niece, and I were all numb, the look of disappointment on the face of my precious niece will haunt me forever. I sent an abject apology letter to all of them. It took us months to heal.

It was a big wake up call. I was doing all this "caretaking" wrong, and I knew it. How could I break free of the ties I had bound myself with for so long? My sisters seemed to have no trouble staying free of these entanglements. They all had their own lives and their own decisions to make about how they care for themselves. It wasn't my place to tell them or anyone else what they should or should not do. I was learning the hard way that it is not my responsibility to heal, save, punish, or control anyone else. I was also learning the hard way that it is up to me and me alone to set these boundaries for myself.

From that experience, I began to question the direction my life had taken. I had to pay attention this time; the people pleasing had to stop. My own children and my own husband needed me, and I had to show my children a better example.

Michael was the tipping point, the last piece of the puzzle. He gave me permission to say, "No more." As with my journeys with Mom, Dad, and Neil, my journey with Michael has provided many lessons for my soul, some of which I am still struggling to learn.

When a person suffers from TBI the way Michael does, they often have no sense of how they affect other people or any understanding of their own limitations. Everything is all about them. Michael has no care in the world for anyone but himself. That's not a moral judgment, just a fact. His brain injury does not allow him to have empathy or put others first; he is not capable of it. He has no boundaries.

I have no boundaries either, but in the opposite way. Michael has no boundaries when taking, I have no boundaries when giving. In this way, Michael is the perfect teacher for a people-pleasing martyr like me. How far down the pit am I going to let myself fall before I pull myself back up again?

Was I enabling Michael? He is vulnerable in many ways and needs help in many things. But am I supposed to sacrifice my well-being and that of my immediate family to help him? Michael is vulnerable, but is he the innocent victim who always needs me riding in on my white horse to rescue him? I have come to realize that Michael *does* know right from wrong. I recently learned that each time he seduced one these young women, he asked them not to tell anyone. He knew what he was doing was wrong! Once I found this out, I, myself, felt a tiny bit betrayed. Was Michael playing me? Not intentionally, but that was the effect. Lessons are everywhere.

I've had to move Michael into a locked men's facility. I spent a tremendous amount of time and effort to ensure that Michael qualified for long-term care. He is now in a wonderful new home. It is clean and he is cared for and safe and so are those around him. I believe that God swept down and gave Michael and me a miracle. Shortly after moving into his new home and after a year of living with his parents, Michael is happy again. I have also found a private fiduciary to take over his finances and help manage his life. The team at his group home is amazing, his case manager a true angel. The new team even found him a new job he loves.

During the year he was with his parents, I had a complete psychological evaluation done, along with medical scanning, and as a result have found a perfect medication to address his impulse control. Now that Michael is settled, as of December 2020, I've made a vow to myself that I am not the family fixer anymore. I may have been broken open, but I am also willfully shedding, to paraphrase Mark Nepo.[25]

Was Michael meant to bring me to my knees? Was he the one intended to make me learn how to choose me? I have always had a difficult time knowing how to be of service without being a servant, without being taken advantage of. I am learning that when we enable people, instead of helping them, we actually hold them back. Maybe I held Michael back by trying to create the life I thought he should have. It turned out to be too much for him. He doesn't see his own limitations, and I wasn't seeing mine. When we enable those who are behaving irresponsibly, we only allow them to continue those behaviors. We're putting more logs on the fire.

When something or someone shows up in my life, I know our Lord is communicating with me. Michael showed up to rock my world. I had to learn how to balance what I truly believe is my duty to take care of others ("to those to whom much is given, much is required") with my duty to become my true self.

Success for me is fulfilling my soul's purpose. I know my service to Michael has helped me to embrace my true self and to realize, as Myla Kabat Zinn writes, "Each difficult moment has the potential to open our eyes and open our hearts."[26] My heart continues to open in my journey with my brother Michael. He has helped me learn that giving at the expense of myself is not really true giving at all.

Chapter 16
HEALING THROUGH SERVICE

My journey with Michael taught me about the power of healthy service. But my call to service didn't begin with Michael, and I'm sure it won't end there either. Throughout my life, I've been aware of the healing power of service, and my opportunities to serve have always shown up when I needed them most. And each time they did, I learned to pay attention. My first call to service began in an informal way with my stay in Brightmoor, when our home—mine and Jimmy's—became the safe place people flocked to when they wanted to feel a sense of community. Brightmoor gave me an appreciation for all the advantages I'd been given in life, all I was able to accomplish, and especially all the people who had done so much to help me along the way. Despite the chaos and hard times of parts of my childhood, I realized our family was still privileged in many ways, and I have always been driven to pay that forward.

Similarly, after I graduated from college and began my career, organizations and individuals who needed my help appeared in my life just when I needed them. I say when I needed them because I needed them as much as they needed me. They became my teachers. I may not have always been aware of it at the time, but they were all perfectly aligned with my life's purpose and helped me heal my wounds. These experiences, these "spiritual whispers," as Oprah calls them, were put before me to bring me to further enlightenment.

After Brightmoor, my work with the Center Against Sexual Assault (CASA), which I wrote about in Chapter 5, was one of my first important acts of service. Not only did I help others heal from the trauma of sexual assault, but I also went a long way toward healing myself. To me, service is a critical step in our journey to heal our wounds and become our true selves. Once we acknowledge our own wounds, we are healed more deeply when we help others who have the same wounds.

After working with CASA for several years, I was looking to help a broader range of people. In 1990, my friend Thaine introduced me to HomeBase Youth Services in Phoenix. I was still managing a large apartment community for another company and hadn't gone into business for myself yet. HomeBase Youth Service helps homeless teenagers by seeking them out on their own turf—wherever they are trying to survive. I have not been involved with this organization for quite some time now, but I do know they continue to provide services in our community. The group organized busses of volunteers to hand out basic necessities—socks and other items of clothing, toiletries, food, and so on. For the kids who want to make a new beginning, HomeBase also offered apartment communities where they can live if they agree to go to school, work, stay off drugs, and undergo therapy.

The homeless teens accepted HomeBase because they knew they would be safe and treated respectfully. We were just people helping people. The staff knew that most of these kids hadn't had the opportunities we had, and it was our responsibility to pay it forward with genuine service. Personally, I knew from living in the streets of Brightmoor how important it was to treat these teens like the beautiful and unique individuals they are, not like specimens in a social experiment. The goal of HomeBase was to give them the chance that many of their families couldn't. It filled my heart when I went on those ride-alongs. It *felt* right to be there.

HomeBase also got me involved in fundraising. All the supplies we handed out, as well as the apartments, weren't free, of course, so we were always raising money to continue and expand our services. I did my share by taking friends on ride-alongs so they could see in person the good work we were doing. Then I invited them to HomeBase fundraisers, where they could make donations. Once they saw the conditions the teens lived in, as well as their spirit in the face of such hardship, they always gave generously.

Now that I have my own family, we prepare the same kinds of care packages for the homeless and keep them in our cars so we can hand them out when we encounter those who need them. It fills my heart to see not only the gratitude of the people who receive these packages, but the look on my children's faces when they hand them out, knowing they have done some good for a fellow human being in need. In high school, my daughter Brianna started a school club called Homeless Not Helpless to prepare the same kinds of care packages.

By reminding me of what I might have become if I hadn't had people to lift me up and root for me—my father, my cousin Donnie, the folks at the school board, my counselor Greg—HomeBase helped me tap into a well of gratitude that enabled me to heal some of my childhood wounds. Watching those teenagers who had the courage to believe in themselves and begin a new way of life opened me up. Giving to these young people brought me back to myself. It was after my experience with HomeBase helping kids and fundraising for the organization that I found the courage to begin my own company and life as an entrepreneur.

Another whisper in my life around this time was a twelve-year-old girl named Frei. She wandered into my office with her family to rent an apartment when I was still a property manager. I must have been about thirty-three. I wasn't married, didn't have children, and was completely focused on my career. The last thing on my mind was developing a big-sister friendship with a twelve-year-old girl.

Her family had just arrived from Australia to begin a new life in America. They arrived at Crown Court, the community I was managing and moved into an apartment, when Frei started showing up in my office. Outgoing, confident, and full of vigor, she walked through the door and sat in the chair across from me. She was finding her way as a girl and young woman and was thirsty for the attention of someone she could learn from. Soul mates recognize each other instantly and unconsciously. They come to-gether to help each other further evolve.

That's how it was with Frei and me. Our relationship began as a kind of informal Big Sister arrangement and it has unfolded over the years to be one of the most substantial relationships in my life. We hung out at the office, ran errands, went shopping, went to the movies, and eventually went on trips together. We would go through many important life experiences in the years to follow. Frei was my maid of honor at my wedding (the third one) and I was her maid of honor at hers. She was even in the delivery room when my babies were born.

At the time I met Frei, her family was going through a difficult time making the transition after moving from Australia to America. The move had taken an emotional tole, and her parents did not have the ability to provide her with the emotional attention that she was accustomed to. They were overwhelmed trying to create a new start while also launching child-care centers in our community. They didn't really express it to me, but I felt they trusted me. In their way, they were grateful that I was there for their daughter.

The girl I met was trying to sort out her new life and looking for direction, just as I had been at her age. I saw a part of myself in Frei, and I instinctively reached out to help her. I didn't understand at the time what an impact she would have on my life, how, like the kids from HomeBase, she'd help me heal wounds from childhood. It was as if by helping Frei I was reaching back into the past to help the lost girl I was at that age. She may not have been as lost as I was, but I wanted to be to her what the School Board at my high school was to me. That's what I mean when I say helping others—service—takes you further along the path of healing.

Frei is now forty-one as I write these pages, a strong, kind, and loving woman. She means the world to me, as does her entire family. I think of her as a daughter. She is an exceptional mother and has chosen the most incredible father for her children. She is very much in love with him and her children. She and her husband have a successful energy conservation company. She has always had interest in medicine and serves on the board of a hospital in Washington. She is a wonderful mother, with very accomplished, driven daughters who call me "Kiki," for which I am blessed.

Frei gave me purpose beyond my career when I was in my early thirties. She was one of the few people in my life who showed me how to be of service without being a servant—without losing myself.

Many years later, a similar whisper ran into my living room when she was four years old. She was absolutely adorable, with beautiful long, shiny black hair and flawless skin that glowed in the perfect shade of brown. Her young eyes were auburn and midnight black. The moment I saw her play, I was instantly drawn to her, even though I had my own family by this time. Her grandmother, Fransisca, was our weekly housekeeper and she also babysat Brianna and Jack from time to time. She had been working with us for over two years but had never mentioned a child.

"Who is this little one, Fransisca?" I said, reaching out to the child for a hug. She came into my arms as if we had known each other for years. Another soulmate.

"Lizeth, my granddaughter," Fransisca said guardedly.

"Aren't your children still in Guatemala? Is she here for a visit?"

"No, she'll be living with me," Fransisca responded. "I'll have to bring her with me from now on."

"Oh," I said, finally understanding why she was being wary. As an immigrant, the subject of borders and children must have been a sensitive one. "We're fine with that, aren't we little one?" Lizeth responded with a big, beautiful smile as I bounced her on my knee.

I would never say no to Fransisca, not because she manipulated me the way Taula did, but because she was a strong woman with an energy that commanded respect. She was always responsible and hardworking, and I had no reason to question or manage her. Fransisca and I are the same age, but the sunbaked lines on her face and her callused hands reveal the vast differences in our journeys. She has worked hard at physical labor her whole life, having lived in Phoenix for twenty years before becoming a housekeeper, picking broccoli in the fields and earning U.S. citizenship. She sends every penny she earns beyond necessities to her children and grand-children in Guatemala.

I would later learn that Lizeth came across the border in Texas. Her mother was arrested and sent back to Guatemala, and Lizeth was given to Fransisca, who was already in the U.S., though her status was complicated. Although Fransisca had been a legal citizen, her citizenship had been revoked when she went back to Guatemala to care for her mother, who was dying. When Fransisca returned to America, she was told to sign a piece of paper she could not read, or they wouldn't let her back in. As a result, she renounced her citizenship in a way I never fully understood (since they let her back in) and was living as a noncitizen for the five years before Lizeth arrived.

Fransisca did not have the capacity to stand up to the system. She never had an education and did not speak English very well. One night when Neil and I were out to dinner, we got a call from Immigrations and Customs Enforcement (ICE). Fransisca and Lizeth had been arrested, and Fransisca had given them my cell number. Neil and I were able to have them released as long as we took legal responsibility and ensured they would appear at their court date.

It wouldn't be until five years later, more than twenty court dates, dozens of appointments with CPS, and over $30,000 in legal fees that finally we helped Fransisca and Lizeth become legal citizens (Fransisca for the second time). The majority of individuals in Fransisca's position would never have the means to fight the system; our system makes that very difficult. I have the final court date etched in my memory: October 19, 2011. The judge, a larger-than-life African American man, looked into the eyes of the legal counsel for ICE that day and said, "God, I only hope my children would risk everything to care for me when I'm old and dying, and you took away her citizenship for that? This woman has never had so much as a traffic ticket and has provided necessary services to the country for years! Stop wasting my time." He pounded the gavel, and after a little more paperwork, Fransisca and Lizeth were citizens.

Fransisca is such a proud woman. She insisted on paying us back as much as she could over the years. She wouldn't have it any other way.

While all that was going on, I noticed that Lizeth's academic skills were not what they should be and were not improving, either. She was in second grade by then and they were living in the Phoenix inner city, not known for its school districts. Lizeth had written me a thank you card. I saw that she couldn't spell fairly easy words and formed her letters like a much younger child. Fransisca let me see her report cards. The school was passing her along with Ds in every class. She was caught up in the cycle of poverty and overburdened schools. Her grandmother didn't have the capacity or the education to change direction.

With Fransisca's okay, we enrolled Lizeth in the public school that Jack and Brianna attended. That first year, we decided to put her back a grade so she could catch up. And catch up she did. Lizeth graduated from high school and is now attending the University of Arizona to get her degree in business, just like me! Fransisca and I moved Lizeth into her dorm room during the summer of 2020. We had a wonderful celebration and continue to celebrate as Lizeth is doing well in school. She loves her new lease on life. Lizeth is another one who is like a daughter to me. We have shared every holiday, every birthday, every milestone together. She and Fransisca will be part of our family forever.

Lizeth hasn't physically seen her biological mother since she was three, but they communicate by Skype regularly. Although she has full citizenship, Fransisca has never felt safe enough to leave the states. As a result, one of Lizeth's dreams is to go back to Guatemala to hug her mother and meet her siblings. When the time comes, I would love to help her do that.

As with Frei, I know that in taking care of Lizeth (and Fransisca), I am taking care of that part of myself that was hurt as a child. Lizeth would have been lost in the system with no education, destined to continue the cycle of poverty in her family. We had a different kind of cycle in my family—a cycle of victimhood and codependence—that I have also been trying to break since I left for college in the late seventies. It is uncanny how God keeps the lessons coming until you get them right.

Much of my service has been devoted to helping those outside my circle, as with CASA, HomeBase, and Frei and Lizeth (though these two have definitely become part of the family). One of our biggest service endeavors as a family, however, has been central to our immediate circle. That's our work in the autism community.

I wish with all my heart that every person with special needs and their families can get all the resources we do. That's why we do everything possible to help. As the bible teaches, "To whom much is given, much is required." And that's why our purpose as a family has been clear regarding the autism community.

Less than a year after we were diagnosed, my cousin Donnie, who knew what we were going through with Jack, introduced us to Bernie Marcus, one of the founders of Home Depot. Bernie had started the Marcus Foundation in Atlanta, which had donated $25,000,000 to another organization called Autism Speaks to begin its journey in the fight against autism. Bernie was close to the founders of Autism Speaks, so he arranged a meeting for us. We wanted to learn as much about autism as we could, and we knew that meant networking with those already in the arena.

It was beautiful summer day in Manhattan in 2006. We had been invited to Rockefeller Center to visit Bob and Suzanne Wright, who had just founded Autism Speaks. Bob was the president of NBC. I was in such a blur those days and so busy trying to get acclimated to our new lives in the world of autism, I had no idea what to expect. I just knew my little boy was in trouble, and I was scared. As far as I was concerned, this was another meeting to get help for my little boy.

As we entered Rockefeller Center, we were taken aback by the security, which seemed more elaborate even than an airport's. That's when I began to realize how big a big deal this meeting was. Neil had had high level meetings like this throughout his adult life, but I hadn't. Neil had even met with the first President Bush once and photos of the meeting had appeared in the newspaper. Was I dressed well enough? How about my hair? My shoes? I wore the best I had that day, but it was by no means designer level.

We went effortlessly through security, where we were greeted by five or six impeccably dressed men and women who escorted us to the top of Rockefeller Center as if we were royalty. There they turned us over to Suzanne Wright, who had come out to greet us. My heart was pounding with the spectacle of it all.

"Welcome! We've been looking so forward to meeting you both," Suzanne Wright said graciously. She was dressed in a classic blue suit I'm sure was very expensive, and her jewels took my breath away, but she embraced us warmly and graciously. We had something in common. She had also been brought to her knees by autism, in her case, that of her grandson.

As we entered the President of NBC's office, I still hadn't absorbed where we really were. The office overlooked Manhattan's skyline in all its beauty and power and was decorated with pictures of some of the biggest stars posing with Bob and Suzanne: Jerry Seinfeld, Dustin Hoffman, Jay Leno, and many more. They had all been standing right here, in this room, on this carpeting, in the same place I was standing. I was stunned and starstruck.

"Neil and Lynn," Bob said in the kindest, most humble voice. "We've been so looking forward to meeting you."

Bob was a gentle man in his seventies, handsome and slim. His nature was sweet and calm. I loved him instantly. Suzanne was more direct and straightforward; she reminded me of my mother-in-law. She even looked a little like her with a similar stature and coloring.

Suzanne got to the heart of the matter. "We want to start by letting you know that we have also been terribly affected by autism. Our beautiful grandson is severely affected, and it's been difficult on the family, especially our daughter. We feel we have to make a difference because we have the resources. We'd love to explore how we can help each other and the whole community. We have to make sure every family receives the services and resources they need." She spoke with great conviction and determination, then went on to tell us about the work they were already doing.

Bob cheered Suzanne on, and in her pauses, asked Neil and I questions about our family and California Closets. We got to know them well and met their family in the months ahead, including their grandson. The pain their family was experiencing was very familiar to us, and we instantly bonded in understanding and compassion. There was a great deal of work to be done and we were honored they had reached out to us to be part the journey. When we left Rockefeller Center on that beautiful summer day, Bette Midler was standing on a stage rehearsing directly in front of us. She has always been one of my favorite actors and singers. In my normal frame of mind, I would have been mesmerized, but on this day, I could take in nothing more. I was in a euphoric state of gratitude trying to process what we had just experienced.

This was not a perfunctory one-off meet and greet. After that day, we worked with Bob and Suzanne quite a bit, attending conferences together at which Neil and Bob spoke. We even went to Washington, D.C., with them to lobby for the Combating Autism Act of 2006, where we met with Senator Hillary Clinton. We had such adventures with Bob and Suzanne and so many other wonderful people we've met along the way. It felt good to find direction, to meet people who wanted to do their best to make a difference. We wanted to be a part of that and made sure that we were.

We also connected with another great advocacy organization, Cure Autism Now, and worked closely with them. In fact, Neil the negotiator played a big part in helping Cure Autism Now merge with Autism Speaks. We felt good using our experience and talents to help others walking down the same path. In our work with these organizations, which included fundraising, learning, teaching, and speaking about our experiences, we began to heal ourselves and transform our experience into something that could do much good. We entered a whole new world and loved forming friendships with those who were also guided by service.

Once we became more educated about autism, we began to work with newly diagnosed families. When we were first diagnosed, many special people helped us, and we want to pay that forward by reaching out and helping other families. Every time we comforted another family, I felt like I was putting a soft blanket of love around myself. Hearing our personal experience helped them to begin putting the pieces of the puzzle together and to make a plan for their child and their family. We understood how they felt and were blessed to have the time and financial ability to help. Our work within the autism community became central to our lives and remains so to this day. The need to be of service helped us find a way to a deeper purpose for ourselves and our marriage.

We enjoyed our work on the national stage, but perhaps the work we find most fulfilling is right here in Phoenix with the Southwest Autism Research & Resource Center (SARRC). SARRC was founded in 1997 by our friends Denise Resnik and Raun Melmed. When we were first diagnosed, we turned to SARRC to get us through the initial learning curve. We went to SARRC for information, and we received plenty of that, but we also received lots of love, acceptance, and understanding. Denise Resnik is my biggest hero, one of the greatest teachers I've met. Denise even founded First Place AZ, the next chapter in our Jack's life that will give him the opportunity to begin his own journey in a life that will begin to unfold as a result of the skills he will learn as a resident at First Place. First Place serves as a transitional center for those affected by autism from living in the family home to living on their own. It is a two-year program where each resident learns life skills such as vocational training, cooking, financial skills, transportation skills, cleaning, hygiene, social skills and much more. The accommodations are set up like real college dorms, work-out rooms, yoga, a pool and many planned activities. Our family and certainly Jack are so fortunate that we are able to benefit from the work that Denise has done to create the next step for our Jack and those that are transitioning to a more independent life. She has been a major leader in the autism community in Arizona and around the world. Today Phoenix, Arizona has been given the title of the most autism friendly community in the world. I believe we owe that title to Denise Resnik and the all the faithful heroes that she has asked to join her on this journey.

Even now we help Denise out any way we can. Neil's many skills in negotiation and persuasion and my abilities to put on events have been a great boon for SARRC, particularly for the Walk for Autism, its biggest fundraising event. Autism Speaks had its first Walk in 2005 in Phoenix, and by 2006, Neil and I took it to the next level. Neil with his masterful negotiation skills convinced Autism Speaks to partner with SARRC, Neil and I managed the walk. We had 2,500 walkers and raised $150,000. Today in 2021, we have over 20,000 walkers each year, and the walk has raised over $10,000,000 to serve the autism community. We have both served on the board and been a part of many national and local events over the years. Neil is a superstar of fundraising and has raised over $1,000,000 for autism causes. He has a unique ability to make an ask, whether from a huge corporation or an individual. He rarely hears no.

Here's a little story of what that really means.

When Neil and I were married, we had over 300 guests at our wedding. Neil learned that some of them hadn't given us a wedding present (I paid no attention). Neil looked up the rules from Ms. Etiquette and found that guests had a year to give the newlyweds a gift. After that year passed, Neil emailed each person who hadn't given us a gift and informed them they were on the Loser List, and if they wanted to get off the Loser List, he'd be happy to accept a gift even at this late date. You have to understand, Neil is a prankster, and everyone knows this. He gets away with these kinds of things because he's funny and generous and a blast to be around. Believe me, we received a slew of new gifts after that email!

He applies the same tactics to fundraising for autism. You don't want to be on Neil's Loser List! Every year our friends know they must pay what we now call the "Balter Tax," which has become part of everyone's annual budget. We have always played a big part in putting on the walk every year, but in 2011, the year we were the actual committee chairs, was something special. I put on a kick-off party to motivate everyone to begin their fundraising, build their teams, and start work on committee tasks and activities.

We had an old-fashioned dinner movie theater in North Scottsdale, Farrelli's Cinema Supper Club, that has since been torn down. At the time, the theater was decorated with the glamour of old Hollywood. The stage was elegant with its polished floorboards and grand, old-world curtains hiding the movie screen. An intricately carved frieze circled the wall just below the ceiling, and old school movie posters hung on the walls. In keeping with the theme. I requested that everyone dress in the old Hollywood style. As each guest entered the theater, they were all greeted by a photo shoot with "Elvis" and "Marilyn Monroe." We all marveled at the creative Hollywood doubles: Frank Sinatra, Bette Davis, Doris Day, Dean Martin, Bette Midler, and the like.

Once the guests were seated, Neil and I kicked off the show as Sonny and Cher. The music of "I Got You Babe" blared as we made our grand entrance. I wore a bright orange jump suit and enormous chunky high heeled shoes, with a dark slickly combed wig that fell past my waist. Neil wore an orange suit with gigantic black lapels that were almost as big as his gold pendant, and a five-inch-wide belt.

"We would like to welcome you all to the 2011, Walk Now for Autism, Sonny and Cher show," announced "Ed McMahon" in his seventies business suit.

"Honey," I said in my deep Cher voice. "One of the members of our audience asked me for a donation today for a very important cause. Do you have any money?"

"No, I'm a little short today."

Neil is taller than Sonny was, though not much, and I had on the highest shoes I could still walk in and patted the top of his head. Everyone laughed.

Our banter continued while the "Beat Goes On" began to play.

Neil as Sonny looked Cher up and down with a frisky look. "Honey, I'm feeling the love, and I have something exciting in mind."

"Oh, Darling, no, not tonight. I have a headache."

"I mean more exciting than that," Sonny said.

"You mean there's something more exciting than that?" Cher said, in surprise.

"Yes, it's the Walk Now for Autism 2011!" The audience cheered.

"The Beat Goes On" continued to play as we introduced a leading doctor in the field of autism to get down to the real reason we were there.

We had a blast. In addition to our Sonny and Cher sketch, we showed a pre-produced video on the big screen. Performers included our friends the Costas' talented son, AJ, who put on a sketch showing how much fun fundraising could be and the dance company Brianna was part of, Arizona Angels, owned by my friend Amy. The Arizona Angels have raised many thousands for autism by performing each year at the Walk.

Being a part of the fight against autism in these ways has brought many blessings to our lives and a bit of fun as well. I don't mean to make light. The ordeal many families undergo when a family member is affected by autism is real and often painful. But I have found in my life—and Neil and I have found in our life together—that a sense of humor is a gift from God that can carry you through trials that might otherwise tear you to pieces.

To this day Neil and I continue to meet with newly diagnosed parents to guide them through the initial shock of an autism diagnosis and the tremendous learning curve required. We are still active in the Walk each year. Neil attends each committee meeting and continues to be the top fundraiser. Neil is also developing a class for newly diagnosed dads called Daddy Bootcamp. In general, fathers have a harder time than mothers accepting the challenges of autism and what it takes for their child to adapt and succeed. Perhaps this is because even today in the twenty-first century, mothers do the bulk of the caretaking and see the effects of autism more clearly. Many men stay in denial longer. Because early intervention is critical, Daddy Bootcamp is designed to bring fathers up to speed more quickly. Neil is working hard to make this valuable class a reality. I am blessed with a husband who has looked autism in the face and has truly been a hero for our son Jack and the broader autism community.

We will be forever grateful for the blessing of being a part of a community of people who give back and take such good care of one another. Many of our friends who don't have children with autism have also stepped up and worked hard in the fight. We have seen much good in our journey through autism, but we still have a lot of work to do! When we were diagnosed, one in 160 children were affected. Today the ratio has risen to one in fifty-eight. Helping families and raising money for the larger organizations at the forefront of the fight against autism has given Neil and me a greater purpose in our own journey. I couldn't think of a better example of healing through service.

A great thing about travel is that you get to go to some incredible places, where profound, history-changing events have taken place, events that inspire you to even greater service.

In 2010 we visited South Africa to attend YEO University in Cape Town, where we had the honor or meeting some of the heroes of the fight against apartheid, such as Dennis Goldberg and Helen Lieberman. Many of those who spoke at that YEO event had spent more than twenty years in prison to fight for what they knew was right and good. I was deeply moved by their wisdom and love and the nobility of their sacrifice.

I was even able to work at one of the townships in Cape Town with Helen Lieberman. Townships are typically the underdeveloped, racially segregated urban areas in South Africa. We all helped to create a space for the Mamas (the grandmothers) to care for their grandchildren while their daughters worked. It was small, about 500 square feet in a beaten down structure on a dirt road, fenced in for our safety. We cleaned, repaired, and painted whatever we could get done in a day. After we were done with the renova-tion, Helen had the twenty of us privileged white women serve the Mamas a meal in prayer before we left. The tears flowed down the faces of those elderly black women who had never been attended in that manner by white women. It was a divine experience I will cherish forever.

Our next stop was Soweto, where I drank in the energy of what had occurred there in 1976 when black high school students protested against the decree forcing black schools to teach at least half of the time in

Afrikaans, the language associated with the oppression of apartheid. As many as 700 students died that day, with thousands wounded. The event was a tipping point and a rallying cry in the fight against apartheid.

While in Soweto we also visited the house in which Nelson Mandela lived from 1946 to 1962, not far from where the 1976 uprising had occurred. I felt the courage of his sacrifice pass into me as I walked through the places where he and other warriors had lived and performed their brave acts. God was whispering to me the whole time.

Although life was hectic in the years I was dealing with my cancer and Neil's, Jack's autism, Michael's challenges, my own addictions, when I needed peace and fulfillment, I turned to service. I felt I had to honor what was important to my purpose no matter how much it added to my already busy life.

One of the most fulfilling service projects I was involved in was Kids Who Care, for which I volunteered for about three years, from 2012 through 2014. Founded by Barb Greenberg, Kids Who Care is a nonprofit that teaches service-learning in the schools. To work in the classroom, I went through certification training in Arizona State University's Service-Learning Program.

Service-learning combines classroom lessons with in-person community service, for example, reading to the elderly, working in a food bank, packing backpacks of school supplies for underprivileged kids. The goal is to create an intersection between the classroom and the community, thereby teach-ing kids compassion and empathy as well as organization and management skills in a hands-on way.

Each participating classroom chose a nonprofit agency to create a project for, and then designed a project plan laying out all the steps, materials, and roles needed to get it done, as well as who would do what tasks. The founder of Kids Who Care and I went into the classroom to guide the children throughout the project, acting as a liaison between the students and the nonprofit. Once the students completed the project, they wrote a report and made a presentation to their class, which the teachers graded.

To teach the students the value of such efforts, I developed a program called the ABCs:

- **Accepting differences:** Learning to acknowledge that differences exist and that differences give us our unique and interesting characters.
- **Being good to one another:** This is an anti-bullying program; learning that not only should we not attack others who are different, we should actively honor and protect those with differences.
- **Community service:** Putting values of compassion and cooperation into action in the community.

We worked with kids in schools throughout the Phoenix area, from affluent schools to schools in low-income areas, empowering children to make a difference in the world. The organization creates a culture of service and emphasizes the importance of giving no matter what our circumstance in order to promote a braver and kinder future. To create a safer future for everyone, it's important for young people to experience the value of service and care. Seeing the joy the students felt when they gave to others filled me with joy. I served on the board as well during that time; it was a wonderful experience that I will cherish forever.

Our family also started working with Homes of Hope, which we were brought into by our friends Phil and Dave and their families. This organization was founded by one of the most loving families I have ever met, Sean and Janet Lambert, who have taught us all the meaning of purpose, because they live it every day. Homes of Hope is part of Sean's larger ministry, Youth with a Mission (YWAM), whose goal is to transform the lives of the poorest of the poor throughout the world. Through Homes of Hope itself, more than 130,000 volunteers have built more than 6,300 houses for poor families in twenty-three countries around the world.

Each year we take Brianna and Jack to Mexico to build a home for a family. With twenty-five or so volunteers, each build takes about two days. The volunteers are accompanied by staff members and a translator. While building the house, we get to know the family and the other villagers. All the children play together—those of the volunteers, those of the family we're building the house for, those of the village. As kids do, they create a bond that it is hard to put into words. The memories for all of us will last a lifetime.

This experience has nurtured and blessed our family. It reminds us how fortunate we are to live as we do in one of the most affluent countries in the world, where we benefit from all the medical advancements the west has to offer, not to mention strong education, more than adequate food, effective water and electric utilities, a solid infrastructure, and so on. It has given our children the opportunity to learn about themselves and other cultures and to respect how much we have been given. Working with these families is a gift we give ourselves as much as the families.

We still try to participate in Homes of Hope every year. Despite his pain some years, Neil shows up and does his best. It's all worth it to see the joy on the faces of those determined families who have been sleeping on dirt and living in tin or cardboard boxes as they walk through their new front door with their children. Because they now have a home, the children in these families are finally able to attend school and change the cycle of poverty. To be part of the program, each family must show proof of employment and purchase their own land, which often takes many years. That's how they show buy-in, so the house isn't just a handout. The houses are built for families who are ready and determined to work for a better life.

My daughter Brianna and I also joined National Charity League, a mother-daughter charity you commit to for six years, from seventh grade through twelfth. It is a philanthropic organization dedicated to community service, leadership development, and cultural experiences, and has been a reward-ing way to spend time with Brianna. We must log a number of hours of service a month and attend an array of meetings to teach the girls etiquette, meeting and party planning, and how to serve on committees. Each month there is a calendar of events to choose from and each one must be done by mother and daughter together. One activity we both loved was packaging food to be sent to third-world counties for Feed My Starving Children. Brianna and I have met many wonderful friends through this organization.

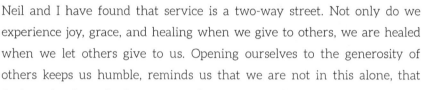

Neil and I have found that service is a two-way street. Not only do we experience joy, grace, and healing when we give to others, we are healed when we let others give to us. Opening ourselves to the generosity of others keeps us humble, reminds us that we are not in this alone, that God works through the acts of others. During the eight years that Neil has been ill, God has been talking loud and clear. We experienced many hardships but also many miracles. We received the love and support from many beautiful people. I felt the same way I did when my brother was hit by the truck; everyone in our lives is showing up to be of service.

It reminds me that we are all here to make life as easy as we can for one another. It is through giving and receiving that we heal. I knew how badly I've needed to heal all these years, both by receiving and giving service. We truly needed the love and support of everyone around us. And I also know that working with all these organizations and many others helped me push through the hard days. Reaching out to others took us out of our pain and helped us feel good by extending a hand to others who were in the same pain. If we are listening, our path will lead us to this kind of service that heals while bringing us closer to our true selves.

Chapter 17
WHAT DEATH CAN TEACH US

Neil and I came face to face with our mortality first with my breast cancer and then with his multiple myeloma. Death. We're talking about death, which scares the hell out of most people. But not me, not really. Don't get me wrong, I have a healthy respect for death. It marks the end of this life-time. It's graduation day for this session of our earth school. It's our passage back into spirit, back into our soul state. But it's for that reason I don't fear death. The soul is pure.

That doesn't mean I want to go quite yet. I have great affection for this lifetime and the people in it, the ones who love me and I them (especially Neil, Brianna, and Jack), others who have been my teachers. I don't think I'm done yet. I have many more lessons to learn.

In fact, death itself has taught me many lessons.

One of the first lessons occurred on Tuesday afternoon, May 13, 1980, at Western Michigan University when I was in college. I had decided to stay for the spring session to focus on one of the more difficult accounting classes I needed for my business degree.

I always found it easier to study in the library in one of those cubicles you lock yourself into, so I didn't have any distractions. After walking inside the building, I signed up for a room, got the key, then headed up to the fourth floor to set up for an afternoon's work. I had a beautiful view of the business campus with its old-world charm and lovely Tudor architecture. It was cloudy, the wind was blowing, and then it began to rain, but nothing out of the ordinary. Every so often, I looked up to watch the swaying trees our campus was so famous for, red and white oak and magnificent red maples.

It was turning into a nice cozy day, perfect to help me focus on my work. I was immersed in my books and making great progress when all of a sudden, I was ripped from concentration by the piercing wail of what could only have been a siren, but a siren with a sound I had never heard before. It wasn't the sound of an ambulance, police car, or firetruck. I looked outside, where everything had gone still, not a sound or movement, the trees no longer swaying, not one leaf trembling.

"Hurry, Hurry. Get out of there!" a lady screamed over the siren as she pounded on my locked door.

I opened the door without a word. The woman—I recognized the librarian from the first floor—grabbed my hand and pulled me behind her. The floor was empty, since it was the summer session and later in the afternoon. Thank God she remembered I was up there. I followed her down the flights of stairs until we reached the first floor with maybe twenty of us left in the building. Everyone was pulling or sweeping books off the center shelves. We were told to get on the floor, while a group toppled the metal shelves and laid them on top of us, creating a kind of protective cage. Soon after, we heard the roar of what sounded like a huge train pass by, shaking the old brick building hard. We couldn't be sure it wouldn't come crashing down on top of us. But the building held, and within minutes the stillness returned. Nobody spoke as people raised the shelves and crawled out from beneath them. A hand reached out to me— the same woman who had risked her own life to rescue me from the fourth floor. I was grateful! My spirit guides in the form of this woman were watching over me that day.

That was the only tornado I have ever been in. It was one of the biggest natural disasters in Michigan history and one of the few tornadoes that ever had a direct hit on a city's downtown. A large swath of downtown Kalamazoo was destroyed, every window of the nine story Industrial State Bank (ISB) building shattered. Gas and electrical fires burned, trees were ripped from the ground, cars were upended, buildings crumbled. In the end, there was over $50 million in damage. Five people were killed, seventy-nine injured, and more than a thousand made homeless in our little Kalamazoo community.

What I saw when we left that library, my heart pumping, stayed with me forever. It looked like the pictures of Stalingrad or London during the blitz from my history books. Nature had spoken and I gained a profound respect for its power. I am not so self-centered that I believed God was speaking directly to me with this tornado, but I got his message loud and clear. I was given this lifetime as a gift, and it could be taken away from me at any time. Use it wisely. A lesson I've always tried to follow.

The tornado was a powerful reminder of my own mortality in an abstract way. The first experience of death that affected me profoundly in a personal way was my second cousin Stacy's death from cancer when she was eleven years old.

Stacy's father was my father's cousin Donnie, who was named after my dad. Donnie and his family lived in a beautiful home in the Atlanta area in Marietta and had a second home on Lake Lanier, a reservoir fed by the Chattahoochee and Chestatee rivers. I visited both homes quite often, but the one on the lake was my favorite. The house was right on the water and had tennis courts and a dock, where they kept the boat they took out on the water just about every day. They were an upper middle-class family and very well respected in their community. I loved to visit. Their life always seemed so alive and fun.

My father had a second home in Atlanta with Priscilla, his second wife, just down the road from Donnie, his wife Marty, and their girls Kristi and Stacy. (Kristi is like a sister to me now and has lived close by for many years.) Dad lived on the Chattahoochee River in a spectacular home overlooking the water, a lifestyle he enjoyed after leaving my mother. I spent the summers there, and I loved being a part of it. It was so different from my life in Michigan.

And though I loved visiting my father in his new home, I was troubled by some of his choices, mainly, his marriage to Priscilla, with whom I had a complicated relationship. She always put me down, criticized me, made sure I knew that she was first in my dad's heart, not me. When we were together, I had to cater to her whims, jumping to soothe her when she was upset, walking on eggshells lest I be the one to upset her. I wasn't allowed to have needs, let alone talk about them. She was like a stepmother in a Grimm's fairy tale.

Stacy and I took long walks on the heavily treed pathways along the lake. She was nine and I was twenty, but she was much more evolved than I could have dreamed of as a young girl. She had a knowing peace that radiated from her like that of a saint in our old Roman Catholic missals. She had straight blonde hair, was always tan, and her radiant blue eyes drew you to her as much as her gentleness. I could talk to Stacy about anything, but especially Priscilla.

"I'm angry that me and my brothers and sisters aren't welcome in Dad's life. It's difficult to have a stepmother who hates how close Dad and I are." I would go on and on about how Priscilla had my father wrapped around her little finger and resented his children because we not only took his time, as she saw it, but took his money as well.

"Lynn, you can't control how anyone thinks or how they treat you. You can only control how you respond and how it affects you. Don't let anyone have that control. Each of us is doing the best we can to learn and to grow."

Stacy had a close relationship with Priscilla. In fact, her mother and Priscilla had become best friends. Stacy knew I was confused about that. Priscilla was another gaslighter in my life, expert at showing people who mattered to her only what she wanted them to see. They thought I was the crazy one, that I had it in for Priscilla because she was my stepmother. They didn't see what I saw.

"Your anger will only make it worse," Stacy continued. "She'll never understand what you feel. The only way you'll feel better is if you forgive her." Stacy said this with the grace and wisdom of someone much older, and it worked. She was always able to soothe me. I never questioned how a nine-year-old was able to do that. She just did.

One day when she was ten, she told her fourth-grade teacher she had a bad headache. "I don't feel well," she told the teacher. "I think I need to go home."

There was a test that day and her teacher wasn't buying it. "Take your test first, then we'll send you to the nurse."

"I really don't feel well. I have to go home," Stacy insisted.

The teacher made her take the test, then sent her to the nurse. The nurse sent her home, but the headaches only worsened. After several doctor's appointments, she was diagnosed with brain cancer. After the diagnosis, she said, "They don't think I am lying now, do they!" She never lied and was insulted that someone thought she had.

In the following months, we watched Stacy go through chemotherapy and watched her parents and sister suffer along with her. Although Stacy grew puffy from steroids, and her long, beautiful hair fell out, she never complained, and she wasn't afraid. She had come to a place of peace beyond understanding. When I visited her in the hospital toward the end, she consoled me (and everyone else) even as she suffered from so much pain I couldn't bear to watch.

During one visit, I was there with her father. Her teacher had sent a card along with cards from the entire class. Stacy was blind by this time, and Donnie was reading her the cards. "Honey, your teacher says she is so honored she was able to have you as a student and that you taught her so much." He went quiet for a moment, then he added. "You've taught me so much, too."

Though she couldn't see, Stacy looked directly into her father's eyes and said with love and wisdom, "Not enough Daddy. Not enough yet."

Donnie cried and held her tiny hand. "Honey, I know, I know. I have a lot to learn, and I want to keep learning. I'm so grateful for you."

Donnie and I both knew what Stacy meant. Donnie put great store in status and money and all their trappings. Ever so gently and with great love, as was her way, Stacy was trying to nudge her father onto a higher path.

An overwhelmingly powerful energy entered the room, put us all into a kind of trance. This wasn't a child talking. This was Spirit speaking through a child. God's divine intention filled the room. Time stopped, as did my breathing, and I felt a space between my physical body and my spirit. I wasn't afraid. I was grateful, accepting. God was embracing Stacy, letting her know he was ready to take her home. I felt her enlightenment grow, then flow onto to me like a gentle wave. It was then that I knew everything was as it should be—that everything always is as it should be, that God is here on earth with us and within us all. I was honored that he had extended to me the comfort of his loving arms as he embraced our beautiful spiritual teacher, eleven-year-old Stacy. Stacy passed away six days later.

Stacy taught me that death was not something to be afraid of. It is all beautiful, even our passing. I was also blessed by Stacy's Dad, Donnie, my dear cousin when he passed. He was more like another father to me and when he passed, he let me know that he was alright. He was more than alright; he was home. I had just returned from Greece and went straight to bed. It was September 28, 2009, and I fell into a deep sleep after our long journey home. Donnie had been diagnosed with late-stage cancer only weeks before. While I was away my cousin Kristi, his daughter had let me know that he had taken a turn for the worse and it would not be long before he passed. While fast asleep, I awakened to the gentlest flutter of love that swept throughout my body. The rush that flowed through me radiated with the energy and vibration of Donnie. Without question, I knew it was him. He said goodbye for now and gave me the gift of knowing how much he loved me as he soared to the kingdom of heaven.

I woke up abruptly and told Neil that Donnie had passed. Neil calmed me until I fell back asleep. The next morning, I received the call, Donnie had passed. Since having had these blessed experiences, I haven't been afraid of death. I'm certain that it has to be more magical than we could ever imagine.

In 1987, I visited Detroit for my ten-year high school reunion. I had taken off a week of work and left early on the Saturday morning the week before the reunion and planned to return the following Sunday, so I could get to work on Monday. Sometime during that week, my sister Michelle talked me into going to a party with her on the Sunday I was supposed to leave. I checked in with my boss to get my PTO extended, and she agreed. I called the airline and changed my flight, but I didn't think to tell anyone. I had no one to answer to, really.

The party was at a very high-end home on a beautiful lake with boating and water skiing and panoramic views. It was a beautiful day in August, and the sun shone all day. The water was crystal clear and the people I met, all friends of my sisters, were a blast! I felt like I was in an episode of the *Lives of the Rich and Famous*. We left the party at about 8:00 that night after spending the entire day there. We got into the car and smoked a joint, something I hadn't done since I was a teenager. I wasn't accustomed to smoking pot, so it hit me hard. We giggled as we reminisced about our perfect day and funny things from childhood.

I walked into the house, and the phone was ringing. Michele was unpacking the car, so I grabbed the phone in my euphoric and relaxed state, confused at the panic on the other end of the line.

"Lynn, Oh My God, is that YOU?" Mark yelled into the phone.

Mark and I had worked together in the restaurant when I first moved to Phoenix and had remained good friends. "Yes, Mark, I'm fine. What's wrong with you?"

"I thought you were dead. It's really you. Are you okay?"

"Why would you think I was dead?"

"Your plane crashed! Everyone's dead."

I got that prickly feeling on the back of my neck. "I'm fine, Mark. I changed my flight. I'll give you a big hug when I get home."

I couldn't quite wrap my head around what he had just told me, so I turned on the TV news and watched in amazement and shock as they showed the crash site on a freeway just outside the airport. I fell to the floor in front of the TV while my sister now fielded phone call after phone call. I hadn't told anyone in Phoenix or in Michigan that I had changed my flight. It was August 16, 1987. Northwest Flight 255 crashed at 8:46 p.m. The only surviving passenger was a five-year-old girl. A total of 148 passengers perished along with six crew members and two people on the ground.

I was numb, thinking how close I had been to being on that flight. Thank God I liked parties. It was otherworldly, like I was watching my own funeral, feeling the grief—and the relief—of everyone who called. I couldn't really bring myself to console them. Michele had to take care of all that. I woke up at three in the morning and broke down, weeping hard for all those beautiful souls lost in the crash, one of them in a seat that had been meant for me.

The next morning my father took me to the airport. It was the same flight from Detroit to Phoenix with the same flight number. As the car approached the overpass into the airport, we could see the wreckage on the freeway below. My father visibly trembled as we took it all in. As we walked through the airport, we passed the families learning about their loved ones. That could have been my father and sister. My dad held me tight before I entered the jetway. When I took my seat, there was such stillness. Priests, rabbis and nuns made their way through the plane comforting us. Some of the people on the flight had been on stand-by the night before.

I lost two friends on that flight, one from high school and one from college. Matt Mclaughlin was twenty-nine. We had spent a lot of time hanging out in high school. Matt was from a big family, his sister Ruth was a year younger, my age. Their large house on top of the hill in Northville, Michigan was a happy place for me, as was their cottage in Northern Michigan. We had some great parties there. We also lost Steve Brosnan, a college friend. He was twenty-seven. I remember many nights partying with Steve in Kalamazoo.

There was such tremendous loss for so many. Years later, I read about an author who lived in Munds Park who had lost her two young girls on that flight. Now that I have children, I can't imagine how she survived.

No one spoke to each other for the entire three hours from Detroit to Phoenix. We held hands and prayed in honor of those who were gone.

Why had I changed my flight? It was more than the party. About two days before, I had felt God's touch in the same way I had in the hospital room with Stacy. I was thinking of changing the flight, and I just had a feeling that I should. So I did. My lessons for this lifetime were not over.

And afterwards, of course, as with the tornado, I knew how close I had come to death, which helped me appreciate the time I was given on earth.

When we were in South Africa in November 2010, once we were finished with our YEO commitments in Cape Town, our next stop was Zimbabwe with our friends Dave and Sherry Steele. We stayed at the Victoria Falls Hotel, an elegant, a five-star hotel that had been visited by royalty for many years.

We decided to go white-water rafting down the Zambezi River. I really didn't put much thought into it or ask any questions. I was accustomed to following Neil's lead. He always makes the travel plans and I go along with them. We had gone diving with the sharks in Cape Town, so I thought, compared to that, how bad could this be?

It is no wonder that Victoria Falls is one of the seven natural wonders of the world. It is absolutely breathtaking in the power and beauty of the crashing water falling more than 350 feet. (Victoria Falls is twice as high and twice as broad as Niagara Falls.) It was a perfect day to view the falls and then go rafting. The sky shimmered with the sharpest blue, reflecting the crystal radiance of the water as it fell to the river.

I realized just how tall the falls were when, to get to the starting point of our rafting trip, I descended every foot of it by means of the 936 steps to the canyon with only metal handrails to hold onto. I have jumped out of a plane, but this was different. I was terrified. I couldn't look down at the enormous gap between me and the earth below. The only thing between me and possibility of falling to my death were those few metal bars. When my feet finally touched the earth at the bottom of the canyon, I pried my trembling hands from the railings and said to myself, *I made it! The rough part is over.*

How wrong I was!

The falls were to the left of us, where we all noticed a hippopotamus had fallen from the top. Not a good omen. We began our journey just past the roar of the falls as it poured into the Zambezi River. A group of about fifty people were going down the river that day, with about twenty guides. There were three or four other boats, each boat carrying twelve to fifteen people.

We were accustomed to hiring our own private guides on all our adventures and this was no exception. It was just the four of us and our guide, Rudo, in our boat. He steered the raft and told us about the history of Zimbabwe as we went. Many of the other guides, Africans in their twenties and thirties, were in the water on small kayaks. They were all in amazing shape with muscles that gleamed in the sunlight. I did wonder why there were so many of them and why they were in the water.

As we began our journey down the river, I was captivated by its beauty and serenity as it flowed through the deep canyon, and how the water reflected the trees and the mountains from the surrounding bluffs.

"We are now approaching our first rapids called The Wall," Rudo said, as he motioned for us to hold on.

Sherry and I were in the front of the boat, and Dave and Neil in the back. When we saw what was ahead, we looked at each other in fear and disbelief. My body tensed and with my hands, still sore from our descent to the river, I gripped the rope at the front of the raft as tight as I could.

The roar of the rapids came before we felt anything. Then the raft jerked forward, the water gushing and twisting around us, spinning us so fast my heart pumped with adrenaline. I'm sure it took only a few minutes to get through the rapids, but it seemed endless to me, endless terror. This was not what I had in mind. I wanted out! When I looked over at Sherry, I saw that she felt the same way.

"Neil, I have to get off the raft," I called out in real panic after we reached the calmer water. The rapids were triggering some kind of PTSD in me.

"Lynn is right! This is crazy!" agreed Sherry, who had almost drowned once before. Despite the chill of the water and the sun overhead, her face was white with fear. She hadn't wanted to go in the first place. Neil had convinced her it would be fun. "Rudo," Sherry addressed the guide directly. "Are there more rapids like this one?"

"I am sorry to say Miss Sherry," he said in a professionally calming voice. We weren't his first scared passengers. "There are many ahead. Please prepare. It will be fine."

"Can't we get off the river?" I said, trying to sound authoritative rather than terrified. "I can't do this!"

"I am sorry Miss Lynn. It is a three-hour ride, and there is no way out except to continue."

There was that damn calm voice again. What it told me was that we had to ride it out, quite literally.

As soon as my nerves settled from the first run, I heard the next set of rapids ahead. My body shook, as I once again held the ropes against me with as much strength as I could.

"We are now entering the rapids called Between Two Worlds," Rudo said, commanding us to hold on tightly.

The water hit us with a force that tossed us up and off the raft as if we were ragdolls. I went in the water and was pulled beneath the raft. I bounced against the rocks and for a brief second, I was able to hold on to something to slow me down. In that moment, I saw the same terror in Dave's eyes before the turbulence engulfed me again. Just then, a hand latched on to my life vest and pulled me onto a kayak. It was one of the guides. That's why there were so many of them! He paddled me to the other side of the rapid. Then he helped me get back on the raft, though I would have much rather stayed with him.

I looked to be sure everyone was all right. Sherry, Dave, and I were all overwhelmed and comforting each other, while Neil, to our amazement, was hooting and howling about how much fun he was having.

There were eight rapids in all. We had only passed through two of them. I was a prisoner to the river. About then, I started shutting down.

The only experience I could compare it to was the rape. And that's no exaggeration. I felt the same sense of helplessness and physical terror as when that monster raped me in the desert. I couldn't get away; I was trapped. I had to get through it. This was not fun.

We got through the next two rapids in fear, but we were able to stay on the raft. My fingers and hands felt as if my bones were being pulled apart, like I was being subjected to some medieval torture device. Then came the Stairway to Heaven. I held on for a second before being abruptly thrown into the center of the rapid. I spun in the water trying to find space for a quick breath before I went under. I slammed hard into another rock, which knocked what little air I had left right out of me. You know that feeling like your lungs are going to burst and you're never going to breathe again? That's how I felt. When my legs started kicking in panic, I was rescued by another guide who brought me to the other side of the rapids on his kayak.

While we were going through a calm area, it occurred to me that I hadn't seen anyone else fall from their rafts. "Rudo, why are we the only ones flipped off the raft?"

"Miss Lynn, you all wanted a private boat with no weight, so that is what happens. I thought you wanted a big adventure!" he said. Neil was grinning beside him. I should have known.

We survived the rest of the rapids by gritting our teeth and holding on for dear life, and on my part, by shutting town. When we went through The Devil's Toilet, we were able to climb on a rock and walk to the other side. I would have fallen to my knees and kissed the earth, but I was too sore and catatonic.

When we arrived at the hotel, Sherry and I went back to my room. We wanted nothing to do with Neil, who had put us through this terror. We sat on an ottoman at the end of the bed, held each other in our arms, and rocked back and forth. It was the same shock and powerlessness I had felt after the assault. I had been captured and trapped again, this time by the river, and I could not get away. I had to surrender to terror to survive. And I had survived. Intellectually, I knew I was safe. Emotionally, I was still gripped by terror.

I later learned later that there are six classes of rapids, six being the high-est, and we had experienced Class 5.5. I also learned that there are crocodiles in the Zambezi River. A few years later, I met a man had also been a guest at Gulf Breeze. He had worked for three years as a guide on the Zambezi and told me that several people had died rafting on the river. He saw one person attacked by a crocodile. I'm grateful I never saw a crocodile on our trip. My terror in the rapids was plenty for me, thank you very much. I felt vindicated that I wasn't crazy after all—there had been real danger to be afraid of. Neil in his "Go-go-go!" bravado had tried to convince me other-wise. What I felt was real!

This experience reminded me of two lessons: one, that I was a survivor. I could survive rape and I could survive near drowning. And two, that I had a long way to go to learn how to take care of myself. I let Neil talk me into this experience against my better judgment, and then he belittled, disregarded, and dismissed my feelings of terror while we were on the water and afterwards. Neil said he had compassion for Sherry because he could see that nearly drowning years before would have made it a terrifying experience for her. The experience was bad enough for me, but Neil recognizing Sherry's trauma while dismissing mine made it much worse. Feeling helpless and powerless in your own body is a kind of death in itself, and I allowed someone I loved to put me in that position (though I don't think he thought it would be that dangerous). This was another whisper telling me to learn to take care of myself, a whisper I was not listening to—yet.

On July 19, 2017, I woke up terrified and hyperventilating. I had dreamed that I died in a bad car accident. It was so real. Afterwards, though, there had been a deep peace. Since I often learn important things from dreams, I take them very seriously.

"Are you okay? What's going on?" Neil said groggily, coming out of his own deep sleep.

"I just died in my dream. Oh my God, it was terrible. I was in a really bad car accident.

The car was spinning and there was a terrible crash. I saw the whole thing so vividly. There was a lot of noise, and I was trying to stay clear of the other cars on the road."

"Calm down, Honey, it was just a dream. It's okay," Neil said, so we could go back to sleep.

The next day, Neil left on a trip to Canada, and I stayed home with the twins. We were leaving the following day to go to our second home in Munds Park to get out of the 110-degree heat of a summer in Phoenix. It can be twenty-five to thirty degrees cooler in the majestic mountains and jagged pine trees that surround our home there. It's my magic place, the place I go to breathe deeply and exhale.

Munds Park falls between the red rocks of Sedona and the rustic town of Flagstaff. With its single gas station, a little party store, and an unpretentious country club, you feel as if you're in Mayberry RFD, where everyone slows down, whether they're walking or riding their Rhino ATVs, and smiles. Our club was built in 1959 and has the feel and décor of those times. It includes a golf course, a restaurant, and a bar with lots of games and entertainment. The ice cream truck with the magical sounds of the sixties winds its way through the neighborhoods. We all love it there. Our little piece of heaven.

It was July 21, our big old Suburban packed and ready to go. It's only an hour and forty minutes from our home in Scottsdale to Munds Park. Brianna was bringing her best friend Kaila. Jack was in the front seat next to me. Brianna and Kaila were in the second seat. Our dog Cooper along with our guinea pig were in the back with a pile of groceries and luggage.

Traffic was heavy that day, a Friday. We weren't the only ones getting an early start on the weekend. We headed north on I-17 just before rush hour and had barely made it outside Phoenix when Jack and I began arguing about his urgent need to have Burger King. I heard the screech of tires to my left. The car in that lane was moving into ours, but we must have been in its blind spot, because it was about to sideswipe us. I overcorrected, time slowed, and everything unfolded as in the dream. The dream had warned me, so I knew what to do. I recall very clearly thinking, this is not a dream, but follow the dream. Stay away from the noise, which I knew meant traffic. Focus. I steered away from the traffic across three lanes, the car launched into the air and spun to the other side of freeway, stopping only when we crashed into the cement barrier at seventy miles per hour.

I can't remember anything after that until I came to and looked at Jack to my right. The airbags had gone off and he was spattered in blood. My autistic son looked at me with a calm eye, not a shred of fear and in the most knowing tone, said, "Mom, it's okay. We're going to be just fine." I twisted to look behind me. The girls were screaming, but they were alive! That was my peace. The kids were alive. Jack was right.

The girls continued screaming. Jack was trying to calm us. I saw Cooper try to climb over the seat to Brianna, so he was okay too. The car seemed to be on fire under the hood. I couldn't get out my door. The girls couldn't get out either. I looked out the window at all the people running toward the car, some with fire extinguishers, others with their phones or tire irons. I don't know what they did, but they got us all out and put out the fire.

Someone called the police. Within minutes arrived fire fighters, police officers, and an ambulance. The police and the fire fighters made sure we were all safe, including the pets. It dawned on me that the man in the other car may have not been as lucky, but just then a man appeared before me, crying. He told me he was the other driver, and he didn't even have a dent in his car. That's good, I thought. That's good.

A witness told me later we actually flew through the air! Others said they couldn't believe we made it to the other side of the freeway without hitting anyone or getting hit ourselves. All the other cars had managed to steer clear of each other as well. It was a miracle. As I held my children to comfort them, I knew we had been touched by God. We had more lessons to learn in this lifetime.

The EMTs thought I might have a significant neck injury, so I was taken to the hospital in the ambulance. The police stayed with the children until Kaila's dad Gary drove up from Phoenix and took them to the hospital. Gary said the kids and the pets were standing on the side of the road on that 110-degree day when he arrived, and though his daughter was banged up, he found some humor in the fact that Jack had climbed back into the wreck to get his electronics, which he held onto firmly until Gary put them safely in his car. Gary has shared many times since that day how totaled that Suburban was. It shook him to his core to look at it and revel in the miracle that we were all okay. Once the Suburban reached the auto salvage yard, the employees that worked there said they had never seen a car in that condition that did not have passengers without serious injuries or death.

I ended up being fine. I had pulled the muscles in my neck with no nerve or spine damage. We were all fine, except for the guinea pig, who died later that night. He was seven years old and had led a full life. We gave him a sweet ceremony and buried him in the backyard.

We were still banged up and sore, so we spent the next several days recovering at home in Scottsdale, perhaps just a little more tender with each other because of what we'd been through.

Coming close to death—whether spiritually, as with Stacy, medically, as with cancer, physically, as with the tornado, the whitewater rafting trip, and the car accident, or psychologically, as with the missed plane crash—acts like that brick to the head Oprah talks about.

Any day could be our last.

That's a cliché, but as with many clichés, it begins in truth. Any day could be our last. What are we going to do with it? If we are granted this lifetime to learn our lessons and heal our wounds, how far have we come? We often tell ourselves, Ah, I'll get to that. I've got plenty of time. The fact is none of us know how much time we have.

Today is the day. What are we going to do with it?

That's what I've learned from my scrapes with death and what I think we can all learn from death. Not to be afraid of it, but to respect it and allow death to teach us a greater appreciation of our purpose in this lifetime.

Chapter 18
FINDING PEACE IN THE MIDST OF COVID AND CANCER

Speaking of close calls, in May 2018, we received another miracle. After two stem cell transplants, 528 chemo treatments, and dozens of infusions of daratumumab, we were told Neil was showing tremendous progress in the clinical trial and there was a chance he could go into complete remission. In early 2019, a bone marrow biopsy confirmed it. Neil was cancer free.

The clinical trial had worked, and it became a standard treatment for late-stage cancer, saving lives all over the world. More good news: if the multiple myeloma returned, Neil would be able to receive the same treatment again, unlike the bone marrow transplant, which one can undergo twice only. Doctors have kept a close watch on him with regular bloodwork and yearly bone marrow biopsies.

God was really getting my attention now. We had another chance. What were we going do with it? The thirteenth century Persian poet Rumi wrote, "Through love all pain will turn into medicine."[27] To me this means that the love of two souls joined together in this lifetime to learn their lessons together will help each other rise above the pain to heal.

Neil's medicine had healed his physical pain. Now it was time for us to face the emotional wounds we had covered over for too long. Neil's miracle gave me permission to ask for what I needed: to be given the space and time to take care of myself. Gulf Breeze had been a good start, but I needed to do more work. I was carrying too much resentment and guilt and feeling trapped in unhealthy patterns. I didn't feel good physically or emotionally. It was time for me to go inside myself to heal and stop trying to heal from the outside. I had to find my way back to myself.

For the first half of 2019, I did just that. I had more of the space I needed to heal, and I made a good start of it. I read more. I meditated. I exercised. I turned inward toward my true self and worked on strengthening my resolve to live according to my true nature, not what I thought people wanted me to be. But the road on life's journey is never a straight one. In August of 2019, Michael was accused of assaulting the young woman, I had to move him out of his apartment, and I had to deal with the stress and fallout that followed. Then in January 2020 Neil relapsed. The most recent bone marrow biopsy showed the growth of multiple myeloma once again.

Neil and I had been getting ready to travel to an EO conference in Sydney, Australia, with a first stop to visit friends in New Zealand. We received the news just before we left and decided we needed some time to process it, so we kept it to ourselves. The remission period had been short, and we both felt powerless and frightened again. As if that wasn't enough, COVID-19 had just made its way into the news, but no one knew how serious it would become.

We had a wonderful time in Auckland, and then Mangawhai, New Zealand, at a private resort called Tara Iti Golf Club. It had been built by an American billionaire, and each member is handpicked to maintain the club's laidback, intimate vibe. Our friends are members, and each couple in our group enjoyed their own five-star cottage. Tara Iti is a magical place. The sea and the rugged mountains and beaches of white sand took our breath away while we shared elegant meals overlooking the manicured golf course with its greens and bunkers laid out like a necklace of jewels. While we did genuinely enjoy ourselves, every once in a while, Neil and I looked to each other for strength, knowing what we faced when we returned—doctors, tests, infusions, the world of cancer once again. We kept it to ourselves, as if that way we could put off the inevitable reckoning.

Then before COVID-19 got real, we flew to Australia and enjoyed Sydney for a few days. The EO conference had been cancelled two days before it was meant to begin. The keynote speaker had been Elizabeth Gilbert, whom I had heard speak before, and I was sorry to miss her. Her human approach to spirituality appeals to me. With news of the virus spreading, the Australians began acting strangely—they were buying stores out of cleaning supplies, bottled water, canned goods, and toilet paper. *These are some pretty crazy Aussies*, I thought. *Who hoards toilet paper?* Little did I know that our American compatriots were doing the same thing back home!

Neil and I were fortunate enough to get a flight home before the borders closed. Once we returned, the doctors recommended holding off on Neil's treatment with the virus spreading, since Neil's immune system would be compromised. We knew Neil couldn't wait too long, though, and a PET scan in July revealed it was time to begin treatment, even with the threat of coronavirus. That's when we had to tell people. This time we decided not to make a huge announcement on CaringBridge, Facebook, and the like. Everyone was going through enough with COVID-19. We shared the news only with the twins, our families, and our closest friends.

After Neil began treatment, more news about COVID came out. A medical report revealed that with multiple myeloma Neil would have about only about a 60 percent chance of surviving if he contracted the virus. We were already being very careful, but this heightened our fears.

Meanwhile, as Neil's treatment progressed and Michael's situation headed in the right direction as well, life had calmed down enough for me to continue working on myself. I had done deep energy work in the past with an intuitive consultant, teacher, and healer named Mary. My work with Mary over the course of several years had helped to heal trauma and unconscious beliefs. She could tap directly into my energy field by working over the phone and each time my sessions with her would take me to a place of deep spiritual discovery. Once I was blessed enough to work with her in person as she shifted the energy within me with a full-on spiritual surgery. Mary helped me understand that my soul had decided that I would recover in this lifetime from my shadows of victimhood—that I had to work hard and pay attention. My experiences with Mary have been a gift that I will cherish forever. I also began to recognize her gift in others as I grew through her teachings.

I had a phone number of a woman I had met in La Jolla a few summers before, Cathia, a meditation guide and spiritual teacher. She works in Sedona with five other spiritual teachers, one a shaman. Her soul had spoken to mine, and I had felt drawn to her instantly, but life had gotten in the way, so I had never contacted her. Now she kept showing up in my thoughts, and I knew there was a reason. I called her and began to work with her and her partners. Each meditation I had with them took me deeper. Each time I found more stillness within, felt closer to myself. The panic of feeling owned, imprisoned, and controlled by past experiences was lifting as I gave myself permission to go within myself and find peace.

After one of my meditations with the group, I went outside on our deck and continued the meditation on my own. It was September 2020, and I was alone at our home in Munds Park, my safe and magic place. Hundreds of pine trees hug the house and deck, providing an umbrella of peace and serenity. As I breathed in the fresh mountain air, the pressures of life dropped away, and I felt the lightness and tranquility I feel nowhere else. The crows in the pines, those embodiments of strength and wisdom, those symbols of life magic and mystery, called out their mantra: caw-caw-caw. They took me deeper into nature, the stillness and comfort spreading over Munds Park in the stars that radiated the energy of our oneness, the brilliant supermoon rising against the darkening sky. I stood drinking in the moonlight sky, absorbing the divine energy as my soul soared in its perfection, the gift of life God has created for us. I always feel his gifts even more deeply when I'm there, a heightened sense of empathy, love, joy, and wonder.

It is difficult to express in words the flow of life I felt within me that night. I had only seen a supermoon once before, at Gulf Breeze. I believe the moon is like God and each one of us; we experience it in slivers, but the whole of it is always there. We are always home. That evening I knew I could be exactly who I am, but only if I let go and allowed it to happen. I wasn't trapped. I had a choice. I could learn and listen.

The next day my writing flowed through me as if guided by Spirit.

Around this time, I had another deeply spiritual experience, but it needs some background.

I was close to my mother-in-law, Roberta, a wonderful spiritual teacher for me. She lived in Las Vegas, which suited her. She was a woman of large stature, both in body and in the respect she commanded. She was brassy without the least bit of insecurity. Her clothes were Vegas flash with animal prints and the big jewelry to match. Her hair was thin, straight and blonde, always styled with flair, and she had long, elaborately sculpted nails. When Roberta was at a party, she commanded the room, holding court with her direct and loud wisdom. You either loved Roberta or you didn't.

We certainly had our power struggles at the beginning of our relationship. She expected me to jump when she needed something; she told me how to decorate my house; she asked me how I was spending what she called "my husband's money." We had a big blowout once because I stood up to her about something minor. Jack had just been diagnosed, I was tired, and I blew up at her, which you simply didn't do with Roberta. She screamed and yelled at me. I yelled back and called her a bully. She called me two weeks later and apologized. She said she had asked her girlfriends if she was a bully, and they told her that she most certainly was! She told me she would never do that to me again. I gained her respect that day, and she was true to her word—she never treated me that way again.

She could be quite overwhelming, but people listened. Truth is truth and Roberta knew truth. Over the years of my marriage to Neil, when she sensed trouble, she said these words: "Do you have any idea how many women would like to have your life? Never let them win." She pointed that long finger at me.

"How do they win?" I asked.

"They only win if you leave, you idiot!" She used the word *idiot* quite often. "Men are just stupid men honey. They don't even know when they're being played by another woman. Protect what you've got. Protect your family. Don't let the stupid little things take that away."

In 2017, Roberta was diagnosed with stage-four lung cancer and decided not to undergo treatment. Our family took turns visiting during her last months. We wanted to make sure the twins had some time with her before she became too ill. It was toward the end of October when our son Jack was able to spend time at her home in Las Vegas. He knew it would probably be the last time he'd see her.

"Grandma, my fourteenth birthday is coming up on November 19, and I want to make sure you can get my gift before then, in case you die." Jack sat next to her on her bed and waited for her response. In his literal, autistic view of the world, this was a perfectly reasonable thing to say.

"Well, Jack, that's a very important question. What do you think you deserve this year? Have you been doing well in school and listening to your parents?" She smiled without the least bit of irritation.

"Yes, I've been good. I have a new iPad in mind. All you have to do is give me your credit card number, and we'll be all set. And since we have that all taken care of, can we discuss my inheritance now?"

"Oh, boy, I feel like I am in an episode of *Atypical*," Roberta laughed. "That's my beautiful grandson." *Atypical* is a popular Netflix show about a teenage boy with autism. We all loved that show and found much of it true to life.

A few weeks before she passed, I went to Las Vegas to help care for her. Neil, his brother Craig, and I took turns during the last weeks of her life. I had just flown in from Phoenix. She was in hospice and had a few friends visiting when I arrived. I went immediately to work to put things in order, checking what food she could still have, arranging gifts and cards from friends, managing what friends could visit and when, and making sure she had everything she needed. It's what I do. Roberta felt the energy of my need to please immediately. She knew me well.

"Who do you think you are? Joan of Arc?" she asked. "You can't make everything better. Stop trying to save the world! Now, get over here. *I could use your help."*

I stood beside her and didn't question her judgment. She was showing me what was important—that I couldn't rescue everyone; that I needed to spend more time rescuing myself. I had learned to appreciate her pithy wisdom, however harshly it might be delivered. Since she passed away, I miss her blunt, enlightened guidance.

She used to talk to all of us that way—direct, brassy, hardcore. She didn't put up with any nonsense. We knew she loved us very much, though. Not long before she passed, she told me she would give me a sign when she was on the other side. "A feather," she said. "Like a French feather." Later she said her last words to me: "You are okay, Lynn. You have guides that protect you. They are always there for you. Trust that, keep learning to grow closer to yourself. I love you very much!" She held my hand with compassion and watched the tears slide down my face. That was the last time she was able to speak to me.

She died shortly after on November 13, 2017. I was honored to be with her when she passed.

Roberta had been gone for over two years, and I hadn't seen the feather she promised. I missed my mother-in-law dearly, and I looked and looked for that sign, trying to rediscover that connection with her. I needed the wisdom she gave me when I was off track.

It had been a week since I had had the deep meditation in Munds Park. I had closed up the Munds Park house and returned to Scottsdale to get the twins set up for online schooling. This was September of 2020, and the pandemic was raging. The first day I was back, I looked down in our backyard, and there it was, a flashy Vegas leopard-skin French feather. Of course! I picked it up and held it in my hands as if it was a newborn bird. *She's here*, I told myself.

That week I found two other feathers just like it. They appeared as I glanced at something else. Roberta was enfolding me in her love and guidance, bringing me to a new level of awareness on top of what I had achieved through meditation. She was telling me I was on the right track.

So now I knew I was on the right track, but Neil was still undergoing treatment, and though I had moments of peace and transcendence, like the meditation session and Roberta's feathers, it didn't take long for me to be thrown back into the maelstrom of fear, uncertainty, and anger about the future.

Neil's treatment was going well in general, but there were unavoidable side effects that caused tension, stress, and conflict in the family. The intramural therapy using daratumumab was working again, along with an oral chemotherapy drug called pomalyst. Neil was also prescribed dexamethasone, the same steroid used for COVID-19 patients. The dexamethasone heightened Neil's feelings of anxiety, aggression, and frustration. Neil could not control the cancer, the virus, or Jack's autism, but he could control me. Because COVID-19 was a threat to his weakened immune system, that became the locus of his control. We were told by his doctors that if he were to be infected by the virus that he would literally have about a 30 percent chance of survival. They even assured us he would have a bed available to him immediately at Mayo Hospital if he tested positive. He was terrified. Who wouldn't be? As a result, he monitored where I went, what I did, who I saw, how close I got to other people. (If I ever got closer than six feet, he'd have a major meltdown.) He watched how I wore my mask, how often I was tested, how I handled groceries, how I monitored the children and their friends, how I washed my hands, how I cleaned things in the house. I was under surveillance twenty-four seven.

One day he found out that one of Brianna's friends had been exposed to the virus, and he just lost it. All day long, he screamed at Brianna. Then he screamed at the rest of us. Then he screamed at Brianna some more. I told him he was scaring the children. "Tough," he said. "My life is more important than any 'feelings' they may be having right now." I was saddened and angered by his narcissism. His fear, the terror of covid, coupled with his cancer, had taken over his sense of balance. He was terrified.

I called Neil's best friend to talk some sense into him, but that didn't work. I had some wine, and after a whole day of Neil's yelling and berating all of us, that evening it began again. I lost it myself and fought back, which should never happen with my guard down. I'm not saying I shouldn't challenge Neil, but when I have a few glasses of wine, my response can be unhealthy and unproductive. The conversation became very heated and occurred in front of Brianna. She had already been quite upset all day, so this only added to her anxiety. On this day, October 28, 2020, I decided to become stronger and healthier. Caring for myself and stopping the cycle of old patterns had to become my priority. Since that day, I have felt a deeper sense of strength within myself to change the cycles that had become ingrained within me. I still enjoy relaxing with a glass or two of wine, but I know that reaching for a glass of wine is never the answer when I'm angry. I am working hard to learn to go within myself, control my reactions, and eliminate the need to numb myself or to find courage in a bottle.

Please understand that I realize that alcohol addiction is a serious matter. It can kill wonderful people and destroy lives. I saw that firsthand at Gulf Breeze, and I do not take it lightly. Is eliminating anything that we even question that can bring us closer to our true self a better choice? In all honesty, there have been far too many times that words spill from my mouth when the effects of alcohol have taken over, words that I would have chosen much more carefully or at a different time. I am still certainly working hard on this lesson. I am still evolving, still trying to find the strength to be more conscious, to eliminate the need to reach outside myself for comfort when I am upset or triggered.

One of my biggest accomplishments in this lifetime will be to learn to be aware of when I'm in danger of falling into the role of a victim or allowing anything outside of myself to affect how I treat myself or others. I am quite aware that this is a lesson that I am still trying to overcome.

We were more worried about Neil surviving COVID-19 than the cancer at this point and lived in perpetual fear. If any of us did the wrong thing and contracted the virus, it could kill Neil. We were all terrified of being the one to make that mistake. As a result, we were hypervigilant with ourselves and each other. *That's not six feet! Your nose slipped out of your mask! Did you wash your hands? That wasn't twenty seconds. You get to see your friends, why don't we get to see ours?* You get the idea. We were picky and pissy and playing the blame game. We were all stressed out. Arguments broke out. I think that terrible night had taken its toll on all of us.

Something had to give. One afternoon after that October blowup, I sat the family down for a talk. "We have a serious problem," I began, once we were all gathered in the family room. "We all need to take a breath and have an honest discussion. It's about your father and his health."

"Mom what's going on? Is everything okay?" Brianna was hiding beneath the pillows of our sectional.

"Everything's fine. But I know we're all terrified that Dad will get the virus. I know you're both aware of the risks to Dad and are doing everything in your power to follow the rules. It had been a lonely and difficult time, especially for seventeen-year-olds.

"Let's talk practicalities. Dad and I have worked hard to put things in place to make sure you're both taken care of when we're gone someday. But that's not happening anytime soon." I raised my hand to stop their protest. "But none of that means anything if we do not have an emotionally healthy family. I am concerned that if, God forbid, something ever happened to Dad as a result of this virus that the three of us would blame ourselves until the end of time. But believe me, if your father gets this terrible virus, it will NOT be anyone's fault. We are all going to make mistakes by standing too close to people, or not having our masks in place, or forgetting to wash our hands. Dad has made several mistakes himself in the last week."

"What did he do, Mom? You were the one who had a friend in the back-yard visiting. You both had on masks, but you didn't look six feet apart," Jack said, as he paced from one side of the family room to the other. Jack often paced. It calmed him when he was anxious.

"Jack, Brianna, this is exactly what I'm talking about. We aren't prison guards. We can't blame each other. My friend Meg was visiting from Montana, and we were careful, but you're right, maybe the table was only four or five feet apart. That's not ideal, but it's not the end of the world. We're all going to slip up, make little mistakes. Dad makes mistakes himself. This is too much pressure to put on each other." I looked to Neil for confirmation.

"Mom's right kids. I could get it anywhere. I've been getting massages. I rolled down my window without a mask and bought a shirt from a lady at the lake. She didn't have a mask and was right next to me. I could get this from a gas pump. We just have to be as careful as we can. If it happens, it happens. It won't be anyone's fault. Except the virus's."

This talk calmed us all down and made it easier to establish more realistic behaviors. We made the rules less complicated and made sure each of us understood our parts. Neil stayed by himself in Munds Park as often as he could. We gave Brianna some breaks to be with her friends and her boyfriend as long as she quarantined and tested afterwards. On the doctor's recommendation, Neil and I decided to sleep in separate rooms until he and I were vaccinated. We all fell into a better groove, and the tension level in the house fell dramatically.

Neil continued treatment until December 2020 when we received the miraculous news that his multiple myeloma had been contained once again. His levels had dropped to zero. He was in remission. We wept and prayed in gratitude. We are all now fully vaccinated and are even more grateful that we weathered another storm. Neil was safe.

Chapter 19
WRITING TO BE FREE

For me, the COVID quarantine came with a silver lining. I'm not dismissing the real tragedy, sorrow, and economic devastation it has brought to much of the world, but because the quarantine forced me to stay at home, it compelled me to look inward. It forced me to take care of myself.

We couldn't travel. We couldn't entertain. We couldn't have company. We couldn't see extended family. We couldn't leave the house unless it was essential. Without all these outside commitments, I was able to slow down. I slept longer. I exercised more. I lost weight. I meditated. I wrote parts of this book. I did Qigong (pronounced chee-gong): Chinese exercises and spiritual practice involving body movement, breathing, and meditation. I felt healthier than I had in a long time. I spent time with my family and enjoyed the children. I lived at my own pace, and it was a revelation! I was able to find what I needed through quiet and alone time.

My own pace = peace. I wasn't reacting to external demands. I acted from my core self, from what rose within me. I felt a tremendous freedom. It wasn't selfishness—it's not like I did whatever I felt like whenever I wanted to. It wasn't self-indulgence. It was self-care. I still had duties; I still had commitments. The transformation was more about what fueled me. I was learning to do things, not to please others, with the frantic anxiety that creates *(Is this what they want? Am I doing it right? Am I doing enough? Do they like me?)* but in alignment with my soul, my true self *(Is this healthy? Does it feed my soul? Am I doing this from a place of strength or weakness? Love or fear? Am I serving the other's true self or acting as a servant to their ego and greed?).* I was learning to live exactly as who I am.

It has become clear to me that all this—my life until now—has been about learning how to take care of myself. I spent much of my life trying to live up to what I thought was expected of me, what I thought pleased others, what I thought would earn their love, and I had never learned to care properly for myself. Each of my life lessons was created perfectly for me. I will continue to face one crisis after another until I finally learn to love myself enough to say *No*.

Remember, it starts with a pebble, then it becomes a stone, then a boulder, and suddenly the brick wall falls on you. You don't have to say *No* all the time or in an unkind way, but when you are depleted at the expense of yourself, no one wins. I became so depleted at times that I melted down. Since I left Gulf Breeze, I had two major bathroom floor moments and several other tea kettle blowups.

I knew that after I left Gulf Breeze, I had to teach the people in my life that to be my true, healthy self, I had to untie the binds of unreasonable expectations and codependence. The problem was, I hadn't given myself permission to untie them. I wanted others to untie them for me. I continued to need the approval of others and had forgotten—or never fully learned—that first and foremost I need the approval of my true self. I can no longer allow myself to be anyone (and everyone) else's piece of clay. I am learning to mold the clay myself in my own image, to use my pain to grow instead of letting it dominate my life. My prayer is simply to learn how to stop betraying myself. I continue to evolve, and strive to stop looking for validation outside myself, in the pleasing of others.

I decided to write this book shortly after returning from Gulf Breeze in 2017, and I've been writing it ever since. As I wrote each chapter, I sometimes suffered in trying to write well enough to bring the reader into the experience. I had to let each word, each sentence, each chapter move through me in its own way and time. Many times, writing the words brought me right back into the experience, and I had to face it all over again, to relive it, and that came with a certain amount of PTSD. The book has taken this long to write because of the ocean of emotions it brought up, as well as the natural challenges and duties of life, along with my inability to say *No* in the face of the challenges and needs of others.

As I wrote and meditated, I came to realize that the purpose of my suffering and pain was to introduce me to myself. As the chapters unfolded, a little at a time, I realized that these words were my life. Nobody could take that away from me. I was in control of where the words took the story and became more in control of myself as I gave myself permission to keep writing. Each time I healed enough to begin again, each new chapter brought me a little closer to my true self.

I finally understood that I was really the only one who could lift me up and give myself permission to untie the binds that had held me for so long. I had been choking. I had been suffocating. I realized the relationship I had with others is determined by the relationship I have with myself. The world mirrors our shadows. If we are unhealthy, we draw to ourselves those who are unhealthy, those who will continue to hurt themselves and others if we enable them, those who will bleed us dry. If we are healthy, we draw to ourselves those who are also healthy, those who will truly benefit from our help and truly help us in return, those who will grow along with us to become their true selves.

The ultimate destination of our life journey is to love ourselves first and then to love one another, to treat each other as we would like to be treated. We must learn to understand when too much love hurts others. And by too much love, I mean unhealthy, dysfunctional, enabling love. This is not real love at all. Sometimes loving too much or doing too much can take the power away from those who have their own lessons to learn. The difference between enabling and being of service to those who are more vulnerable than we are ourselves is a fine line. I am slowly learning to walk that line.

Those in our lives who do not let us love ourselves are not healthy for us, nor are we healthy for them. The only ones we must put before ourselves are our children. They are our responsibility, to love and nurture above all else until they are adults on their own. After which, of course, we still love them but must learn the hard lesson of letting them fly on their own. It is much easier to raise a healthy child than to repair a broken adult.

One of the most important examples we can give our children is how we treat ourselves. Giving ourselves the same love and compassion we give our children shows them the way toward wisdom and happiness, a path they can follow all their lives. Neil has done a good job of showing our children self-worth and self-care. I haven't always done the same, though I'm doing much better now. It's never too late to grow.

For example, I have found that to the path of forgiveness is one of the most important ways we can align with our true selves. It has been one of my biggest struggles. Intellectually, I know how important forgiveness is and that it gives us a tremendous amount of strength and peace when we are able to forgive. Lewis B. Smedes puts it this way: "To forgive is to set a prisoner free and discover that the prisoner was you."[28] I strive to set my prisoner free.

When I think of forgiveness, I believe I must first and foremost continue the journey of forgiving myself for the many times that I have not reacted in grace toward others. I pray that I will continue to grow in my quest of being conscious of my reactions and choose both the words and the appropriate times to discuss sensitive matters. When doing so, I pray that I can act in love and kindness instead of coming from fear. I know that I have hurt the people I love when I have not responded appropriately. I send each one of those individuals love when my memory takes me to those places and hope that in forgiving myself and learning from those mistakes that I can heal myself and those I have hurt in the magic of know-ing that, as Maya Angelo Says, "When we know better, we do better."

My mother is also on top of the forgiveness list, as she has had a profound effect on my life. She pushed me into the role of an adult way too early in my childhood and set me on the path of people pleasing and codependence. I believe that I have found a special place within myself that does forgive her. Mom never had the capacity to do it any other way, but her mark is deep. Mom and I have healed in many ways since my bathroom floor experience in Spain. I finally recognized the gravity and depth of my scars and the critical need to forgive my mother in order to heal myself. I know now that in our journey together, we both have done the best we could. She is beginning to understand that I can't always jump to help her and in her last years, she has really stepped up.

Throughout most of the pandemic, Michael has lived with Mom, since I couldn't very well have him in the house with my teenage daughter. Mom has been a hero. He lived there for almost a year while I applied for long-term care funding through the Department of Developmental Disabilities of Arizona and appealed his case three times. But finally, I did it. Michael has long-term care funding and is now living in a beautiful home with a caring and wonderfully competent group of angels working with him. They even found him the job he loves with RISE. He is a greeter at the front desk. It's like a YMCA for the disabled, and he is happy.

I am very proud of Michael and very proud of my mom and stepfather. Throughout this period, they have been wonderful parents, though they are both elderly and it wasn't always easy for them. They had the opportunity to reconnect with their son and take over the responsibilities they had left to me for so long. This is something that they and Michael both needed—to be reminded of the love they had for each other in their roles as mother and father and son. Michael had missed Mom, and though he wouldn't have been able to put it this way, he had felt a little abandoned by his mother and father. For Mom's part, she realized how much her son needed her and did her best to make up for lost time. I know Michael will always cherish that time he had with them.

Mom told me about a conversation she had with Michael recently. Michael had fought with one of my sisters during a family gathering. "Michael, the most important thing in life you can do is forgive," she told him. "It will take the pain away. When we forgive others, we open our hearts to them and understand what they are not able to give. We all do the best we can from where we are. It's not personal to you. She [our sister] loves you, Michael. We all have wonderful parts of our personality, but we also have characteristics that can be difficult for ourselves and others. If you can find it within yourself to tell her you're sorry, I promise it will make you feel better."

Though she was relating a conversation she had had with Michael, I knew that at some level she was talking about her and me as well. She started crying and told me she knew her body was giving out. Then she let me know how grateful she was for all I had done for Michael and that she knew how much of a burden she had put on me. She acknowledged my childhood and the role of caretaker and fixer I have always had in the family. Though she didn't say it directly, she was asking my forgiveness.

On May 17, 2021, mom fractured her hip and was rushed to the hospital. My twins' graduation from high school was three days later. I, of course, realized that I had to drop everything and be there for mom with long days at the hospital both before and after their graduation. I was exhausted for their graduation ceremony and a large party that I gave them on May 22nd. The party turned out great, but Brianna knew how exhausted I was and that I was not myself. Mom's health was already quite bad before she fell. The fracture made it much worse. Caring for her had taken a huge toll in those weeks. She required a great deal of care and was difficult to handle.

As I write these sentences more than seven weeks after her hip fracture, I have had the miracle of reflecting on my thinking within this book. I now know that I had to walk the walk and take my own words seriously. I have taken a big step back, for example, and have let go of the lead role within our family. I am learning. I am saying "NO." Mom has been frustrated with my change in behavior and has even become quite angry several times.

I believe it is our responsibility as our parents age to make sure that they are comfortable and cared for. The first three weeks were serious. I felt it was my responsibility to make her care my priority, but once she was out of the hospital, I gave myself permission to share as much time as possible with my children before they moved out a month later to begin their journeys at CU (University of Colorado Boulder) and at First Place.

I provided professional care for Mom on the days I was away so that I was sure to do my part. My sisters and my brother Donnie and his wife were amazing and took on a great deal of the responsibility and time needed to care for my mother. It wasn't easy for them, but they stepped up, showed up, and helped me understand that they have always been there. I just wasn't ready to let them be responsible before now. I have come to under-stand that I was my own captive. It was always up to me to take better care of myself. But this time, I did it. I said "No," and my siblings have shared the responsibility equally.

Sharing my journey with my mom within these pages, has come with concern—concern that some of the people I love the most will feel pain in some of the words that I have written regarding our mom. I believe and pray that when my sisters and brother Don read through the pages of this book that they understand my struggle more clearly and that these words have not been written to harm anyone, but to tell the truth because truth heals. I believe it's okay to discuss our shadows within ourselves and our families. We are all here with the sole purpose to evolve. Truth evolves.

I know my mother won't be here much longer. I know she loves me dearly. I have forgiven her and myself. She might be confused and frustrated with me now, but I wanted to be sure that I reacted in a healthier manner before she passes, for my own good, to change the cycle. She did the best she could with the tools she had, and I know she is becoming closer to her true self as she approaches the end of this lifetime. She has some beautiful qualities and some shadows, as we all do. After all, what I know for sure, is that in our soul state, I chose her to be my mom.

Neil is another one for whom I have to learn forgiveness, and thereby, learn to forgive myself. I have to forgive him for unconsciously repeating the patterns he learned growing up, just as I have to forgive myself for repeating my own destructive patterns from childhood and letting myself succumb to his as well. Part of my journey to love myself is to continue to grow and learn in my marriage.

I love Neil dearly. I know we will continue to walk through this journey together. I couldn't have walked through this lifetime without him. There has been darkness, but also light. The medicine is in the pain. Neil and I are not afraid to face it, to walk through the pain to find our purpose. We are rising above old belief systems to accept each other's separate strengths and weaknesses. My prayer is that we continue to accept one another with love and compassion.

The souls of Neil and I came together to help each other grow. We have complementary strengths and weaknesses that are helping us evolve toward our true selves, individually and together. I don't think that happened by accident. Neil has been a vital part of my growth. By his example, he showed me how to care for myself. He may have sometimes treated me as if he was the parent and I the child, but that helped me learn to advocate for myself. Both Neil and I have become more aware of these unhealthy patterns.

Every relationship has its peaks and valleys. Those ups and downs are part of the growth. The fear and uncertainty of the pandemic and Neil's relapse brought this out in full force. We both fell into our old comfort zones. Driven by his fear, Neil tried to control me with his anger and his criticism. Unable to stand up for myself and ask for what I needed in a healthy way, I turned to suppressing my feelings or sometimes finding courage in a bottle. This was a divine indicator that Neil and I still have some work to do in bringing the patterns of our shadow selves into the light so we can resolve them. To some degree, we are still undergoing the power struggle Harville Hendrix writes about, but we're making progress. Now we both understand how important it is for each of us to resolve this struggle. That hasn't always been the case. We continue to learn to treat each other as we would like to be treated. It is my prayer that when one of us is scared, the other shows up; when one of us is at our worst, the other is at their best. We are both learning how to have a more spiritual and equal partnership.

After completing this book, I told Neil that I would like him to read the first copy before putting it out into the world. We made a decision that we would not discuss it until after he had read the whole thing and had some time to reflect. It was never my intention, but as a result of this book, Neil was able to deep listen in a manner that would only occur if you were reading a book. Without the pre-planned response that naturally can occur when discussing feelings verbally and the ability to process the feelings that would unfold as the chapters revealed my inner most thoughts, Neil was able to listen and grasp the gravity of our life together in a manner that had never been possible before. Since he read a draft of this book, our relationship has gone to a whole new level of understanding and depth. Neil's response and reflection that has come forth from this book is a gift that I will be forever grateful for. We have had beautiful insights and wonderful adjustments as a result. Neil is my soulmate. As I send this book out into the world, our twins have both graduated from high school and on to their next chapter. Neil and I are on to our new chapter together as well, and I couldn't be more excited. Neil's new motto is "Sixties are Go Go, Seventies are Slow Go and Eighties are No Go unless you Go Go." We are all set to Go Go.

Our twentieth wedding anniversary was on October 27, 2021. We have grown tremendously over the years. I couldn't be prouder of him. He has given his blessing to publish this book and that took the courage and the confidence that he has always embodied in such a glorious way. Neil chose me when he agreed to let this book fly wherever it might land. We renewed our vows in Boulder Colorado on October 17th, a surprise to Neil. Neil, Jack, and I went to Parent's weekend for Brianna at CU and on our last morning, we took a very special hike. Jack, Brianna, Neil and I as well as our Colorado based side of the family (my niece and nephew, Barb and Garrison) came along for the special surprise. My brother-in-law Craig and my sister-in-law, Barb had to be out of town, but would have certainly participated otherwise.

We hiked along the Ute Range View Trail of Flagstaff Mountain to Realization Point, which overlooks the majestic Rocky Mountains at the

Continental Divide covered in the deep green splendor of the pines. It was a perfect sunny fall day, we were all enjoying our hike and our time together. As we approached the mountain top, the lyrics from our wedding song, "It's a Wonderful World" by Louis Armstrong echoed over the trailhead, I loved watching Neil's expression as he realized what song was playing. Rabbi Alan, his lovely wife and our photographer, Shannon were waiting as we arrived. We were all prepared with our beautiful stories of our years together and prayers for the special day. As Neil continued to realize what was unfolding, I saw the same eyes and love before me that we shared on our wedding day twenty years before. At the end of the ceremony, in traditional Jewish fashion, we broke the glass, with a champagne toast, as we celebrated each other and our next chapter to-gether. There wasn't a dry eye. We told wonderful, emotional and funny stories. I loved watching Jack and Brianna. I knew it meant a lot to them as well. We had found our way to a deeper purpose together and what better place than the perfection of "Realization Point. " I know, great name, couldn't have been more perfectly chosen. I will be forever grateful for choosing the person that has helped me the most to find myself, and in that, we have found each other.

Each experience in my life has brought me closer to letting go and letting God. I believe we must flow with life and trust God's plan. I know there is natural order, and we cannot resist it. We must learn the lessons meant for us in this lifetime. Sometimes the natural order needs a reset, and the pandemic has done that in many ways, both at home and in the world at large.

The September before the pandemic, Jack had grown obsessed with telling anyone who would listen—teachers, therapists, friends, and family—that a terrible recession was coming the next Spring. At every family meal, he talked incessantly about it, trying to prepare us. We got tired of hearing about this wild paranoid fantasy of his, as we saw it, and told him to knock it off—that he was way too negative and anxious about something that wasn't going to happen. Neil got to the point where he was going to punish Jack if he didn't stop. Jack just looked at us like a Buddha—no judgment, no frustration, just a deep understanding and certainty that he knew what was coming.

I don't know how he knew, but Jack was right. The pandemic brought with it great change, and we learned from him not to resist, not to force anything but to go with the flow of God's love. There's been a natural cleansing that was needed to get our attention. The pandemic is cracking open lost values. A massive spiritual awakening is occurring. We are all shifting, reframing our lives, weighing what needs to be adjusted and released. Relationships will shift, and necessary changes will occur. Karma will be rebalanced. We are becoming more aware of our neglect of the ill and elderly, the mentally ill, the poor, the planet with its disappearing plants and animals, our dismissal of peace and compassion.

I am grateful to be a part of this shift, to experience along with everyone else the oneness of Spirit. I have always felt God's presence. Even as a small child, I could go within myself to be with him no matter what was going on at home. I remember going for long walks in the woods, where I caught butterflies in all the colors of the rainbow and relished their beauty. I climb-ed the lush trees with their golds and greens, each branch bringing me closer to the top of the world. I loved being alone where it was always safe, listening to the birds sing and watching them soar through the sky in freedom. Nature has always been healing for me. I was sometimes gone for hours, nestled by myself in the trees surrounded by the comfort of God and the magic of nature.

I still love the magic of the outdoors. I have been a big hiker my whole life. As a single adult, I was up by five most days to hike one of the many mountains in the Sonoran Desert, and I still try to do that when I can, especially when we're in Munds Park. I love the majestic golds and oranges of the desert sunrise, the pickets of Saguaros up and down the mountains, the perfection of their white cactus flowers with the bright yellow stamens, the smell of overripe melon wafting on the soft desert breeze.

I keep myself in better shape both mentally and physically when I give myself this sacred time. When I'm in the woods or mountains, I'm home. It's my sacred place, my healing place. On my desk I have a photo of an incredible view from my favorite hike at Crystal Point in Munds Park, it has the caption "Turn Up the Quiet." It was a gift from a sweet friend. That was our mantra whenever we hiked together. When I need to breathe, I just look at that special picture. When I'm centered in the magic of nature, I know that all is well, and I'm all right.

God hit me hard in some respects in this lifetime, each time trying harder to give me the opportunity to learn my lessons. I'm still here despite some close calls. I'm grateful he never gave up (though I'm sure he never gives up on any of us). I still have lessons to learn, much growing to do in my relationship with myself and those I love. God has a plan. I just have to follow his lead and trust in him. It all happens exactly as it must, so our spirit can elevate to a higher consciousness, to our higher purpose. I have yet to achieve my full purpose, and I look forward to continuing my journey to discover it.

Thich Nhat Hanh teaches, "As you practice building a home within yourself, you become more and more beautiful."[29] I'm certainly still building that home within myself! James Baldwin puts it another way. "Your crown has been bought and paid for. All you have to do is put it on your head."[30] What these two profound statements tell me is that it's all inside us, the bad and the good, our shadows and our true selves, and that no one else can live our lives for us so why should we let them?

As I continue to evolve and grow, I'm beginning to worry less about what others think of me and more about what I think of myself. Writing this book is all part of the process, part of the journey to my true self. By remembering where I've been, I hope to leave all that baggage behind and forge my way forward with greater strength and clarity. I'm writing to be free. This book is part of the home I'm building within myself, part of the crown I'm putting on my own head.

ACKNOWLEDGMENTS

I would like to thank the following people for their love and support throughout my life and while writing this book.

My mom. You are the mother I chose in my soul state to provide the experiences that would lead me closer to myself in my quest to become whole. I Love You Mom.

My husband and Soulmate Neil. You have supported me throughout the process of writing this book. The courage and vulnerability you have demonstrated in support of my interpretation of the beautiful journey we have shared has opened us to a deeper understanding and love for one another.

My children, Jack and Brianna. You are the two people in the world that I am most proud of. Both of you are my light, my strength, and my most cherished gift in life. It is a privilege and honor to be your mom.

All my friends and family who have supported me in my journey while writing this book. Your love and support have meant the world to me.

My editors, Laura Bush and Charles Grosel. Thank you for your magnificence, talent, and undying patience with a first-time author. I certainly couldn't have done it without you.

ABOUT THE AUTHOR

Born and raised in the suburbs of Detroit, Michigan, Lynn Balter began learning the lessons that would bring her closer to her true self, a journey of self-discovery, at a very young age. After attending Western Michigan University and earning her Bachelor of Business Administration degree in 1982, she moved to Scottsdale, Arizona, where she began her career as a property manager, then a real estate agent/broker, and a successful entrepreneur in the vacation rental industry. The years passed, the lessons continued, every time bringing her closer to healing the wounds necessary to further her growth. She married Neil Balter, her soulmate and a self-made entrepreneur in 2001. One year later, they became the parents of twins, one of whom has autism.

Lynn's journey to discover her true self is a story of surviving childhood trauma, sexual assault, breast cancer, addiction, divorce, a diagnosis of autism, a crisis of traumatic brain injury, co-dependency, gaslighting, a "cancierge" (caregiver of late-stage Multiple Myeloma), business and bankruptcy, and near fatal accidents all perfectly intended for her growth, the growth that would continue to align her personality to her soul (her true self). With each lesson learned, Lynn also found peace and enlighten-ment through her love of spiritual teachings. Service and philanthropy have been key in healing the wounds necessary in her quest to become whole.

In 1996, Lynn earned membership in the Young Entrepreneurs Organization (now EO), where she met her husband. She and Neil have helped raise millions of dollars for Autism Speaks and the Southwest Autism Research & Resource Center (SARRC), both internationally recognized nonprofits. Over her lifetime, Lynn has volunteered and served for numerous nonprofit organizations, including the Center Against Sexual Assault (CASA), HomeBase Youth Services, SARRC, First Place AZ, Kids Who Care, Homes of Hope, National Charity League, and Epi Hab, an organization that creates jobs for special needs individuals with epilepsy and other special needs.

NOTES

1. Lao Tzu, *Tao Te Ching*, trans. D.C. Lau (New York: Penguin, 1963), 58.
2. Gary Zukav, *The Seat of the Soul* (New York: Simon-Schuster, 1990), 35.
3. Oprah Winfrey, *The Wisdom of Sunday –Life-Changing Insights from Super Soul Conversations* (New York: Flatiron Books, 2017), 80-81.
4. Zukav, *Seat of the Soul*, 81.
5. Earvin "Magic" Johnson, *Safe Sex in the Age of Aids* (Ottawa, ON, Canada: Golden Bridge Books, 2001).
6. Kahlil Gibran, *The Prophet* (New York: Alfred A. Knopf, 1923), 11.
7. Joseph Bailey, M.A., L.P., *Slowing Down to the Speed of Love* (New York: McGraw-Hill, 2004), 202.
8. Bruce Lipton, Ph.D., "The Jump from Cell Culture to Consciousness," *Integrative Medicine: A Clinician's Journal* 16, no. 6 (December 2017), 44-50.
9. Harville Hendrix, Ph.D., *Getting the Love You Want* (New York: St. Martin's Press, 2001).
10. Debbie Ford, *The Secret of the Shadow: The Power of Owning Your Whole Story* (New York: Harper Collins Paperback Edition, 2003).
11. Thomas W. Phelan, Ph.D., *1-2-3 Magic* (Illinois: Child Management Inc., 2003).
12. Elisabeth Kübler-Ross, M.D., *On Death and Dying* (New York: MacMillan Publishing Co., Inc., 1970), 38-112.
13. Jennifer Carroll, *Cool 2 Be Me!: Bigsbee's Unbee-Lievable Journey to Fly* (New York: Morgan James Publishing, LLC, 2005).
14. Christopher Hartwell, *Exit Wounds: Overcoming Unprocessed Pain* (Texas: Brown Girls Publishing, 2014), 285, Kindle.
15. Bailey, *Slowing Down to the Speed of Love*, 109.
16. Hendrix, *Getting the Love You Want*.

17 Oprah's Super Soul Sunday. "Oprah and Mark Nepo, Part 2." 432. OWN, November 10, 2013, https://www.oprah.com/own-super-soul-sunday/full-episode-oprah-and-mark-nepo-part-2-video.

18 Brené Brown, *Rising Strong: How the Ability to Reset Transforms the Way We Live, Love, Parent and Lead* (New York: Random House, 2017), 64.

19 Brené Brown, interview with Tim Ferris and Dax Shephard, *Unlocking Us with Brené Brown*, podcast audio, December 16, 2020, https://brenebrown.com/podcast/brene-with-tim-ferriss-and-dax-shepard-on-podcasting-daily-practices-and-the-long-and-winding-path-to-healing/.

20 Sydney Banks, *The Missing Link: Reflections on Philosophy and Spirit* (Washington: Lone Pine Publishing Ltd., Partners Publishing, International Human Relations Consultants, 1998), 19-20.

21 Michael Singer, *The Untethered Soul: The Journey Beyond Yourself* (California: New Harbinger Publications, Inc., 2007), 83.

22 Rick Lawrence interviewed by William Paul Young, "William Paul Young on the Goodness of God," YouthMinistry.com, https://youthministry.com/william-paul-young-on-the-goodness-of-god.

23 Hendrix, *Getting the Love You Want*, 306.

24 Oprah Winfrey, *The Wisdom of Sunday: Life-Changing Insights from Super Soul Conversations*, 126-127.

25 Oprah's Super Soul Sunday. "Oprah and Mark Nepo, Part 2." 432, 00.22-3.03.

26 Myla and Jon Kabat-Zinn, *Everyday Blessings: The Inner Work of Mindful Parenting* (New York: Hyperion, 1997), 8.

27 Roya R. Rad, MA, PsyD., *Rumi & Self Psychology (Psychology of Tranquility): Two Astonishing Perspectives for the Art and Science of Self Transformation: Rumi's Poetic Language Vs. Carl Jung's Psychological Language* (Illinois: Trafford Publishing, 2010), 21.

28 Alex A. Lluch, *Simple Principles for a Happy and Healthy Marriage* (California: WS Publishing Group, 2008), 152.

29 Thich Nhat Hanh, *How to Love* (California, Parallax Press, 2015), 20, Kindle.

30 Toni Morrison, "James Baldwin: His Voice Remembered, Life in His Language," *The New York Times Book Review*, December 20, 1987, 7, 21.